The Seed-Starter's Handbook

Other Books by the Same Author

Vegetables Money Can't Buy
Working Wood (Written with Michael Bubel)

The Seed-Starter's Handbook

by Nancy Bubel

Illustrations by Robert Shetterly
Photographs by Mike Bubel

 Rodale Press   Emmaus PA

Printed in the United States of America on recycled paper

Library of Congress Cataloging in Publication Data
Bubel, Nancy.
    The seed-starter's handbook.

    Bibliography: p.
    Includes index.
    1. Vegetable gardening. 2. Seeds. 3. Plant
propagation. 4. Organic gardening. I. Title.
SB321.B9   635'.04'31   77-25332
ISBN 0-87857-209-0

Grateful acknowledgement is made to the following publishers for permission to reprint copyrighted material:

Lea and Febiger: *Vegetable Growing* by J. E. Knott. Copyright © 1955 by J. E. Knott. Reprinted by permission.
John Wiley & Sons, Inc.: *Handbook for Vegetable Growers* by J. E. Knott. Copyright © 1957 by J. E. Knott. Reprinted by permission.
Sierra Club Books: *The Unsettling of America* by Wendell Berry. Copyright © 1977 by Wendell Berry. Reprinted by permission.

Grateful acknowledgement is made to J. F. Harrington, Department of Vegetable Crops, University of California, Davis, CA., for permission to reprint previously published tables and to Dr. Garrison Wilkes for permission to reprint exerpts from his article "The World's Crop Plant Germplasm—An Endangered Resource" from the February 1977 issue of *The Bulletin of the Atomic Scientists*.

4 6 8 10 9 7 5 3

To My Parents,

Milton and Grace Hangen Wilkes

We lose our health—and create profitable diseases and de-pendences—by failing to see the direct connections between living and eating, eating and working, working and loving. In gardening, for instance, one works with the body to feed the body. The work, if it is knowledgeable, makes for excellent food. And it makes one hungry. The work thus makes eating both nourishing and joyful, not consumptive, and keeps the eater from getting fat and weak. This is health, wholeness, a source of delight. And such a solution, unlike the typical industrial solution, does not cause new problems.

The "drudgery" of growing one's own food, then, is not drudg-ery at all. (If we make the growing of food a drudgery, which is what agribusiness does make of it, then we also make a drudgery of eating, and of living.) It is, in addition to being the appropriate fulfillment of a practical need, a sacrament, as eating is also, by which we enact and understand our oneness with the Creation, the conviviality of one body with all bodies.

Wendell Berry
The Unsettling of America

Contents

Acknowledgments

In referring to our debt to those who have gone before us, a wise man once said, "We stand on the shoulders of giants." This is especially true, I think, in gardening, where we have been both enlightened by the experiments of learned men and supported by the faithful efforts of obscure dirt-gardeners who have saved and selected seed and cared for the soil over the centuries.

In preparing this book, I've received generous help—in the form of correspondence and printed matter—from Dr. R. J. Downs, Phytotron Director at the North Carolina State University at Raleigh; Dr. Robert F. Fletcher, Extension Specialist in Vegetable Crops at Penn State University; Dr. O. A. Lorenz, Chairman, Department of Vegetable Crops, University of California at Davis; Dr. Raymond Sheldrake, Professor of Vegetable Crops at Cornell University; and Dr. H. Garrison Wilkes, Botany Department, Boston Harbor Campus of the University of Massachusetts. Dr. Garrison Wilkes, Dr. James Harrington, and Dr. James Edward Knott have kindly permitted me to quote from their work. Any errors or misinterpretations, though, are mine alone.

In addition, R. Gregory Plimpton of Atlantic and Pacific Research, Inc., has supplied me with much helpful information. Kent Whealy, originator of the True Seed Exchange, Forest Glen Roth, Director of the Abundant Life Seed Foundation, and Lawrence Hills of the Henry Doubleday Research Foundation have answered my inquiries in a spirit of kind cooperation and allowed me to quote from their writings.

When Rob Shetterly, Art Editor for *Farmstead* magazine, agreed to do the illustrations for the book, I was flattered, having long admired his work. When I saw what he had done, I was thrilled. Thanks, Rob.

I'm grateful, too, to my husband and children, who good-naturedly endure my absentmindedness when I am "with book." And to my son Greg, who deserves an award for perseverance for his typing of the whole much-spliced and corrected manuscript for publication.

Nancy Bubel

Introduction

Since 1957, when we tried (and failed!) to grow radishes in a windowbox outside our third-floor apartment window in Philadelphia, my husband, Mike, and I have been learning about growing vegetables. We got off to a slow start. I had only vague memories of the Victory Garden my parents grew for a few years in our New England backyard, and an insistent yearning to begin a garden of my own. Mike had grown up on home-raised vegetables—a surprisingly limited variety of them though, mostly grown from seed his mother had carefully saved from one harvest to the next: cabbage, potatoes, beans, carrots, beets, dill, cucumbers, sunflowers. Later, during a stay in Germany, he had taken a course in gardening at a free university of sorts. Mike wanted a garden too.

When we moved into our first house, we bought digging forks and shovels almost before the ink was dry on the deed. And we started, that first year, with tomatoes and beans and many flowers. It took us several years to progress to planting a garden that we could eat from all summer, but by 1970 our vegetable garden was carrying us year-round. Today we hardly ever buy a vegetable. Our year-round vegetable self-sufficiency is due in large part to starting seeds early indoors and making continuous outdoor plantings of varieties of food chosen for quality and ease of storage.

Along the way, we've learned a lot about how and when to start different vegetables. Experience—trial and error—has helped. Older relatives and neighbors have been generous with advice and lore, and we never start a new gardening year without thinking fondly of our different mentors over the years, and how much they have given us. Reading about gardens and gardening, seeds, plants, soil, and insects has given us a framework that often points up relationships between what we've observed and what we've been told.

Mostly, though, we've muddled along, taking longer than it now seems we should have to see and use the full potential of a piece of ground and a packet of seeds.

That's why I decided to write this book—to help other gardeners to make that jump between dabbling and self-sufficiency sooner and more easily than we did. At the same time, I hope that experienced gardeners will find here some insight into possibilities never considered, into alternatives and experiments in areas of gardening where the final word has yet to be written.

Consider this book, then, a *manual* of procedures, giving you the step-by-step how and when of various planting techniques. Look too, in every chapter, for the principles—the "why"—on which these techniques are based. And count on finding at least a few open-ended questions that might challenge old suppositions or suggest new growing frontiers.

There's no *one right* way to do most of these things, you know. There are a good many workable options open to you in planting seeds. I've tried to suggest the range of possibilities. The choice is up to you.

Let this book be smudged. Let it be marked. It's meant to be used. I hope it will make a difference in your garden. And, ultimately, on your table.

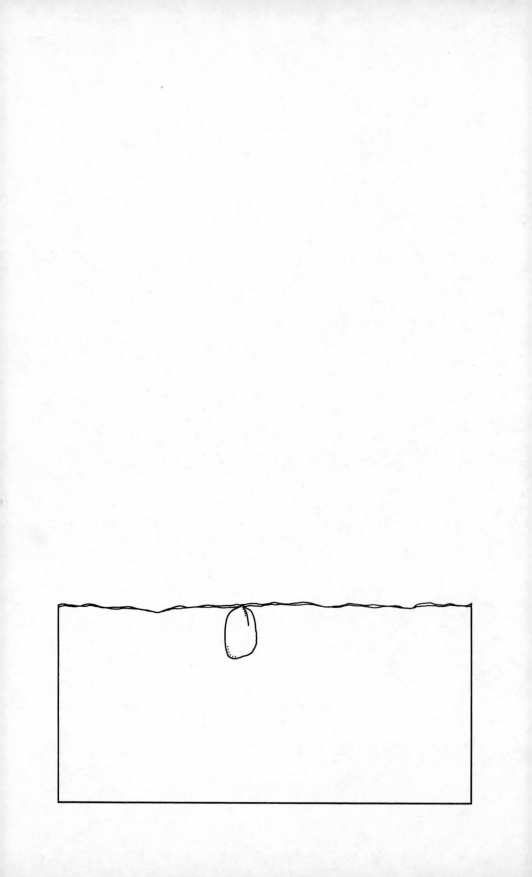

Section One

To own a bit of ground, to scratch it with a hoe, to plant seeds and watch the renewal of life—this is the commonest delight of the race, the most satisfactory thing a man can do.

Charles Dudley Warner

1
Why Start Your Own?

Security and adventure might be considered opposites in some situations, but the gardener who raises plants from seed can have both. Security, that confidence in the future that springs from one's own ability, forethought, and preparation, and adventure, the soaring sense of "anything is possible" and "there are so many interesting things to try," are well known to those who grow new varieties, experiment with new methods, and dabble in plant breeding and seed saving.

Skill in raising vegetable plants from seed is to us the very cornerstone of gardening independence. Choice of seed and careful handling can bring you not only earlier harvests but better vegetables. You can select varieties of food known to keep or process well so that the winter eating season, for which we gardeners are always planning, will be a time of abundance. At the same time, good eating will be yours all summer long from the selection of fresh vegetables you've planted for their superior quality.

While I suspect that I'd continue to raise my own seedling plants even without a good excuse, because I just plain enjoy the process, when I stop to think about it I realize that there are all kinds of good reasons for nurturing one's own plants from seed.

1.   You can get a much earlier start in the garden, and therefore put fresh food on the table sooner, when you've grown flats of cabbage and tomatoes, eggplant and peppers indoors for setting out when weather mellows. Naturally, the sooner you can begin picking from your garden, the greater your yield for the year.

2.   Varieties of plants offered by commercial seedling vendors represent but a tiny fraction of the possibilities open to you as a gardener. Buying started plants severely limits your options for raising vegetables of special flavor, keeping quality, insect or disease resistance, and extra nutritional value. If, for example, you want to grow Caro Red tomatoes (extra high in vitamin A) you'll have to start with seeds. Looking for special gourmet foods like globe artichokes, watercress, Japanese melons? It's back to the seed catalogs. Peppers that are hot, but not too hot? Start your own Hungarian wax plants. Delicious, mild, sweet Golden Acre or

2

Flats of various vegetables, ready for planting out, all raised from seed.

Jersey Queen cabbage? For those you need to start with seeds. Cauliflower that needs no blanching? Start from scratch.

3. Seedlings you've grown yourself *can* be super seedlings. If you do all the right things at the right times, you'll have the best that can be gotten. And you'll know that your plants have well-developed roots growing in good soil that's not been hyped with chemicals to give the plants a short-lived artificial high. You can even plant organically raised seed to give your plants an extra running start on excellence.

4. By raising your own plants, you minimize the chance of introducing soil-borne diseases to your garden. Club-root and yel-

3

lows of cabbage, anthracnose, tobacco mosaic, and verticillium and other kinds of wilt are some examples of plant diseases you may escape importing if you grow your own. Of course, you must use uncontaminated soil and, especially in the case of mosaic and pepper, eggplant, and tomato seedlings, avoid handling tobacco around the plants.

5. You'll save money. Well, maybe. Certainly for the price of a dozen greenhouse tomato plants you can buy a small handful of seed packets, each of which will give you plants to share, to sell, or extra seed to save for the following year. There are so many interesting plants to grow, though, that once you start raising seedlings you might find that you tend to put some of that saved money back into seeds of other kinds. But since you're likely to eat even better as a result, you may well consider that you're still far ahead. And, since you can grow more plants than you need from a packet of seed, you can afford to choose only the best from those that sprout, to carry on for the garden.

6. Creative satisfaction ought to count for something too. From settling a well-chosen seedling in a pot of its own carefully prepared soil and watching it grow greener, sturdier, and leafier, to picking and eating the peppers, eggplants, or other nutritious food the mature plant finally bears, you know you've been in on it all the way, and you can see that your skillful care has made a difference.

7. At the very least, planting seeds indoors is a good cure for the winter doldrums, those bleak, cold days when February seems like a permanent condition and you feel you just must do something to nudge the season into turning. Choose your earliest plantings judiciously, though. You don't want them to be past their prime when you set them out in the garden. Onions, chives, peppers, and house plants like coleus and geranium are good candidates for beginning the season.

2
First the Seeds

You have in your hands an array of seed packets and perhaps a few jars of seed you've saved yourself. And you're anxious to plant, to get a start on the growing season that still seems far away. (March followed February last year too, and despite outward appearances, we're confident that the usual order of spring will also prevail this year.)

Take a minute now, if you will, to be aware of what the seed really is, before committing it to the soil. Dry, flaky, hard, smooth, warted, ridged, powdery, wispy. These distinctively shaped particles may look as lifeless as the February garden patch. Don't be deceived, though. Seeds don't spring to life when you plant them. Seeds *are* alive.

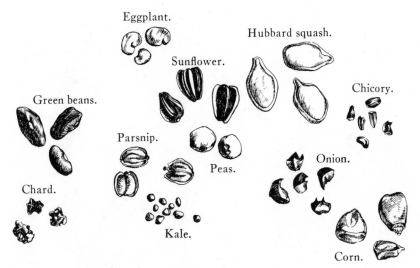

A variety of seeds, enlarged.

Often referred to as symbols of beginning, seeds are living guarantees of continuity between generations of plants. Inside even the most minute, dustlike grain of seed is a living plant. True, it's in embryonic form, possessing only the most rudimentary parts, but

5

it lives. Nor is it completely passive. At levels that we can't see, but laboratory scientists can measure, seeds carry on respiration. They absorb oxygen and give off carbon dioxide. They also absorb water from the air. Seeds need a certain minimum of moisture within their cells, in fact, in order to make possible the metabolic processes by which they convert some of their stored carbohydrates into soluble food. Thus they maintain their spark of life—dim though it may be—until conditions are right for them to complete their destiny as germinated plants.

The Botanical Facts

By strict botanical definition, a seed is a ripened fertilized ovule containing an embryonic plant and a supply of stored food, surrounded by a seed coat. In practice, though, gardeners use many seeds which are actually fruits (the mature ovary of a flower containing one or more seeds). A kernel of corn is really a seedlike fruit. Carrot, dill, and fennel seeds are, technically, dry, one-seeded fruits.

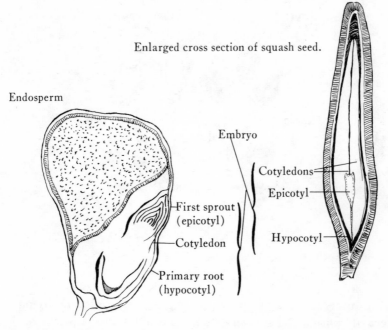

Enlarged cross section of squash seed.

Endosperm

Embryo

Cotyledons

Epicotyl

First sprout (epicotyl)

Cotyledon

Hypocotyl

Primary root (hypocotyl)

Enlarged cross section of kernel of corn.

Seeds, then, are completely self-contained. They possess, within the boundaries of the hard, dry coat that protects them, enough food energy to carry them through their dormancy and into the support of the plant. They have all the enzymes they'll need to convert this stored food into a form their tissues can use. And they carry within their cells the genetic information that directs what they will be, and when, and how.

Let's look at an example. Not a typical seed, perhaps, but one in which it is easy to see the parts, and their arrangement, that are common to all seeds. The good old garden bush bean is the favorite of botanists for this purpose, since its size and structure make it possible for us to see clearly how it is formed.

If you soak a bean seed in water for a few hours, the hard outer coat will slip off easily. The bulk of the bean that you now see is composed of the cotyledons, the two identical fleshy halves that comprise the "meat" of the seed. These rudimentary leaves— unusually large and thick in the bean—contain stored fat, carbohydrate, and protein. Both cotyledons are attached to a rudimentary stem, and they curve protectively over a tiny leafy bud. The root tip, on the other end of the seed, will elongate into the first root of the plant when the seed germinates.

Any seed you plant, no matter how tiny, wispy, or irregular, will possess these features: cotyledons, the plant's first leaves (sometimes one, more often two), a brief stem, a leafy bud, and a root tip. Most seed-bearing garden vegetable plants are dicots, that is, they possess two cotyledons. Monocots, with just a single cotyledon, are represented by the grass family (*Gramineae*) which includes corn, wheat, rye, and other cereal crops. Beans, tomatoes, celery, cabbage, and other vegetable seedlings germinate with two "wings"; corn, wheat, and other grains send up the familiar single grasslike spear of green.

In many seeds, some of which are important food crops in their own right, the stored food is not contained in the cotyledons, as in the bean, but in another layer called the endosperm, which surrounds the embryo. This part of the seed varies in different species. It may consist of starch, oil, protein, or waxy or horny matter, but whatever its form, its function remains the same—to nourish the seed from the time of its maturity on the parent plant to the beginning of the next growing season when conditions will be favorable for its success as a plant in its own right. Often, of course, the tasty endosperm is

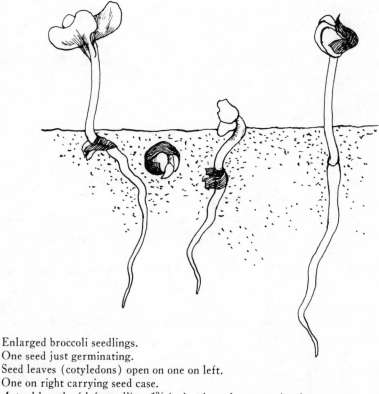

Enlarged broccoli seedlings.
One seed just germinating.
Seed leaves (cotyledons) open on one on left.
One on right carrying seed case.
Actual length of left seedling, 1¾ inches from leaves to tip of root.

what we're after when we raise the crop, as for example, buckwheat, corn, wheat, and rye.

Just to keep the record straight, cotyledons may in some cases synthesize nourishment needed by the seed; they may also both store and synthesize food. If you find that fact surprising, reflect that there is more—much more—that we don't yet know about seeds.

We know very little about the origin of seed-bearing plants as we grow them. Charles Darwin called it an "abominable mystery." Spore-bearing plants existed first, followed by gymnosperms like the evergreens, which shed their seeds bare, unencased. Angiosperms, flowering plants in which the seed (encased in an ovary) is more fully protected, appeared suddenly during the Cretaceous period (roughly 100 million years ago). Eventually they dominated the more primitive spore-bearing forms of green life, probably partly because the well-developed seed embryo, clinging to the parent plant until thoroughly mature, had the edge over the naked, randomly shed seed. Still, we know so little.

But we know enough of the internal workings of the seed to stand in awe at its variety, its toughness, its practical simplicity.

Dormancy

We're just beginning to appreciate too how much is still unknown about dormancy in seeds. If you've ever tried unsuccessfully to start a row of lettuce in midsummer heat, you have an idea of how a dormant seed behaves. It refuses to germinate, even when it is otherwise viable, when it lacks the right temperature, moisture, and oxygen supply that would ordinarily favor germination. Something has blocked the seed's response to these usually effective stimuli.

Although it's annoying to miss a seeding you've counted on, the ability of seeds to remain dormant, in varying degrees, has contributed to the survival of seed-bearing plants as we know them. Certainly a plant that needs 90 days of warm weather to mature will be doomed to failure if it sprouts as soon as it matures at the end of the summer, shortly after the first frost. Lettuce, likewise, has less chance of success under random conditions when sown in hot, dry soil than it does in the moist, cool surroundings that promote its quick growth. Dormancy, then, is a protective device, designed to assure the continuity of the species.

A seed may be dormant because its embryo is still immature, its seed coat is impermeable to water or to gases, its coat is too unyielding to permit embryo growth (although this is rare), or because of a metabolic block within the embryo. Often, more than one of these factors is operative.

Breaking Dormancy

As a gardener, it is often in your interest to try to break dormancy in certain kinds of seeds. Since you intend to give the plant special care and optimum conditions, you can often do this and get away with it. For example, you are anxious to raise a fine bed of lettuce to eat with your midsummer tomatoes—a real mark of gardening expertise—how do you give your lettuce seeds the message that it's all right for them to sprout?

Studies of seed in research laboratories have furnished valuable clues to the interruption of dormancy. The period is relative, not absolute. In fact, there seems to be general agreement among a number of scientists who have studied this phenomenon that the whole question of seed dormancy must be considered a matter of balance between the growth-promoting and growth-inhibiting substances that are found in all plants.

So how do you tip that balance in your favor? Here is what the experts have discovered:

1. Chilling the seed often breaks dormancy.

2. Subjecting the seed to light—even a dim continuous light or a sudden bright photoflash—will sometimes help, especially with lettuce. The light needn't be intense. Germination depends on the total amount received. The dimmer the light, the longer exposure necessary.

3. Exposure of some seeds to red light (660 nanometers) promotes seed germination. Experiments with lettuce bear this out. Far red (730 nanometers) has been found to inhibit seed germination. Practically speaking, this means that hard-to-germinate seeds will often do better under fluorescent plant lights (see chapter 10). There are some seeds, for example, that won't germinate when shaded by leaf cover above them, probably because the leaves filter out helpful rays while allowing the inhibiting far-red light to reach the seeds.

4. Experimental studies have shown that the application of gibberellic acid often promotes germination in dormant seeds. Gibberellins (growth-stimulating substances secreted by plants) are found in a wide variety of plants, particularly in the seed and bud tissue. Commercial preparations are sold by several seed companies. See "Sources for Some Items Mentioned in the Book," page 355.

Dormancy is seldom a problem in home gardening, except for some heat-sensitive seeds like lettuce and celery. If you save your own seeds, you'll find that carrots and parsnips, for example, need a month of afterripening following harvest, before they'll germinate. Beans, mustard, and many other vegetable seeds never go dormant. Seed you've purchased has had time, of course, to undergo any necessary afterripening in the months between collection and planting.

3
Choose Your Medium

The first step in starting your seeds on their way to being the plants they really want to be is to prepare a growing medium that will nurture the seeds through the critical germination and seedling stages. The stuff to which you entrust your seeds should be:

- Free from competing weed seeds, soil-borne diseases, and fungus spores.
- Able to absorb and hold quantities of moisture.
- Not so densely packed that vital air is excluded.
- Naturally derived and free from any substance you would not want to put in your garden.
- Noncrusting.

Since the physical conditions of their surroundings—warmth, moisture, air, and light—are more important to germinating seedlings than the nutrient content of the soil, these first mixtures in which you plant your seeds needn't be rich—in fact it's better if they're not—but they should be light, spongy, and moist.

Three Favorites

I've had good results planting seeds in each of the following three media.

Vermiculite is a form of mica which has been "popped" like popcorn by exposing it to intense heat. The resulting flakes are light and capable of holding large amounts of water. Be sure to buy horticultural vermiculite, not that sold for the building trade, which is coarser and often contains substances toxic to plant roots. Horticultural vermiculite is a completely natural product and a wonderful soil conditioner. It is especially useful for sowing fine seeds.

A mixture of equal parts of vermiculite, *milled* sphagnum moss, and perlite. This makes a spongy, friable seedbed that promotes good root development. Perlite, despite its plastic appearance, is a natu-

11

Three widely available ingredients for seedling-raising media.

Mixing bagged potting soil, perlite, and vermiculite.

ral product, a form of volcanic ash, and while I do not like to use it alone, as I do vermiculite in some cases, it is a fine component of this seed-starting mix. The moss must be milled sphagnum, which is very fine, not peat moss, which is too coarse for small seeds and tends to dry and crust. Mix these three components together thoroughly *before* dampening. A large old tub or bucket set on newspaper makes the job easier and spillage less of a problem. When moistening this and all other soil mixtures, I like to use warm water because it is more readily absorbed. This seems to be especially important for mixtures containing sphagnum moss, which tends to float on cold water in a dustlike layer that takes ages to soften and swell. It is also a good idea to prepare your soil mixture several hours before you intend to plant seeds. Then, if you *have* added too much water, you can simply pour off any that puddles on the upper surface, before planting the seeds.

A three-layer arrangement composed of torn shreds of sphagnum moss put down first and well dampened, then a one-inch layer of good soil, either loam from the garden or potting soil, topped by a

*Peeling a "scalp"
of moss from a
rock in the creek.*

13

Gathering moss from rocks by our creek.

Separating wads of moss into small, manageable shreds.

half-inch layer of vermiculite. The bottom layer of moss should not be finely milled. I use clumps of moss gathered in our woods. The air spaces trapped by the ferny fronds of the moss promote excellent root development, I've found. I am very careful, though, to tear up the wads of moss into small pieces, so that individual plants can more easily be removed when it's time to transplant them. There is some evidence that sphagnum moss exerts a mild antibiotic effect which would help to control bacterial diseases of seedlings.

Alternative Media

I'd not recommend starting seeds in plain garden soil, since it tends to pack and crust when kept in shallow containers indoors. In addition, unsterilized garden soil may harbor fungi that cause damping-off, a disease that makes young seedlings shrivel and wilt at soil level, and sometimes even interferes with complete germination. Soil in which such diseased seedlings have been grown must be pasteurized (see page 18) before another batch of seeds is planted in it.

15

There's nothing absolute about these mixtures that I use, though. Other gardeners have obtained good results with the following seed-starting media. What you choose may depend partly on what is easily available to you, and on your personal reactions to the feel of the stuff.

Other options are:

- Equal parts of milled sphagnum moss and vermiculite.
- One part milled sphagnum moss and two parts each of vermiculite and perlite.
- Shredded moss alone (well dampened beforehand).
- A cube of sod—turned grass side down—works well for the planting of larger seeds like squash, melon, and cukes, and supports the seedling until it is planted out in the garden.

Feeding the Seedlings

Neither vermiculite, perlite, nor sphagnum moss contains the nutrients necessary to support plant growth. Seedlings growing in these substances, or mixtures of them, must be fed regularly until they get their roots in real soil. (See chapter 9.)

Such liquid feeding, carried on over a period of weeks, amounts to hydroponic culture, with the growing medium serving only to hold the plants upright and condition the roots. We like to give our seedlings the benefit of the more complex interactions taking place in real soil, and so we transplant them, eventually, to a growing medium.

Potting Mixtures

There are all kinds of potting mixture recipes from which to choose. Here are some options, along with a few hints about their suitability or limitations:

1. Equal amounts of:

    - Commercial potting soil or leaf mold.
    - Sphagnum moss or peat moss.
    - Perlite or sharp sand.

This is the formula for potting soil that Thalassa Cruso recommends in her book *Making Things Grow Outdoors* (Knopf). For fast-growing seedlings, I like to change the proportions to two parts soil or one part soil and one part compost, mixed with one part moss and one part sand or perlite. As originally formulated, for house plants, the mixture is a bit lean to support strong seedling growth.

2. Equal amounts of:

- Compost.
- Good loamy soil.
- Sharp sand, perlite, or vermiculite, or a mixture of all three, totalling one part.

3. A rich mixture, good for lettuce and cabbage transplants, is:

- One part leaf mold.
- Two parts loamy soil.
- One part compost or rotted, sifted manure.

4. One part (one-quart measure, for example) of each of the following:

- Loamy soil.
- Perlite.
- Vermiculite.
- Milled sphagnum moss.
- Sharp sand.

This too is mostly physical support for the plants. Transplants growing in this mixture must be fertilized often.

5. Another mixture is:

- Four parts loamy soil.
- Two parts peat moss or sphagnum moss.
- Two parts leaf mold or compost.
- Two parts vermiculite.
- Six teaspoons dolomitic limestone.

If you want to formulate your own potting mixture from what you have or can readily find, you'll probably be on safe ground if you include each of the following:

- Soil, preferably loam, for nutrients.
- Sand or perlite for drainage. Gravel may also be used in the bottom of a solid container, but not as part of a soil mix.
- Compost, leaf mold, vermiculite, or moss for water retention.

A part, of course, can be any measure of volume ranging from a teacup to a bushel basket, as long as the measurement used is consistent. I'd suggest making up more soil mix than you think you'll need, while you have all the ingredients assembled. Mix the components thoroughly as you go, just as if you were making granola.

Heat Treatment

Commercial potting soil is usually sterile, but garden soil is, of course, teeming with organisms. Most of them are beneficial. If you've had trouble in years past with damping-off and other fungus diseases attacking your seedlings, or if you are reusing soil from last year's seedlings, you might need to heat-treat your soil.

Before heating the soil, moisten it thoroughly so that small puddles form when you press your finger into it. Bake the soil in metal pans in a preheated 275°F. (135°C.) oven. Small amounts, a gallon or so by volume, should be ready within 30 to 40 minutes. Larger quantities, a half bushel or so, may need to remain in the oven for 1½ hours. It is important that the soil be wet. The steam generated by the water penetrates the spaces in the soil. Dry soil takes much longer to treat and smells much worse.

A meat thermometer inserted in the soil will indicate when the brew has arrived at the proper temperature to kill off offending organisms. Damping-off fungi, for example, die at 130°F. (54°C.), and 160°F. (71°C.) kills most other plant viruses and pathogenic bacteria. Avoid overheating the soil, for you want to retain as many of the more numerous helpful soil microorganisms as possible. Also, in soil that is held at temperatures above 180°F. (82°C.) dissolved salts are released, which then become toxic to plants. Even at 160°F. (71°C.) some salt-releasing soil break-down begins.

George Abraham, author of *The Green Thumb Book of Fruit and Vegetable Gardening* (Prentice-Hall), says that you can also kill off most soil pathogens by heating the soil in a pressure cooker for 20 minutes at five pounds of pressure. Pouring boiling water over a flat of soil does not sterilize it, but effectively kills many microorganisms. Soil that has been baked should be rubbed through a hardware cloth screen to break up the clumps before using.

Temperature Necessary
to Kill Soil-Inhabiting Pests

Pests or Group of Pests	30 Minutes at Temperature	
Nematodes	120°F.	(49°C.)
Damping-off and soft-rot organisms	130°F.	(54°C.)
Most pathogenic bacteria and fungi	150°F.	(65°C.)
Soil insects and most plant viruses	160°F.	(71°C.)
Most weed seeds	175°F.	(79°C.)
A few resistant weeds, resistant viruses	212°F.	(100°C.)

From *Organic Gardening Under Glass* by Doc and Katy Abraham, Emmaus, PA: Rodale Press, 1975.

I do not routinely heat-treat my soil, but if you need to do it, now you know how. (Plan a picnic supper or a weekend trip, because the kitchen will smell *awful!*)

Helpful Hints

Perhaps the following hints will save you a bit of trouble too.

1. The time to collect good garden soil for spring seed start-ing is in the fall, before it freezes solid. Even if you're lucky enough to have a winter thaw at the time you're doing your planting and transplanting, the soil is likely to be mucky, and you may not be able to dig very deeply either.

2.   There's leaf mold and leaf mold. Make your own seasoned pile for use in potting mixtures. One year I scraped up a bushel of lovely, crumbly, woodsy-smelling leaf mold from the edge of our woods, and put it into my soil mixture. All the seedlings growing in this "special" mixture died. I'm not sure whether the stuff was too acid or toxic in some other way, but from now on I test such soil amendments on a few plants rather than gambling my whole crop of early seedlings.

3.   Watch out for peat moss too. Personally, I don't like the stuff. It's chunky, unmercifully hard to moisten, and it crusts when it dries, making it worse than nothing. I would never use peat moss in a soil mixture when I could get milled sphagnum moss. If you must use it, wet it very thoroughly several hours before you need it.

Some sphagnum moss.

4. Sharp sand, specified in the soil recipes, is coarse builder's sand. Sand brought from the seashore is too fine and too salty. Don't use it for plants. Even lake sand or sand scraped up by the roadside is too fine for our purposes. It will pack into a cement-like mass that is death on plant roots. I know—I've used it by mistake. Once.

5. What would I use if commercial potting mixture ingredients like vermiculite and perlite were unavailable? Equal parts of:

- Compost.
- Good garden soil, rubbed through a screen.
- Torn Moss.

I would not use garden soil alone, for no matter how good the soil, it tends to pack and harden when used indoors in small lots.

4
Containers

Your seeds are ready. Your soil is mixed. Now it's time to comb closets, attic, and cellar for likely discards to hold the soil and provide a temporary home for your growing vegetable seedlings.

The ideal container for starting seeds is no more than two to three inches deep. One that is deeper will only use up more potting soil. A shallow pan, though, will dry out quickly and limit root development. The soil holders you use do not necessarily need to have drainage holes. You can prevent pooling of water around plant roots by choosing the right materials to fill the vessels (see chapter 3). While long, narrow flats fit neatly under fluorescent lights, it's a good idea to set an upper limit for the size of your soil holders. If they are too large, they will be difficult to handle when filled with wet soil, which can be surprisingly heavy.

I've grown seedlings in all of the following kinds of containers, for different reasons and with varying results. Each has its place.

Seedling containers may be purchased, recycled, or handmade.

Some are more useful than others. Certainly it is preferable, all else being equal, to make use of some of the many throwaways that clutter up our daily lives. But there *are* times when a specially prepared device will be more effective than anything else, and it's silly to make do, unless you must, when with a little effort and some scrap wood you could rig up a really fine seedling-care system. At any rate, here's my list of container candidates, briefly evaluated for effectiveness, cost, and useful life.

Eggshells and/or egg cartons. Low cost, but not really much good in the trials I've run on them. The shells can't hold much soil, and they dry out fast. I think it's a mistake, too, to start a child gardener with one of these cute but impractical gimmicks. The learn-

Celery plant in milk carton.

Broccoli seedlings in half gallon milk container, cut lengthwise.

23

ing child deserves good equipment that will help him or her to be successful. Something about planting seeds in eggshells seems to have captured the imagination of armchair gardeners, and you'll see articles in homemaking magazines suggesting the method every spring. Go ahead and try it if it appeals to you. Just don't expect great results!

Cut-down milk cartons. Yes. They're free, good for one growing season, and they fit together well under lights. You can either halve a half-gallon milk carton the long way or cut one side out of a quart carton. If you don't buy milk, no doubt your friends, relatives, or neighbors would save their cartons for you. Even the little pint and half-pint cartons may be used for larger individual transplants.

Aluminum disposable pans. The loaf pans make fine seedling trays. They last for several years, work quite well, and can be had free if you know people who will save them for you, or at modest cost when found at yard sales. The shiny sides of the loaf pan reflect light back on the seedling. One of my best generations of eggplant seedlings was raised in an aluminum loaf pan on the kitchen window-sill. Pie pans are more of a last resort for plants, for they are too shallow to hold enough soil for proper moisture and root development. They're fine for sprouting seeds, though, if you transplant promptly.

Peat pots. A tray of seedlings all neatly tucked into peat pots looks neat and satisfying. I started to use peat pots about 10 years ago and for a while I bought hundreds each season and put each transplant in one. Now I use them much less than I formerly did, for despite the assumption that plant roots will readily penetrate the walls of the pot and find the surrounding soil, I have not found this to be true in all cases. More than once I've uprooted a plant and found its roots pretty well confined to the peat pot. I want more than this for my plants, so I am using peat pots less and less for plants that can be transplanted (lettuce, pepper, tomato, etc.) I still plant some melon seeds in them and occasionally a few cukes. Also, unless grouped closely together, peat pots dry out fast.

Peat pellets, compressed soil pots in netting, seem to offer less resistance to plant roots than the peat pots, if you remove the net at planting-out time. Even though there are air spaces in the net, it often appears to inhibit plant roots. And the soil mixture sometimes contains a chemical fertilizer. They are easy to use, neat, expensive, and can't be reused.

Cut-down plastic gallon jugs have worked fairly well for me, but I prefer the long, narrow cut-down milk cartons, which seem to accommodate more seedlings and waste less space under lights. These jugs are free, lightweight, last two or three years, and may be further recycled by saving the cutoff top to put over seedling plants in the garden for frost protection.

Shoes. Yes, shoes. I tried planting melon seeds in cast-off shoes last year, on the advice of an elderly gardener whose flourishing crops indicate he must be doing something right. The shoes were fun to use and they certainly made a stir when visitors noticed them, but

Cucumber plants in shoe.

I can't honestly say that they made any difference in the plants that grew in them. They didn't seem to hurt, though. The kind of shoe to use is a moccasin or oxford sport shoe with low heels, not a platform or high-heeled shoe. What next!

Market-packs, those rectangular trays made of pressed fiber, seem to me to be preferable to peat pots. The packs are not cheap, but they last for several years, fit together well in storage, and allow plenty of depth for root development. Also, unlike the larger flats, they may be kept on a sunny windowsill.

Flower pots are expensive, long-lasting, and fine for special transplants. They are the best container for starting watercress seeds, since they can be kept in a tray of water so that the soil is constantly moist. Too costly and unwieldy for most transplanting and growing on, though, as far as I'm concerned.

Household discards like chipped enamel broiler pans, rusty cake tins, or lopsided dishpans make good containers for groups of transplants. Old refrigerator crisper drawers work well too, especially for lettuce and other leafy crops grown under lights in winter, since they hold plenty of soil.

Cottage cheese cartons cost nothing and outlast at least one use. I use them mostly for give-away seedlings, since in my setup the round planting shape wastes space under the lights. They do fit on most windowsills, though, which can be a boon to the gardener without lights. Incidentally, you'll probably need to provide some protection—a tray or foil liner—to prevent spills and splashes from spotting your windowsills.

Foil-lined berry boxes are a rather makeshift arrangement, but I've used them in a pinch, and the foil held the soil pretty well. You're lucky if these last through one season, but they're cheap, because you can use third-hand foil.

Flats. My favorite. When you raise your own seedlings, there is no such thing as too many flats! A flat is nothing more than a four-sided frame made of scrap wood about three inches wide, with slats nailed across one open side—a shallow, topless box. The bottom

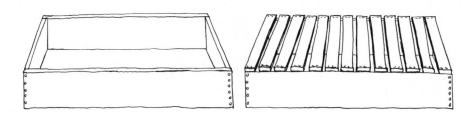

Making a flat. Nail slats across bottom, ⅛ to ¼ inch apart.

slats should be spaced one-eighth to one-fourth inch apart to allow for drainage. Most flats are rectangular, since that's the most efficient shape.

Six 12 by 18-inch flats will fit on each shelf of a 26 by 48-inch, double-bank fluorescent light cart. I wouldn't recommend making flats any larger than about 14 by 18 inches, or they'll need extra bracing to hold the weight of all that soil, and then they'll be too ungainly to handle. Flats are basic. Make as many as you can find time and materials for. You won't regret it.

Commercially made plastic trays, just the right depth (two inches) and a handy length (usually 18 to 20 inches), are costly but long-lasting. I avoid buying plastic as much as possible, and I have used only one of these—the one that came with my first growlight. In all fairness, I'd have to say that it's pleasant to use, but no better than the wooden flats, and I'm reluctant to recommend that you purchase anything made of plastic, which as you know requires petroleum for its manufacture and distribution.

Like most gardeners who can't resist starting enough plants for the whole neighborhood, my spring seedling setup is a motley arrangement of all the flats I can muster plus representatives of most of the other kinds of containers mentioned above. Which just about sums up my advice for other seed-starters! Use what you have, but aim for a growing supply of long-lasting, cheap (or free) wooden flats.

5

Sowing Seeds Early Indoors

I've been starting spring-plant seeds indoors in late winter for some years now, and I'm still learning—still making mistakes too. Once in a while the cats will knock over a flat of transplants. Then I must start all over again. And quite often I experiment with a new vegetable or flower, which shakes up the routine a bit.

But in general I've worked out a pattern for this yearly ritual. I no longer worry about whether the seeds will come up. I know now that they will, if I keep them warm enough. I no longer start my tomatoes in early February, since I've learned it's better to set out plants that are in active growth rather than overblown specimens I've been holding for three weeks until the weather was right. Neither do I sow seed as thickly as I once did, although this bad habit of the amateur gardener dies hard. It has to do, I suppose, with a lurking reluctance to trust those seeds. And only time and repeated sowing and harvest can soften that inner uneasiness, leading to the respect for each seed that gives it sufficient room to grow.

My Timetable

It is all too easy, when you have a severe case of the Februaries and long for an early start on spring, to get out the flats and the soil mixtures and start a whole batch of spring vegetables. Now, that's perfectly all right, if you can chalk the whole project up to experience or winter indoor recreation and start another batch later at the right time. Or if you live in one of those benign climates where frost won't hit after early April. But most of us would rather try to do it right the first time. So here's a little timetable to give you an idea of safe indoor starting times for your spring-planted vegetables.

- Onions—Sow 12 to 14 weeks before safe planting-out date.
- Peppers—May be planted 8 to 12 weeks before the date of the last expected spring frost.
- Eggplant—8 to 10 weeks before the last frost.

- Tomatoes—6 to 8 weeks before the last frost.
- Lettuce—5 to 6 weeks before the safe date to plant out (lettuce needn't be frost-free).
- Cole crops (cabbage, broccoli, collards, etc.)—5 to 6 weeks before the safe planting-out date (after danger of severe weather but while nights are still cold).
- Cucumbers and melons—2 to 4 weeks before the last expected frost (but don't plant out until the weather is warm and settled).

Having said this, I must admit that I do some fudging on these planting dates when I start pepper seeds in late January, about 16 to 18 weeks before our mid-May frost-free date. I can get away with this early pepper planting for two reasons: 1) I raise my seedlings under fluorescent lights, which keeps them from getting leggy and out-of-hand; and 2) The seedlings are kept quite cool, so they remain stocky and strong.

When I raised my seedlings on sunny windowsills, I started them well within the range of traditionally recommended times given on the table above—if anything, a bit on the late side, since late-winter sun is still quite weak and it's not until well into March that you can expect old Sol to do much for your windowsill plants.

The date you choose for starting your plants, then, will depend on the variety you're growing, whether you'll raise the plants in a greenhouse, on a windowsill, or under lights, and the average frost-free dates in your growing area.

A Sowing Checklist

Now that we've settled the when, let's go on to the how. Here's a checklist of seed-sowing steps.

1. Gather your equipment—the flats or other containers, planting mix, seeds, watering can, newspaper, labels, and markers you'll need.

2. Prepare a work space where you'll have room to knock things around. Spread a layer of newspapers over the area. It's easier to gather up and discard the papers than to mop up spilled potting soil.

3. Go over your seed packets and write out a label for each one, before you plant the seed. You won't believe, till you've done it, how easy it is to mix up different seed lots even when you're sure you'll remember. And if you plant five kinds of peppers and eight kinds of tomatoes as I do, labeling the seed flats is doubly important. A hot pepper seedling looks no different from a sweet bell pepper seedling, and you may want to plant out 10 of one kind but only five of the other.

For labels, I use wooden popsicle sticks broken in half, just because I have them on hand. Our friend Charley, for whose gardening expertise I have great respect, uses cut pieces of metal venetian blind slats. That's what *he* has on hand. I've also quite often simply glued scrap paper labels to the sides of wood flats (glue new labels right over the old ones next year) or clipped tags to plastic containers to identify my plants.

If you do any kind of experimenting with different fertilizers, kelp sprays, chilling treatments, or soil mixtures, of course, accurate labeling (and record keeping) are even more important.

4. Now prepare your flats. Spread a layer of newspaper on the bottom of each flat or container that has drainage holes or slits in the bottom, to keep the soil from sifting through. If the spaces between slats are wide enough, wedge in a "caulking" of torn shreds of moss.

I always spread a layer of torn moss (gathered from our woods) over the bottom of any container in which I start seeds. The moss serves as an insurance cushion, soaking up extra water so that it doesn't puddle around the roots, and at the same time holding this moisture in reserve so that the flat doesn't dry out too fast. It *is* important to tear the moss into small pieces, rather than leaving it in big wads, so that each seedling may be easily separated from the others at transplanting time. Although most experts recommend punching drainage holes in all seed planting containers, I have found that in many cases my seedlings have done quite well in containers without drainage holes, *as long as I've put this cushion of moss on the bottom.* I thoroughly dampen the moss before adding the second layer.

Next I spread a layer of planting mix (see recipes, chapter 3) over the moss, moisten it thoroughly without saturating it, and firm it well. The final layer is vermiculite which has been soaked for an hour or so to absorb its full capacity of water. Sometimes I plant seeds in plain vermiculite, omitting the moss and soil layers. The seedlings that are started this way must be transplanted sooner to a soil mix containing nutrients.

Fill the flat or container to within about a half-inch of the top. A deep container, half filled, will both shade the plants and interfere with ventilation of the seedlings.

Finally, firm the top surface of the planting medium, preferably with a flat object like a board or a brick. Now the small seeds won't tumble too far into the crevices.

5. **Ready to plant** the seeds? Good!

Scarifying helps to hasten germination of hard-coated seeds like morning glory or New Zealand spinach. Just nick the outer seed coat with a knife or file, but don't cut deep enough to damage the embryo.

Presoaking cuts several days' germination time for slow-to-sprout seeds like carrot, celery, and parsley. I've had good luck planting these seeds after having poured just-boiled water over them, draining when cool, and mixing with dry sand to avoid clumping. Some gardeners put such seeds in small muslin bags to soak overnight before planting. Other seeds like peas and beans will sprout sooner if presoaked for a few hours in warm water. Presoaking isn't necessary for most seeds you'll be planting indoors, though.

You can either scatter the seeds over the entire surface—especially when using a small container—or you can plant in rows, usually a good idea when raising seedlings in flats. At any rate, give each fine seed at least one-eighth inch of space from its neighbor; medium seeds need one-half inch of room and large seeds one inch.

Getting the seeds to go where you want them can be tricky, but the knack comes with practice. To disperse fine seeds, try sowing them from a salt shaker. Medium-size seeds like tomatoes, which may come only 20 or so to a packet in the case of some hybrid varieties, may be placed exactly where you want them with a fine tweezers. According to most of the pictures you see, the real experts sow seed by tapping it lightly directly from the seed packet. I always feel that I have better control over distribution of the seed by taking a pinch of it in my fingers and then gently rotating thumb and forefinger to gradually dislodge the seeds. For another method

31

Sowing seeds in flats of fine soil.

Precise placement of seeds—here using treezers—helps to prevent crowded straggly seedlings and makes better use of expensive seed.

that gives excellent control with practice, crease a piece of white paper and pour the seeds into the "valley," then gently tip the paper so that the seeds run down the V onto the soil. If all this is new to you, you might want to practice by sowing a few batches of seed over a piece of white paper so that you can check to see what kind of distribution you're getting.

6. Cover the seeds, except for very fine seeds, which may be simply pressed into the soil. The rule of thumb is that seeds should be covered to a depth of three times their size; a one-eighth-inch seed, then, would have three-eighths inch of soil over it. I hardly ever put more than one-half inch of soil over any seed, and that only for larger seeds. For indoor sowing I simply press a one-fourth-inch layer of fine, light soil or vermiculite over the seeds. This last layer needn't be wet. If the planting medium on the bottom is well soaked, the top will soon become damp too. The good thing about pre-soaking the growing medium is that then it's not necessary to water the planted seeds from the top. If you've ever tried this procedure, I'm sure you've found as I have that it's a surefire way to relocate all your carefully spaced seeds. If for some reason you do prefer to top-water your seedling flats, either use a gentle spray from a rubber bulb sprinkler with a flat, perforated nozzle head, or spread wet burlap over the flat and water through that. In that way you'll avoid the flooding that would carry seeds willy-nilly to the corners of the flat. I often water small flats of seeds by dipping my fingers in a bowl of water and flicking them off over the soil.

Be sure the top layer of vermiculite or whatever is pressed firmly over the seed so that the seed is closely surrounded on all sides.

7. Cover the flat (or other container) with one of the following:

    a.   damp newspaper or burlap,

    b.   scrap piece of used aluminum foil,

    c.   plastic sheet or bag slipped around flat (but watch for mold),

    d.   another seed flat; you can build a stack if your flats are roughly the same size. In fact, the soil surface will receive better ventilation if the flats don't fit exactly edge to edge. (Watch for mold here too. Provide better ventilation if it develops.)

8. Set the whole colony of flats, milk cartons, etc., in a warm place to germinate. We've found the following arrangements conducive to good germination:

- Put flats in the corner behind wood-burning stove, preferably not on the floor, where cool air settles, but elevated two feet or so on a small table or box.
- Set flats on a high shelf above a floor register. Watch for excessive drying, though.
- Small batches of seed do well when set on the pilot light on a gas stove.
- Flats set on top of a turned-on fluorescent light fixture, as on a light cart setup where we have several tiers of lights, receive steady warmth at the ends of the tubes. Once I have the earlies (onions and peppers) sprouted and under lights, I can set the flats of the next germinating seeds on the dark but warm tier above the lighted plants.

An alternative method of indoor seed planting, used by an accomplished gardener with whom I enjoy trading lore, goes like this: soak the container with water at seed-planting time, using a cut-down milk carton or plastic jug. Enclose in a plastic bag and keep the whole shebang good and warm. After three or four days, punch drainage holes in the bottom of the containers (use a pick or knife). Keep warm and covered, but allow to drain and check for mold until you see the seeds have germinated.

Presprouting Seeds

Ever since I picked up the idea from Dick Raymond's book *Down-to-Earth Vegetable Gardening,* I've been presprouting seeds of tender crops like cucumbers, squash, pumpkins, and melons. The first three are planted directly in the ground, after they've germinated, and you'll find more information on dealing with them in Section Three (individual vegetables). Melons too bear earlier if they have a head start indoors. (Some gardeners feel that cucumbers also do, but I've not been convinced of that yet.)

Presprouting melon and other cucurbit seeds has given me a much higher rate of germination than I was able to get when planting two seeds to a peat pot. I suspect that this is partly accounted for by the more constant warmth and moisture received by the specially prepared seed. Whatever the reason, it works beautifully and yields many more plants per packet. I highly recommend presprouting for those crops which need especially warm conditions during germination.

To start the seeds on their way, space them evenly on a damp double layer of paper towelling (or several thicknesses of paper napkin). Be sure that no two seeds touch. Carefully roll up the towel, keeping the seeds as well separated as possible, and tuck the rolled cylinder into a plastic bag. If you label the rolls, you can put more than one variety in the bag.

Put the bag full of damp, rolled, seed-filled towels in a warm place. I use the gas stove pilot light or the warm top of a fluorescent plant light fixture.

Check the seeds each day. Nothing will happen for several days, but germinating seeds do need a certain amount of oxygen,

Seeds to be presprouted should be evenly spread on a damp paper towel.

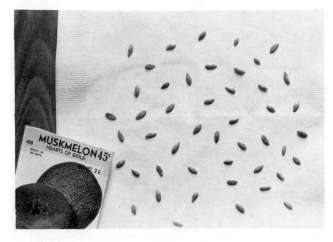

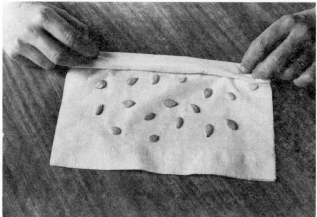

Roll up the paper carefully so that the seeds don't tumble together.

Tuck the rolled, moist paper containing the seeds into a plastic bag and put it in a warm place until the seeds have germinated.

Planting pre-sprouted cucumber seeds in a peat pot.

and the small amount of air that wafts in when you peek at the seeds will do them good.

The first sign of germination in cucurbit seeds will be the development of the root. Be sure to remove your sprouted seeds from their incubator before the root hairs grow together and tangle. If one should grow through the towel—and this often happens— just tear the towel and plant the damp shred of paper right along with the seed.

Plant the presprouted seeds in a good rich potting mix that you've scooped into individual containers and premoistened. Cucurbits don't take kindly to transplanting, not with those fleshy, sappy, easily bruised roots, so your plants will stay right in these containers until they go into the garden. I do use peat pots for melons, as well as an occasional shoe as I mentioned in chapter 4. Some gardeners like the compressed peat pellets for these seeds. Individual half-pint milk cartons work well too, since the bottom may be easily removed and the whole plant clump set in the hill.

Cover the presprouted seed root lightly but firmly with soil and set the pots under lights immediately (or put them on your sunniest windowsill).

6

Germination

If you've ever lost track of a flat of germinating seeds, as I have, and discovered them too late—when the thready white stems had grown an inch before putting on pale little leaves—then you've no doubt ruefully muttered, as I have, "Out of sight, out of mind." It *is* easy, in the busy spring rush, to overlook flats of planted seedlings tucked away in out-of-the-way corners. For that reason, I like to keep my flats together, rather than scattered, and in a place where I'll see them every day and remember to check on them.

The Process of Germination

What's going on in those flats while we wait? We commonly think of germination as being equivalent to sprouting, and it's true that the final test of complete germination is the emergence of a growing root or leaf sprout from the seed. Yet the process by which a dry, dormant embryo quickens into tender, new green growth begins well before we have visible evidence of the new root or leaf.

The first step in the process of germination is the absorption of water by the seed. This is a necessary preliminary to the internal changes in the seed that trigger growth. The uptake of water by the seed (called imbibition by botanists) depends in turn on the content of the seed, the permeability of its outer layer, and the availability of the necessary amount of liquid. Seeds that contain a high percentage of protein imbibe more water than those that are high in starch. (Only under very acid or hot conditions, which don't exist in nature, will seed starch swell with water intake.) Seeds with hard coats, like morning glories, will absorb water more readily if their hard outer shell is nicked with a file. And, naturally, the seed depends not only on the presence of moisture in the soil, but also on close contact with soil particles, to permit sufficient water uptake. The fact that a seed has absorbed water is not, by the way, proof of its viability. Even dead seeds can imbibe water.

As the seed swells with water, it develops considerable pressure, pressure which eventually ruptures the seed coat (which has already been softened by the surrounding moisture) and eases the

*These seeds
have germinated.*

eruption of the root. These are the physical effects of the seed's absorption of water.

At the same time, internal metabolic changes are revving up life in the seed. Changing its chemistry from neutral to first gear, you might say. For one thing, as water is absorbed by the seed tissues, food stored in the endosperm is gradually changed into soluble form, ready to be used as a component of new tissue.

In order, though, for the starches and proteins in the endosperm to dissolve, they must often be changed into simpler forms—the starches into simple sugars like glucose and maltose, and the proteins into free amino acids and amides. The enzymes, necessary to split complex forms of stored food into simpler forms of usable food, are activated in response to the stepped-up metabolism of the seed. You will remember that even dormant seeds carry on respiration, just as people do. They take in oxygen and release carbon dioxide. The rate of respiration is markedly increased in the germinating seed, both generating and supporting the many interacting internal changes in the embryo.

Enzymes, then, direct the breakdown of certain useful stored foods. Hormones, also present in the seed, control both the transportation of newly soluble foods to different parts of the seed and the building up of new compounds from the components of those that have been broken down into simpler forms. Pea seeds, for example, synthesize new compounds during the first 24 hours of the germination process.

The product of all this stepped-up activity within the seed is new tissue, originating at growing points in the root tip, the stem, the bud, and the cotyledons. This new tissue is formed in two ways: 1) Cells already present in the seed grow longer; and 2) Cells divide to produce new cells, which then elongate.

Soil Temperature Conditions
for Vegetable Seed Germination [1]

Crop	Minimum °F.	Optimum Range, °F.	Optimum °F.	Maximum °F.
Asparagus	50	60–85	75	95
Beans, lima	60	65–85	85	85
Beans, snap	60	60–85	80	95
Beets	40	50–85	85	95
Cabbage	40	45–95	85	100
Carrots	40	45–85	80	95
Cauliflower	40	45–85	80	100
Celery	40	60–70	70[2]	85[2]
Corn	50	60–95	95	105
Cucumbers	60	65–90	95	105
Eggplant	60	75–90	85	95
Lettuce	35	40–80	75	85
Muskmelon	60	75–95	90	100
Okra	60	70–95	95	105
Onions	35	50–95	75	95
Parsley	40	50–85	75	90
Parsnips	35	50–70	65	85
Peas	40	40–75	75	85
Peppers	60	65–95	85	95
Pumpkins	60	70–90	95	100
Radish	40	45–90	85	95
Swiss Chard	40	50–85	85	95
Spinach	35	45–75	70	85
Squash	60	70–95	95	100
Tomatoes	50	60–85	85	95
Turnips	40	60–105	85	105
Watermelon	60	70–95	95	105

[1] Compiled by J. F. Harrington, Department of Vegetable Crops, University of California at Davis.

[2] Daily fluctuation to 60° or lower at night is essential.

Studies done on lettuce seeds, for example, show that cell division begins about 12 hours after germination has begun; the root cells show some elongation at about the same time. In corn, the first change to be observed is the enlargement of the cells, followed by cell division in the root as it emerges from the seed coat. Both kinds of tissue changes are necessary to the normal development of the seedling.

Factors Influencing Germination

Many internal and environmental conditions influence the course of germination.

The condition of the seed. A shriveled seed that has been stored too long, or under poor conditions, will have scant food stored in its endosperm. The seedling that grows from such a seed, if it germinates at all, is likely to be weak and/or stunted. Mechanical injury to the seed during harvesting or drying can injure the cotyledons, stem, or root tip, or produce breaks in the seed coat that admit microorganisms which deteriorate seed quality. The hormones that promote cell elongation are produced by the endosperm and cotyledons. Any injury, therefore, that interferes with the soundness of these hormone-producing tissues is likely to result in stunted seedlings.

The presence of water. Water must be available to the seed in amounts sufficient to start the quickening of respiration that leads to germination. But few seeds will sprout if submerged in water. Some air must also reach the seed for it to absorb the oxygen it needs. Water serves several purposes in the germinating seed. Initially, it softens the seed coat so the root can emerge more easily. Then it combines with stored foods to form soluble forms of nourishment for the seed. As growth proceeds, it helps to enlarge new cells, as directed by the hormones, and serves as a medium of transportation to take soluble foods and hormones to parts of the seedling where they're needed.

Sufficient air. Even quiescent seeds in storage need a certain minimum supply of air. The requirements of a germinating seed are

Days for Vegetable Seed to Emerge
or to Become Seedlings at Different Temperatures

Crop	32°F.	41°F.	50°F	59°F	68°F.	77°F.	86°F.	95°F.	104°F.
Asparagus	0.0	0.0	52.8	24.0	14.6	10.3	11.5	19.3	28.4
Beans, Lima	–	–	0.0	30.5	17.6	6.5	6.7	0.0	–
Beans, Snap	0.0	0.0	0.0	16.1	11.4	8.1	6.4	6.2	0.0
Beets	–	42.0	16.7	9.7	6.2	5.0	4.5	4.6	–
Cabbage	–	–	14.6	8.7	5.8	4.5	3.5	–	–
Carrots	0.0	50.6	17.3	10.1	6.9	6.2	6.0	8.6	0.0
Cauliflower	–	–	19.5	9.9	6.2	5.2	4.7	–	–
Celery	0.0	41.0	16.0	12.0	7.0	0.0	0.0	0.0	–
Cucumbers	0.0	0.0	0.0	13.0	6.2	4.0	3.1	3.0	–
Eggplant	–	–	–	–	13.1	8.1	5.3	–	–
Lettuce	49.0	14.9	7.0	3.9	2.6	2.2	2.6	0.0	0.0
Muskmelon	–	–	–	–	8.4	4.0	3.1	–	–
Okra	0.0	0.0	0.0	27.2	17.4	12.5	6.8	6.4	6.7
Onions	135.8	30.6	13.4	7.1	4.6	3.6	3.9	12.5	0.0
Parsley	–	–	29.0	17.0	14.0	13.0	12.3	–	–
Parsnips	171.7	56.7	26.6	19.3	13.6	14.9	31.6	0.0	0.0
Peas	–	36.0	13.5	9.4	7.5	6.2	5.9	–	–
Peppers	0.0	0.0	0.0	25.0	12.5	8.4	7.6	8.8	0.0
Radish	0.0	29.0	11.2	6.3	4.2	3.5	3.0	–	–
Spinach	62.6	22.5	11.7	6.9	5.7	5.1	6.4	0.0	0.0
Sweet corn	0.0	0.0	21.6	12.4	6.9	4.0	3.7	3.4	0.0
Tomato	0.0	0.0	42.9	13.6	8.2	5.9	5.9	9.2	0.0
Turnip	0.0	0.0	5.2	3.0	1.9	1.4	1.1	1.2	2.5
Watermelon	–	0.0	–	–	11.8	4.7	3.5	3.0	–

Harrington, J. F., Agricultural Extension Leaflet, 1954.

0.0 = Little or no germination

– = Not tested.

more critical. Our atmosphere contains a mixture of gases, with the oxygen portion fairly constant at 20 percent. (Some seeds—certain cereals and carrots—have been shown to germinate more completely in an even richer oxygen concentration.) Seeds also need a certain amount of carbon dioxide in order to germinate, but they don't do well if surrounded by a considerable concentration of carbon dioxide. Cucurbits (squash, melons, pumpkins, and cucumbers) have seed membranes that admit carbon dioxide more readily than oxygen,

Percentage of Normal Vegetable Seedlings Produced at Different Temperatures

Crops	32°F.	41°F	50°F.	59°F.	68°F.	77°F.	86°F.	95°F.	104°F.
Asparagus	0	0	61	80	88	95	79	37	0
Beans, lima	–	–	1	52	82	80	88	2	–
Beans, snap	0	0	1	97	90	97	47	39	0
Beets	–	114	156	189	193	209	192	75	–
Cabbage	0	27	78	93	–	99	–	–	–
Carrots	0	48	93	95	96	96	95	74	0
Cauliflower	–	–	58	60	–	63	45	–	–
Celery	–	72	70	40	97	65	0	0	–
Cucumbers	0	0	0	95	99	99	99	99	49
Eggplant	–	–	–	–	21	53	60	–	–
Lettuce	98	98	98	99	99	99	12	0	0
Muskmelon	–	–	–	–	38	94	90	–	–
Okra	0	0	0	74	89	92	88	85	35
Onions	90	98	98	98	99	97	91	73	2
Parsley	–	–	63	–	69	64	50	–	–
Parsnips	82	87	79	85	89	77	51	1	0
Peas	–	89	94	93	93	94	86	0	–
Peppers	0	0	1	70	96	98	95	70	0
Radish	0	42	76	97	95	97	95	–	–
Spinach	83	96	91	82	52	28	32	0	0
Sweet Corn	0	0	47	97	97	98	91	88	10
Tomatoes	0	0	82	98	98	97	83	46	0
Turnips	1	14	79	98	99	100	99	99	88
Watermelon	–	0	0	17	94	90	92	96	–

Harrington, J. F., Agricultural Extension Leaflet, 1954.
– = Not tested.

thus ensuring a wider range of germination time than is found in some cold-thriving vegetables. In this way, these heat-loving vegetables have a better chance that at least some of their seeds will germinate at a favorable time and avoid chancy late frosts. The oxygen taken in by the seed in respiration combines chemically with its fats and sugars, a process we call oxidation.

As gardeners, we can't manipulate the composition of the air that surrounds us, but we can make sure our germinating seeds are supplied with enough air by planting shallowly, in a loose, friable medium, and by keeping the soil moist but not waterlogged, so some air spaces remain.

Temperature. In general, seeds need warmer temperatures during germination than they will need later when they've grown into plants. There *are* differences in heat and cold sensitivity, though, between the different species. Some seeds, like lettuce, celery, and peas germinate best at low temperatures, while pepper, eggplant, melons, and others prefer more warmth. But extremes of heat and cold inhibit germination of most kinds of seeds. There are, for most seeds, optimum temperatures at which they do best, but the drop in germination with less-than-ideal temperatures is gradual, not abrupt. Seeds that germinate most completely at 75°F. (24°C.) will, nevertheless, put forth some (possibly later and less) growth at 65°F. (18°C.). Some seeds, like dock, tobacco, and evening primrose, need alternating warm and cool temperatures in order to germinate. According to studies done with those plants, it's not the rate or duration of the temperature change but simply the fact of the change itself that is effective.

The most favorable germinating temperatures for garden seeds started indoors is between 75° and 90°F. (24° and 32°C.). That's *soil temperature*. Remember that while the air temperature in a room may be 70°F. (21°C.), a moist flat of soil set on the floor may be cooler than that unless kept near a source of auxiliary heat.

While a soil-heating cable may be used to speed germination of some tricky seeds, it's just one more gadget to fiddle with. If you already *have* a soil-heating cable, I'm sure you'll find some uses for it in starting seeds, but I'd never suggest going out and buying one. There is usually at least one spot in a house—over the furnace or water heater, on top of the TV, near a wood stove or heat register, on a pilot light—where seed flats can be kept warm during germination.

Light. Most vegetable seeds are indifferent to the amount of light they receive during germination. We used to think that darkness was essential to germination, but recent studies don't seem to support that conclusion, except in the case of onion and chive seeds, which seem to be retarded by exposure to light. A few seeds, such as lettuce, celery, and primrose, germinate more completely under some conditions when they receive some light. In the case of celery and amaranth, for example, light promotes more complete germination only when the temperature is higher than that at which these seeds usually germinate best. At the lower temperatures they prefer, exposure to light doesn't seem to make much difference. The lesson from this is clear: when putting in a late planting of lettuce or celery when the weather is warm, press the seeds into moist soil, covering them lightly, if at all, with fine soil—although a few dry grass clippings should be spread over the row to prevent crusting.

Seedling flats, then, can be covered with clear plastic, wet newspapers, damp burlap, or used aluminum foil. Although they don't need light, in most cases exposure to fluorescent lights does seem to promote germination (see chapter 10).

Soil conditions. Apart from the physical conditions of friability, aeration, moisture, and fredom from water-logging, all of which promote germination, there are other conditions in the soil which may affect the outcome of seed planting.

Soils containing a high percentage of organic matter along with many microorganisms may have a higher concentration of carbon dioxide than the surrounding air, and this can affect germination, depending on the permeability of the seed coat to carbon dioxide. Seeds don't need a rich mixture to *start* germinating.

A high salt content, found in some seaside soils, can block germination by drawing water from the seed.

Some seeds respond favorably to a high calcium content in the soil.

Leaf mold from the woods may contain germination-inhibiting substances. Beech tree leaves, for example, develop a compound that inhibits germination after they've been exposed for a winter. The fresh leaves do not contain this compound. Eucalyptus leaves also contain germination-inhibiting substances. As I mentioned in chapter 3, I once killed a whole batch of seedlings by planting them in a mix containing some perfectly lovely leaf mold I had scraped up at the edge of our woods. Leaf mold, on the whole, is great stuff and we use it regularly in our garden and compost pile with no ill effect. But since many of these interactions are still little understood, I no longer collect my leaf mold for seedling mixtures in the woods, but save maple leaves from our yard trees for this purpose. (Leaf mold may also be purchased by the bag.)

Monitoring the Process

Keeping all these factors—light, temperature, water, air—in balance, while we wait for those first spears of green to show, calls for checking the seed flats at least once a day. The soil should be kept moist but not soggy. Air should be allowed to reach the soil surface at intervals, at least enough to prevent the formation of mold on the surface. Although I formerly surrounded each container of seeds with a plastic bag until the seeds germinated, I found that mold often forms on the soil because of poor air circulation, and I now simply cover the top of the flat, without surrounding it with a moisture-proof barrier. If you *do* find mold on the soil, chances are that exposing the flat to the air for an hour or so will take care of the problem.

Then, one day—often, in the case of peppers, just about when you'd given up hope—you'll notice little elbows of stems pushing through the soil surface. At this point, even though the plants aren't

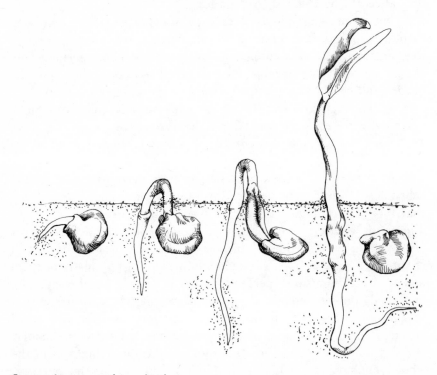

Stages of pepper seed germination.
Actual diameter of pepper seed, approximately ³⁄₁₆ inch.

quite ready to make use of light until their green seed leaves (cotyledons) emerge, I always put my plants under lights immediately. A seedling that must wave around in search of the light grows weak and spindly. Have the light there, ready and turned on, and your seedlings will be able to start in making their own food at the first possible moment.

Germination sounds complex, and it is, when you try to understand what's really happening and consider all the intricately interrelated influences that affect the outcome.

In practice, though, the process is marvelously simple and reassuring. Plant the seed at the right time, in favorable surroundings, and give it moisture, warmth, and some air. Watch for the first sprouts and tend them well. And there you are, regardless of outdoor weather, news forecasts, political shake-ups, or fuel shortages, with fresh, new green life under your roof, the promise of a bountiful garden in the months ahead.

7
What Seedlings Need

The most crucial time in the life of a seedling plant is the period just before it has broken dormancy. Each tentative-looking little plant sprout is rather like a baby. It must have its needs met immediately. If it finds only darkness when its cotyledons break through the soil surface, it will send up a pale, weak stem in search of the light it must have. If the tray in which it is growing dries out, it can no longer enter a holding stage like that it went through as a seed. There is no going back. It has started into growth, and if it is to continue, there must be moisture within reach of the roots and light on the leaves.

Light and Temperature

As soon as the plants have germinated, then, they must be given light, either from fluorescent tubes or from the sun by way of a house or greenhouse window. I try to catch my seedlings even before the whole cotyledon has emerged, when the seed is still just a sprout. This is easier to determine when the seeds haven't been deeply buried. Then when I put them under lights I know they'll have the stimulation they need from the very beginning. (For more about light sources, intensity, etc., refer to chapter 10.)

Temperature requirements of seedling plants are not as critical as light, perhaps, but nevertheless are important. Once the plants are growing above ground, they need less warmth than required for germination. The majority of vegetable plants that germinate most rapidly at 70° to 80°F. (21° to 27°C.) do well when grown at 60° to 70°F. (16° to 21°C.), with night temperatures about 10 degrees lower. Exceptions are mentioned in section 3. Cool growers like lettuce and onions will still flourish when temperatures drop to 50°F. (10°C.).

In a severe winter, seedlings kept in an unheated room must occasionally be moved or covered to protect them from freezing. Undesirably high temperatures may be a more common problem. Although I keep flats of germinating seeds in the warm (70° to 80°F.) corner where heat rises from our wood-burning stove in the kitchen, I move the flats to an unheated back room as soon as the seedlings are up. The temperature in this room averages about 50° to 55°F. (10° to 13°C.) during the late-winter and early-spring seed-starting season. Plants grown indoors in warm rooms put on weak, spindly, sappy growth that is difficult to manage under lights and to prepare for the transition to colder outdoor temperatures. Start seeds warm and grow seedlings cool.

There is, in fact, some evidence that judicious chilling of tomato seedlings, at just the right time, promotes earlier and heavier fruiting. Dr. S. W. Wittmer of Michigan State University found that tomato seedlings kept at temperatures of 52° to 56°F., starting immediately before the seed leaves opened and continuing for 10 to 21 days, developed up to twice the usual number of flowers in the first cluster, and often in the second. Since the position of the lowest group of flower buds on the plant is determined approximately a month to six weeks before blooming, the plant must be chilled during this early stage, before the opening of its first true leaves, in order to induce earlier, lower-on-the-stem flowering.

Other vegetable horticulturists report that peppers may also be induced to form early buds by chilling the plants in the seed-leaf stage. When I read these reports, it dawned on me that I'd been prechilling my pepper seedlings for years, though not through any planned program aimed at early bloom. The peppers *are* in bloom when I set them out in the garden in May, partly because I always start them extra early—in January—and partly, perhaps, because I have inadvertently chilled them at the right time. The back room where my seedlings grow is not much warmer than 50°F. at night during February and much of March, and only in the high 50s, if that, during the day.

This method has not so far caught the interest of commercial growers, probably because it would be cumbersome to carry out on a large scale. One vegetable horticulturist whom I consulted gave little credence to the idea, possibly because his studies have concentrated on large-scale plant-raising operations. We home gardeners, though, are free to fool around with some of these tricks. If they work, that's proof enough for us that the practice is worth trying.

Space

Soon after the seed leaves unfold, conditions often become crowded in the flat, unless you have spaced your seeds with mathematical precision. I know I usually need to thin mine, especially

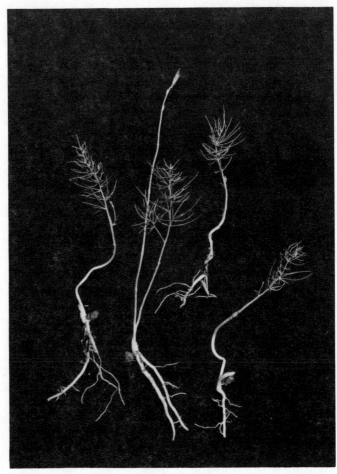

*Asparagus seed-
lings showing
root develop-
ment. Note the
seed cases still
attached to some.*

lettuce and cabbage. And the best way to do this is not to yank the extra plants out of the soil, but to cut them off, using a small embroidery or nail scissors. As you remember, a considerable amount of root growth often takes place even before the green leaves go into operation, and the roots of plants you want to save may be damaged by pulling out neighboring roots.

Superfluous seedlings are just like weeds. Thinning the seedlings, so that their leaves don't overlap, cuts down on competition for light, moisture, and nutrients and also helps to promote better circulation of air around the plant.

There is more going on in the roots of even the youngest seedling plant than most of us ever fully recognize. Roots not only anchor the plant and absorb nourishment, they are also responsible for maintaining the pressure that enables the plant to raise water, against the force of gravity, to its topmost leaves and stems. In many plants, roots give off exudates which help to define and sometimes defend the plant's territory. Roots of all plants synthesize many of the amino acids that control the plant's growth.

Roots are examples of "being and becoming," to borrow Aristotle's phrase (used perceptively by Charles Morrow Wilson in his book *Roots: Miracles Below*). Root growth is continuous. It does not stop, ever, as long as the plant lives. At the same time, root filaments are continuously dying. Root hairs, the tiny fibers that form the point of contact and exchange between the soil and the plant, constantly extend into new territory. They seek moisture, but they also need air. A soil mix that is half solid matter and half pore space, with about half of the pore space filled with water, provides ideal conditions for root growth.

8
Transplanting

By the time they have developed their first true leaves, your seedlings are ready to be transplanted. It's better to get the job done before the plant has a second set of fully developed leaves, because from then on the likelihood is that the stem will be longer and more easily injured, and the roots may be lengthy and trailing and difficult to trace through the soil mix. If you have a great many seedlings to transplant, and you must work gradually because there are also 100 or so other things you must accomplish in a day, then it would be wise to start moving some of your seedlings before the first true leaves are completely developed so the last batch you work with is not too far along.

Some accomplished gardeners prefer to do their transplanting when the seedling is even younger, just after the cotyledons have emerged completely, and the plant is standing upright in the soil. This method does have several advantages:

- It permits you to save almost every plant grown from expensive seed, the kind that comes 12 seeds to a $1.00 packet, since none are lost in thinning.
- It puts the plants into a richer soil mix at an early age and frees your seed-planting trays and mixes for the next wave of plantings.

I have used this method occasionally for selected flower and vegetable seeds, but generally I prefer to thin my seedlings in the cotyledon stage and let them develop their first set of true leaves before transplanting, so that I can choose the very best ones from the flat.

Why Transplant?

Plants that take well to the transplanting process are generally greatly improved by the experience. The following plants not only *can*, but *should* be transplanted:

asparagus	eggplant
broccoli	endive, escarole
cabbage	leeks
cauliflower (carefully)	lettuce
celery (also carefully)	onions
chives	peppers
	tomatoes

Other plants, because of their fleshy or deep roots or their special sensitivity to root insult, should not be transplanted. This group includes:

Chinese cabbage	pumpkins
corn	root crops, except
cucumbers	beets, turnips,
melons	and celeriac
	squash

Those seedlings that move up to this next level in the indoor growing world are improved in several ways.

Stimulation of feeder roots. Some fine roots are broken in the transplanting process. As a result, a new, bushier network of feeder roots is formed. If roots are very long and thready, as in the case of onions, I often prune them to one inch or so, at the same time pruning the top growth to correspond.

Room to grow. Crowded seedlings become weak and spindly-stemmed, and the lack of air circulation between them can promote disease. Giving them more root and leaf space promotes the health and strength of the plant and ensures that the root ball of the plant will have sufficient protective soil around it when you cut the plants apart later to set them out in the garden.

Richer soil. Although seedlings started in soil-less mixes seem to be able to subsist on liquid feedings for quite a while, I like to get my plants into a good soil mixture, so that they can take advantage of the micronutrients and the beneficial interactions in the microscopic soil life, limited as these may be in the small space of a wooden flat.

Selection and evaluation. Discarding a new young green sprout is always a painful process for me. In fact, I usually keep a small container of these extra plants by the kitchen window for a week or so after transplanting, in the hope that some visitor will adopt them. Selection, nevertheless, is a necessary step in raising the best possible nursery plants. No matter how sparingly I try to sow the seed, or how carefully I thin the seedlings, I usually have more seedlings in a starting flat than I will have room for under lights or in the garden row.

And so I choose, as I transplant, the seedlings that appear most vigorous. I look for good green leaves, symmetrical and well developed. Deformed cotyledons sometimes indicate early damage to the seed. Early-sprouting vegetable seeds usually grow into vigorous plants, unless they are retarded by waiting without light for the other, slower seeds to come up. There is, in fact, some evidence that early emergence is an indication of seed vigor and ultimate high yield.

Root growth is as important as top growth in evaluating seedlings. Look for a compact, well-developed root ball. A fringe of well-branched feeder roots will do far more for the developing plant than a single, thready trailing root. It is also difficult to transplant a long, single-filament root without tangling it, bruising it, or doubling it back on itself.

How to Do It

Transplanting is more than a technique. When done well, it involves respect for the young life of the plant, even a certain empathy that can sense the thrust and direction of the tender growing roots, the reach and promise of the unfolding green leaves. The plant wants to grow. It is, you might say, programmed to grow. Having set the process in motion by planting the seed, we now have the opportunity to give each seedling the most careful treatment, so that it will continue growing smoothly on its way to producing our food.

Let's suppose that you have a flat of seedlings that you want to transplant into a larger, deeper flat of richer potting soil. (This is the progression I use in most of my transplanting. As I mentioned in chapter 4, I seldom transplant into peat pots any more, although

I do make considerable use of the reusable market-packs for small groups of seedlings.)

Prepare the flat. Your first step will be to prepare the flat. Spread a double layer of newspaper on the bottom to keep soil from sifting through the drainage cracks. Next, arrange a one-inch layer of torn pieces of moss on top of the newspaper. This is not absolutely necessary, but in my work with young plants I've found that those planted over a torn-moss foundation develop excellent root systems. If you have no source of fairly coarse natural moss, I'd use plain potting soil, but I'd be sure to include some perlite or sand in the mix to promote drainage. Don't use a bottom layer of plain finely milled horticultural sphagnum moss. It's too fine.

Moisten the moss, pat it down flat, and fill the rest of the flat to within about one-half inch of the top with potting soil. Usually I moisten the soil thoroughly before setting the seedlings in their places, although at times I have put the seedlings into dry holes, watered them in, pulled fresh soil over the roots, and then watered again lightly. This unorthodox method has given me equally good results.

The handle of a fork or spoon may be used to prick out seedlings from a flat without disturbing other plants.

Transplants may also be moved into plant bands, which should be wedged snugly together in a bowl or pan to prevent drying. You can make your own plant bands by taping a piece of doubled newspaper about seven or eight inches wide and four inches high around a jar to shape it. While the paper is on the jar, fold in one end as you would a package, but don't tape it shut. Place the tiny paper bags side by side in a pan—an old roasting pan works well—and put one-half inch of soil in the bottom of each bag to anchor it in place before inserting the seedling. The folded-over bottom, if it hasn't rotted away at planting time, may simply be peeled off before setting the plant in the garden.

Prick out the seedlings. Most seed-starting gardeners soon acquire a favorite tool for this purpose. The miniature house-plant shovels that usually come as part of a set are too clumsy for most small, closely spaced seedlings. I use the slim, slightly pointed handle of an old salad fork. Wooden popsicle sticks, pencils, and old screwdrivers can serve the same purpose. What you want is an instrument that will lift out the seedling with the least damage to its roots and those of its neighboring plants.

When possible, remove each seedling from the flat with a clump of soil around its roots.

When seedling roots are compact enough to come up in a relatively dense cluster, it is often a good idea to water the old flat shortly before removing the seedlings from it, so that enough soil will cling to the roots to help prevent transplanting shock. Seedlings raised in vermiculite, which generally falls away readily anyway, or those with long, extensive root systems, won't benefit from prewatering. It's better not to dip the roots of seedlings in water before planting them in their new location. This makes the roots cling together when they should, instead, be individually surrounded by soil.

Remove the seedlings one by one from their old quarters, planting each one before digging up another. Even a few minutes of air-drying will adversely affect those delicate roots. Hold the seedlings by their first leaves rather than by the easily bruised stem, unless there is a large clump of heavy soil adhering to the roots.

Replant the seedling in its new place. You have several options here. You can, as suggested above, set the plants in already-moist-

When transplanting, hold seedlings (pepper here) by their first leaves rather than by easily bruised stem.

ened soil, or in holes of dry soil (over wet moss) into which you pour water, then firm in dry soil and finish with a light watering to further settle the seedling.

Or, if you are putting the young plants into pots, you can tuck a wad of damp moss in the bottom, set the plant on it, half fill the pot with soil, water the plant in, and add enough additional dry soil to fill the pot.

If you're potting up a plant that has long roots, try this: put some soil or moss in the pot and turn it on its side. Position the plant in the pot with its roots spread out on the growing medium, and gradually fill in with soil as you tilt the pot bit by bit back to its normal position. Instead of being coiled around each other, the roots will have more of their surface exposed to soil.

Set the seedlings just slightly deeper than they were in their original container. Tomatoes can be planted as deep as the root will allow. Plants that form a leafy crown, though, like lettuce and cabbage, should not have soil pulled over or into the crown. When settled into place, the first leaves of young transplants should be at about the same level as the sides of the container.

Press the soil gently but firmly over and around the roots. Roots need a certain amount of air, which should be provided by

... If you're potting a plant with long roots. . .
put soil and moss in pot . . . pot on side . . . fill in sod as you tilt pot back to normal position.

good soil mix that is not overwatered, but they also need close and immediate contact with soil particles in order to absorb necessary nutrients.

Except for onions, leeks, and chives, which grow spears rather than spreading leaves, transplants should be spaced at least two inches apart in the flat. Three inches is better for tomatoes, cabbage, and eggplant that won't be transplanted again.

Repeated transplanting, up to three or four times before planting out, produces a stocky, well-rooted plant, but it is not really necessary. Most busy gardeners are content to give their plants one uprooting indoors, and another when setting them out. If you like to experiment, I'd suggest trying an extra transplanting for lettuce, onions, and tomatoes. Eggplants are a bit fussier about being moved and cauliflower is downright neurotic about repeated transplanting, so I'd steer clear of them.

Finally, watch the newly transplanted seedlings for signs of wilting. If they droop, even though you've watered well when planting them, don't pour on more water. The roots are already doing all they can. Instead, help to balance the plant's moisture supply by arranging a tent of damp newspaper over the flat, or by enclosing it in a large plastic bag or covering it with a large roaster lid or other protective layer that will not rest on the plants. Keep new transplants out of direct sun for a day. I put mine back under fluorescent lights half a day after moving them, as long as they show no signs of wilting. Wilted plants should be kept shaded and cool until they perk up, which shouldn't take more than a day or two at the most.

9
Growing On

Your young plants should be showing more new growth within a week after transplanting. The trick now is to keep them growing steadily until it's time to prepare them for planting outdoors.

Watering

It's important to remember, first of all, that soil in containers dries much more rapidly than the deeper, heavier soil you have in your garden. Wilting that lasts more than a day may retard the seedling, so it is best to check the flats every day to see whether they need watering. I usually water my transplants in flats about every third to fifth day. But I base the decision on the condition of the soil, not the time schedule. Short of wilting the plants, it is a good idea to let the soil dry out from time to time. Then the roots are stimulated to grow into the air spaces between the soil particles in search of water.

How do you tell when a flat needs watering? By touch, by feel, and by sight. Touch the soil. Poke your finger into a corner where it won't disturb any roots. If the soil feels powdery or dry, it needs water. When you've been handling flats for a while, you can judge by feeling the weight of the flat whether it has lost most of its water. A well-watered flat is heavier than a dry one. Other than dry soil surface, visible signs like drooping plants indicate a serious lack of water.

Does water temperature and composition matter? I think it does. Our well water is extremely cold, and so I always use tepid water for seedlings of heat-loving plants like melons, cukes, peppers, eggplants, globe artichokes, etc. Water temperature is less critical for the cool-leaning brassicas, lettuce, onions, and such; still, I try to temper extremely cold water to a more moderate 70°F. (21°C.) to avoid shocking the plant. If your water is chlorinated, I'd suggest letting it stand overnight with as much surface as possible exposed to the air—in a bucket or dishpan—before using it to water seedlings. The chlorine won't do the plants any good, and it may kill beneficial soil bacteria. Water that has gone through a water softener should not be used to water plants. It contains potentially toxic amounts of sodium. Some gardeners who are good at planning ahead fill plastic jugs with water and keep them ready so that they always have room-temperature water available for their plants.

Water is powerful stuff. It can nourish your plants, or it can kill. Water is necessary, physically, to maintain the turgidity of the plant so that there is a continuous column of moisture in the cells. It is also indispensable to the intricate intracellular chemical processes that keep the plant growing. But too much water ruins the soil tilth and spoils the plant. Soil that is continuously waterlogged has no air spaces to promote root growth and support helpful soil bacteria. Then other less beneficial organisms take over, rot sets in, and the roots suffer. As you remember, the best potting soil mixtures include moss or some other water-holding medium, and perlite or sand to promote good drainage.

Some expert seedling raisers water their flats from the bottom. This practice supplies water quickly to the root zone and avoids excess surface dampness that can encourage damping-off disease. It is a messy business if you don't have a good setup for it, but if you have a large waterproof trough in which you can partially submerge a flat, or preferably two or three at a time, the method might be

A flat of once-transplanted pepper seedlings.

61

practical for you. Each flat must, of course, have drainage slits or holes in the bottom so that water can be absorbed. Leave each container of seedlings in the water until the top surface starts to look dark.

Bottom watering is really more of a greenhouse refinement, though. I've had no problem at all with top watering of either seedlings or more mature plants. I just take a bucket of water to my plant room and dip a pitcher into it so that I don't need to keep running back and forth to the kitchen faucet. Watering from above also carries nutrients down through the soil to the roots and makes it feasible to top-dress the plants with compost or rich soil if necessary.

If you get to the point, as many of us do, where growing plants are taking over your house, you might want to invest in one of the indoor hoses that will fit on a faucet and allow finger-tip control of the water flow. Such a device can easily reach flats in the farthest corner of a large double-tiered plant light cart like the one I use, in which plants are kept so close to the lights that their containers must be moved in order to water them, since there is no room to fit a pitcher or a watering can between plant and light.

Maintaining Humidity

Humidity—the amount of moisture in the air—is important to plants. They lose a great deal of moisture through their leaves when the air is excessively dry as it can be in both centrally heated homes and in rooms warmed by a wood stove during cold weather. Plants suffer when humidity falls below 30 percent. They do best in the 50 to 70 percent range. Higher humidity, as mentioned above, invites fungus and other disease problems. Misting plants helps, but only temporarily. The best way to increase humidity around your seedlings is to set them on containers of damp moss, vermiculite, or one inch of pebbles in one-half inch of water.

Potted seedlings that spend more than a month or two on this damp bed may send out roots into the moss or vermiculite. You can prevent this by setting a rack or some kind of improvised spacer between the damp bed and the plants. This is usually more of a problem with long-term house plants than with quick-turnover seedlings, though.

Draping a plastic tent over the indoor garden helps to hold

humidity in, although it also cuts down on air circulation. During the winter, air circulation in a heated house is usually no problem since the decrease in air pressure caused by burning fuel causes intake of fresh air, thus keeping interior air in motion.

If you notice green algae or fuzzy mold growing on the soil surface, your plants probably have more water and less air than they need. Run a small fan in the area, remove any plastic covers, and hold off on water for a few days. You might also try sprinkling some powdered charcoal over the soil surface to correct the problem.

Fertilization

Fertilizing, like watering, is a necessity that should not be overdone, or salts will accumulate in the soil to a toxic concentration. It is better to give frequent small feedings than occasional large feedings to very young seedlings. For the first three weeks, in fact, any fertilizer the seedlings receive should be half-strength rather than the full-strength mixture (1½ teaspoons to a gallon of water, for example, instead of one tablespoon to the gallon). Newly emerged seedlings, still in the cotyledon stage, have absorbed enough of the seed's stored nourishment to get them well off the ground. I don't fertilize my seedlings until they've begun to develop their true leaves.

Seedlings growing in nutrient-free vermiculite should receive about two feedings of diluted fertilizer a week. Later, when they have been transplanted to a richer mixture containing soil and/or compost, they can go on a 10-day to two-week fertilizing schedule. I use diluted fish emulsion, a source of trace minerals as well as the three major elements, to feed my seedling plants. The usual dilution, one tablespoon to the gallon, seems to hold true for most of the commonly sold fish-fertilizer preparations. I've found that the labels of these bottles usually become hopelessly frayed and streaked before the contents are used up, so I'd suggest jotting down the appropriate dilutions for different plants while you can still read the label.

Water drained from sprouting seeds, the alfalfa and mung bean sprouts I raise in our kitchen for fresh winter vegetables, is valuable for feeding to plants. I am convinced that the sprout water helps to foster plant growth, although I can't cite any scientific studies as proof. In my one "controlled" experiment, two flats of Elite onion seedlings that I watered-in at transplanting time with sprout water grew thicker, sturdier tops than two untreated flats of the same variety in the same soil. They maintained their advantage until planting-out time. Since gibberellins (growth hormones) are known to be abundantly present in seeds, it makes sense to me to suppose that the sprout soaking and rinsing water might well contain dissolved growth hormones. That's just a supposition, though, for which I have no proof. But I'll tell you this: I save every drop of sprout soaking and rinsing water to feed to my plants.

Some gardeners save their eggshells and soak them in water until the brew develops an odor you wouldn't want in the house. (Leave them on the back porch or in the barn.) The resulting solution, diluted by an equal volume of water, is used to fertilize half-grown seedlings and other plants. Unless you're especially partial to essence of rotten egg, I'd use this stuff on greenhouse, cold frame, and outdoor plants only, but it seems a good use of an otherwise neglected resource.

Light

Plants need light, as discussed in chapter 10, in order to combine air-borne elements, water, and soil-borne food into the raw materials of growth. There's no sense in fertilizing a plant that receives insufficient light (less than 8 to 10 hours a day in the case of vegetable seedlings). The plant can't make use of the food.

If, due to conditions beyond your control, your plants don't receive as much light as they should, keep the temperature low so that new growth will be less spindly. At lower temperatures, plants can tolerate less light.

Plants do a large part of their growing at night. The side away from the light adds more new tissue than the side closest to the light. This is what causes them to stretch and lean in the direction of light. Plants grown at a window should be rotated one-quarter turn each day so that no one side elongates and thus leans too far in any one direction.

10
Light

Seedling plants may have all their other needs met—nourishment, air circulation, correct temperature, water, good growing medium, humidity—but without sufficient light, they will amount to nothing.

People are limited to using the sun's energy in indirect ways, but green plants have the ability to absorb energy from sunlight directly, and to use that energy to make food they can store. Light striking a green leaf sets in motion the process of photosynthesis, the conversion, through the action of chlorophyll, of water and carbon dioxide to simple sugars and starches. For example, $6 H_2O + 6 Co_2 \rightarrow C_6H_{12}O_6 + 6 O_2$ (glucose). Only the green parts of leaves carry on this process. White stripes, blotches, and leaf margins do not contain chlorophyll, and so are not capable of photosynthesis. Red-leaved cabbage, coleus, ruby lettuce, and similar plants contain chlorophyll, but red pigment in their cells masks the green.

Light, although it may appear white to us, is actually a mixture of a rainbow of colors. A full spectrum of light includes the following color gradations, each of which has a different effect on plant life:

Green–yellow light is reflected by the chlorophyll in the plant. Its effect on growth is thought to be negligible.

Orange–red light stimulates stem and leaf growth.

Violet–blue light regulates enzyme and respiratory processes and encourages low, stocky growth.

Infrared (far-red) light stimulates germination of some seeds, but can inhibit others. Its full effect still isn't completely understood.

Ultraviolet light may be good for people, but it exerts a generally negative effect on plants.

Making the Most of Natural Light

If you have a greenhouse, of course, your plants will receive the well-balanced light they need. The quality of sunlight that shines on windowsill-grown plants is the same as that in a glass-enclosed greenhouse, but the intensity is much lower, especially on cloudy and early-winter days when the sun is low in the sky. You can boost the amount of light your windowsill plants receive by positioning shiny metal or flat-white-painted reflectors behind them to bounce the light back on their leaves. Use foil-covered cardboard, shiny cookie tins, or other household findings. The resulting arrangement may not win any interior decorating prizes, but it *does* get more light to the leaves. Try it with eggplant, a real sun and heat lover.

Another problem with raising seedlings on windowsills is that few houses have enough south-facing windows to provide a place for more than a few pots or flats. If you *are* limited to raising your seedlings at the window, choose the kinds of vegetables that most need an early start—main-crop tomatoes, peppers, and eggplants, for example—and sow lettuce, cabbage, and broccoli seeds in the open ground or in a cold frame. You can also raise two generations of indoor seedlings if you put your tomatoes and peppers in a cold frame about the first of May and then use your windowsills for the melons and cucumbers. Where space is limited, you can plant seeds of a tomato like Subarctic directly in the garden rather than raise your early tomato seedlings indoors.

Other ways of getting light to your seedlings, without using power, include the following:

1. A sunny corner in outbuilding or barn, best in mid to late spring in an unheated building.

2. A roof garden, protected by a plastic tent, cloches, etc., can be effective, but may be cumbersome to care for. A flat, black garage or house roof absorbs a lot of heat.

3. A car greenhouse works well if the weather isn't bitter cold at night. By day, the sun-flooded windows will nurture good seedling growth. Use either a junked car or the extra car you swore you wouldn't use since you got your bicycle. It's not practical for everyone, but it works for some.

Artificial Light

Sunlamps might sound like a good light source for seedlings, but any gardener who tries them will find that they are death on plants. The high concentration of ultraviolet rays in the sunlamp interferes with normal plant growth.

Incandescent bulbs produce red light, which, alone, makes the plant grow leggy. They also produce a great deal of heat in relation to the amount of light they give off. It is not practical to try to raise seedlings under incandescent lights. You *will* see special plant-raising incandescent bulbs, often with built-in reflectors, in lighting supply stores. These are used as auxiliary light sources in green-houses or for house plants. They must always be installed in a *porcelain* socket. Care must be taken also to prevent cold water from splashing the bulbs when watering the plants, or the blown-glass may break.

The discovery that plants do well under fluorescent light has made it possible for many more gardeners to get a good early start on the outdoor growing season, and to produce plants as good as any raised in a greenhouse. Plants grown under fluorescent lights develop excellent color and stocky growth. Fluorescent light comes closer than any other artificial illumination to duplicating the color spectrum of sunlight. In varying proportions, according to the type of the bulb, these lamps emit light from the red and blue bands of the spectrum. The tubes give off more than twice as much light per watt of power consumed as incandescent lights.

Fluorescent tubes of various kinds give off different shades of light, including warm white, cool white, natural white, and daylight. The different kinds of fluorescent powder used to coat the inside of the tube account for the range of light quality available.

Reports of plant-growing results at the North Carolina State University School of Agriculture and Life Sciences and at Cornell University, as well as from experienced nonprofessional gardeners, indicate that:

- Plants do well under a variety of tube combinations.
- Special plant-raising tubes are not necessary for start-ing vegetable plants.
- Best results are often obtained by mixing tube colors. For example, use one warm white and one cool white or daylight tube in each fixture.

Cool white tubes emit a bright bluish white light. Warm white tubes have a faint tan or pinkish cast. The cool white tubes are the easiest to find, but most hardware stores will order warm white ones for you if they're not in stock.

Special-purpose plant-raising tubes that are available include the following:

- Grow-Lux.
- Plant-gro.
- Naturescent—a natural light tube originally developed for the textile industry where color fidelity is important.
- Agro-light.
- Power Groove—a tube that has indentations which make the stream of electrons inside the tube travel in an undulating path. The longer trip across the tube results in a higher light output. For example, an eight-foot Power Groove lamp will give off as much light as a nine-foot regular lamp. This extra light output isn't really necessary for raising vegetable seedlings, though.

Special plant growth tubes give more blue–red than green–yellow light. Although there is some evidence that they yield more usable light for the amount of electric power they consume, their higher cost may to some extent offset this benefit.

Incandescent lights were thought to be necessary for flowering in the early days of fluorescent tube experiments, but are now known to be unnecessary. They generate so much heat that they cause rapid drying of soil and air. Although you may find that one of the special plant tubes will give you better results in bringing plants into flower, it is not true that you need an incandescent bulb.

Using Fluorescents Efficiently

You can take your choice, then, among tube varieties, and you can do without an incandescent bulb, but there *is* one thing I'd strongly advise you to do if you are preparing a fluorescent light setup for your plants. Buy the longest tubes you can manage to fit into the space you have, for two reasons:

- Light at the ends of the tubes is weaker than that in the center, and falls off more as the tube ages.
- If my experience is any guide, light space under the tubes is like compost: you never have enough of it. The more you have, the more plants you're

tempted to start, and when they're transplanted, you'll need all the space you can muster.

Tubes are available in 12-, 18-, 24-, 36-, 48-, 72-, and 96-inch lengths. Each foot of length uses 10 watts of power. If at all possible, avoid using tubes under three feet in length; they simply don't put out as much light for the power they use. Forty-eight-inch tubes are long enough to be efficient but short enough to fit conveniently into most household arrangements. A new U-shaped 40-watt tube, the 22½-inch long Mod-U-Lite, gives more light than two 20-watt lamps.

For growing seedlings, your fluorescent light setup should provide 15 to 20 watts per square foot of growing area. A single tube is, in most cases, both insufficient and inefficient, unless you have a long, skinny tray of seedlings under it. A double row of tubes will give enough light to a flat up to about 16 inches wide; and two parallel double rows, like those attached to plant-growing carts, are even more efficient.

If you are buying components and putting together your own light center or centers, you have a choice of the channel tube, a single- or double-mounted tube on a slim metal base, without a reflector, or the more usual two-tube industrial-type fixture with a bent metal reflector. Channel tubes work well on shelves and undersides of cabinets, especially if surrounding surfaces are painted white to reflect more light. Industrial reflector fixtures may sometimes be obtained secondhand, but they are also widely available in lighting supply stores and from household mail-order catalogs.

My first growlight was a 20-watt tabletop stand, a toy that helped me to get through a long northern Midwest winter when snow covered the ground until April. I raised tomato, pepper, lettuce, and pansy seedlings under that little light, and spring came after all. By then, of course, I was hooked. The following year, after moving back to Pennsylvania, to an old house full of nooks and crannies, I had a decentralized system—plant lights on every floor, from the basement to the kitchen to the bathroom. And I began raising all the vegetable seedlings we needed, racing the season to bring the earliest possible lettuce and cabbage to the table.

When we moved to our farm, we accepted a plainer, simpler house because we were hungry for land. Here, in this old house that boasts not a single closet, we need our shelves for books and canned garden produce. So I splurged on a four-shelf plant cart, with four 40-watt tubes attached to three of the shelves.

I've been delighted with the way my plants grow under fluorescent lights. They are stocky and green, with a special bloom to them. My only regret is that the lights consume electric power. I could rationalize that, I suppose, by reminding myself that they take the place of the dishwasher, TV, and clothes dryer we've never been persuaded to buy.

Still, I try to use the lights as efficiently as possible. Dust on the tubes, for example, decreases their efficiency. Use of reflecting surfaces under and around the lights gives the plants more light for the same power output. When painting shelves and reflecting boards use *flat white* paint. It reflects more light than glossy paint.

To get more usable time out of the tubes, avoid turning them on and off more than absolutely necessary. A long burning time after each start is conducive to more economical operation and longer tube life. Most lamps last one to two years (10,000 to 20,000 hours) if turned on only one or two times a day.

It is also possible, I've found, to save electric power by installing fluorescent lights for plants in spots where illumination is needed anyway. For example, we kept a fluorescent light stand on top of the refrigerator where the light it shed helped to illuminate a dark corner and make further lighting unnecessary. We also installed a fixture on the underside of a shelf in the bathroom of our old house, light for the room *and* the plants. An imaginative look at your own home surroundings will no doubt suggest other applications.

Growlight Setups

Not many of us have an entire room to devote to plants. A basement is often the most spacious available area, and that usually works very well unless furnace heat affects the plants or water is not readily at hand. Sometimes a bit of shoe-horning is required to fit lights into an apartment or small home. If you're looking for ways to sneak in another light fixture or two or three, perhaps the following list will suggest some possibilities.

- Use a fluorescent study lamp you may already have.
- Install fixtures on bookshelves or storage shelves.

- Make a closet into a fluorescent light center, with several tiers of lights and storage space for plant supplies.
- Install fixtures on the underneath surface of kitchen cabinets.
- Use a spare bedroom, an enclosed porch.
- Old buffet tables, radio cabinets, and other furniture can be fitted with fluorescent tubes when interior partitions have been removed.
- Once, when plant space really got tight around here, I even tied a 36-inch two-tube light fixture to the underside of a piano bench so that it was suspended a few inches above a flat of plants. A crazy-looking arrangement, but it kept my tomato seedlings going until the cabbage and lettuce on the big cart were ready to graduate to the cold frame and leave room for the next wave of plants.

If your indoor seed-starting space is severely limited, you'd be wise to consider some of the following factors in deciding which plants to start early:

- Those that need a long period of growth to prepare them for setting out.
- Those that are most difficult to find commercially.
- Vegetables you like best.
- Plants that produce well over a long period.
- Fine-seeded plants that might get lost in the garden row.

Seedlings, in general, need more intense light than mature plants. Young plants that develop long stems before their first leaves leaf out need more light. Either they're overcrowded or they are too far from the light. I keep my seedlings extremely close to the light tubes, as close as possible short of touching the leaves to the glass, and never more than three to four inches away for the first three or four weeks after germination. Then, if they are stocky and growing well, I lower them by an inch or two, continuing to lower the flat placement gradually as plant height increases.

It's also a good idea, since light at the ends of the tubes is relatively weak, to trade positions of the various flats of plants from end to the more fully lit center every week or so.

Shelves on my plant cart are adjustable, but I find it easier to jack up the seedling flats by using egg cartons, shallow cardboard cartons, piles of magazines, and other improvised boosters which may be removed gradually as the plants grow. Egg cartons work best: two cartons under a flat raise the seedlings close to the lights; removing one carton then provides a halfway stage for the larger, leafier seedling a week or so before transplanting, ending with removal of both cartons when plant height and development indicate the time is right.

Egg cartons make handy boosters to raise seedling flats closer to lights.

Industrial reflector fixtures, the kind we once used in a basement light center, may be suspended by chains. If you leave enough slack in the chain to raise and lower the light within a 12- to 15-inch range, you'll have a good adjustable setup.

Providing Plants with Darkness

In my experience, seedling plants do very well with 16 hours of light a day, the usual recommended time. I have made do with 12-hour light exposures under limited light space. The lights burned day and night, and the seedlings took turns basking under them for 12 hours at a time. The tomatoes got a bit spindly, but most plants grew surprisingly well on this schedule. Sixteen hours is much better, though. Even 18 hours is not too long, but it's longer than necessary for vegetable seedlings.

Lighting time should not be increased above 18 hours. Too much light will disturb a plant, just as too much water or fertilizer will. The light a plant receives, you remember, makes it possible for the leaves to manufacture starches and sugars, the components of growth. But a period of darkness is necessary for the plants to put these new compounds to use. Plants don't "rest" at night. They digest and grow. Both processes go more smoothly when night temperatures are five to ten degrees lower than daytime levels.

Scientists have concluded that plants are actually attuned to the dark period rather than to daylight. Darkness is indispensable to normal growth. Some plants, in fact, blossom only when nights are long (chrysanthemum and poinsettia); others, like onions, need short nights to develop fully. Most vegetable plants are day-neutral. Their full development isn't dependent on light–dark rhythm of any certain pattern.

The turning off of the lights at night, then, is fully as important as turning them on in the morning. When I shifted two batches of plants under continuously turned-on lights, I was careful to provide "night" for the plants that received 8 P.M. to 8 A.M. illumination by covering them with cartons or newspaper tents during the day.

Fluorescent lamps seem to function best if the temperature doesn't fall below 50°F. Lights operated at around 40°F. may not perform as well. Plants, on the other hand, can better weather a period of light deprivation if they are kept cool, especially at night. According to studies conducted by a group of Russian scientists, the consequent lowering of the plant's metabolism apparently forestalls damage to the reproductive system which would otherwise prevent flowering in plants exposed to more than three days of darkness.

Rapid-start fluorescent fixtures may occasionally develop starting problems if humidity around the light center is unusually high.

Ventilation and promotion of better air circulation usually solve this problem. If you notice that a tube flickers, the starter—a small metal cylinder—probably needs to be replaced. Light brightness decreases with the age of the tube. The tubes themselves give off little heat, but the ballast—the step-down transformer that makes it possible for the lights to use household current—does become warm. Most fluorescent lights have a ballast at the end of the fixture. Some recent arrangements have a remote ballast. Judicious planning of flat placement in relation to the warmer end zones of the tubes can make it possible to utilize this extra warmth to advantage, for example, in germinating seeds or starting sweet potato slips.

The solar greenhouse is, I believe, the next important new direction for the serious seedling-starter to investigate. Conventional greenhouses have never tempted me too strongly because of the necessity for auxiliary heating. Satisfying as it is to work with plants under lights, I am at the same time fully aware that sun-power is beating unharnessed on our house's south side. Important new work is being done on designing practical solar greenhouses for the home. These structures may be trickier to integrate into the average house than fluorescent lights, but they have the advantage of reducing power use and often of helping to heat the house. Tempting indeed, and I am more and more swayed in that direction. Meanwhile, though, I use my lights. And hang my wash out to dry.

11
Problems

Fortunately, seedling plants seem to thrive within a rather generous range of conditions. If your seedlings show compact growth, plenty of good green leaves, short internodes between leaves, and slow but steady growth, all is well.

Occasionally, though, excess or deficiency in one or another of the young plant's life requirements will cause trouble. And a plant in trouble will almost always let you know. If you interpret the problem correctly and treat it promptly, you have a good chance of saving the seedlings. Troubled plants give clues. What should you look for? Check the following list:

Leaf curl. A plant whose leaves curl under, especially in bright light, may be suffering from overfertilization.

Yellowing and dropping of lower leaves is another symptom of overfeeding, although it can also indicate magnesium deficiency. Naturally, you'll decrease the amount of fertilizer your plants receive if you notice symptoms of overfeeding. If the problem is severe, you might need to replant the seedlings in another flat of fresh potting soil. Be sure to leach out the extra fertilizer salts from the soil in the old flat before reusing it.

Dropping of leaves, along with plant stunting, may be caused by leakage of partly consumed gas from the stove or water heater. You can test for gas leaks by buying yourself a bouquet of carnations. If the flower petals curl upward, you've probably got escaped gas in the air. Tomatoes will droop in the presence of gas too. Natural gases like butane and propane don't seem to hurt plants, but manufactured gas does.

Leggy plants with long, often weak stems and large spaces between the leaves growing from the stem may be caused by any one of the following:

- Insufficient light.
- Excessively high temperature.
- Crowding of plants.

Weak, spindly tomato plant needing food and searching for light.

A leggy plant can't be reshaped to conform to the stocky, well-grown ideal form, but there are steps you can take to promote more normal growth from this point on.

First, of course, you'd remedy the cause: supply more light, lower the temperature, thin the plants. Plants kept at a window might need some auxiliary evening light on cloudy days. Then, if at all possible, transplant leggy plants. The root pruning and general mild trauma of being moved will set back their growth a bit. Set the plant deeper in the new container.

Bud drop, particularly in pepper seedlings, may occur if the air is excessively dry. Try setting the flat on a tray of water with pebbles in it, or mist the blossoms with a fine spray of water at least once a day.

Skimpy root growth, which won't be evident, of course, until you transplant, may be caused by any one or more of the following factors:

- Poor drainage.
- Low soil fertility.
- Concentration of excess fertilizer salts.
- Temperature too low.
- Insufficient air space in soil mixture.

Leaf discoloration usually indicates nutrient deficiency.

Pale leaves, for example, in seedlings receiving sufficient light, are a sign of nitrogen deficiency. Tomato seedlings that are severely deficient in nitrogen develop a deep purple veining, especially prominent on the undersides of the leaves.

Reddish purple color on the undersides of leaves appears on a phosphorus-deficient plant. In addition, the plant will often be stunted, with thin, fibrous stems. Soil that is too acid may contribute to the unavailability of phosphorus.

Bronzing or browning of leaf edges can reveal a need for potassium. Brown leaf edges may also appear on plants that are overwatered. (See also table 5, "Soil Deficiency Symptoms and Treatments," page 88.)

The differences between the various symptoms of deficiency are not always clearcut, especially in young plants. Your best bet, if you do notice leaf discoloration that can't be accounted for other-wise, is—in the short run—to give the plant a dose of fertilizer known to contain trace minerals. In the long run, include some com-post in your next soil mixture, or transplant the ailing plants to a medium that contains compost.

Discolored roots are often the result of a buildup of excess fertilizer salts in the soil. Either the plant has been overfed, or overheating the soil in an attempt to sterilize it has released an overly high concentration of soluble soil salts. Replant the seedlings in fresh soil if possible. Your second choice would be to flood and drain the flats several times in an attempt to leach out the toxic salts.

Mold on the soil surface indicates poor drainage, insufficient soil aeration, possible overfertilizing, and/or a lack of air circulation. Remedy the cause and treat the symptom by scratching some pow-dered charcoal into the soil surface.

Insect damage on seedling plants grown indoors most likely means that conditions are not ideal for the plant.

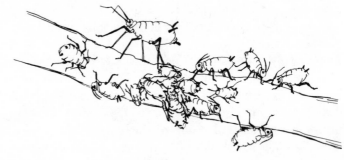

Aphids.
Actual size, four to eight millimeters.

Aphids, for example, will flock to plants that are undersupplied with organic matter. You can deal with the invasion by washing the soft little bugs off the plants with water, or if you want to get tougher, try this spray recommended in *Organic Plant Protection:* soak tobacco stems in warm water for 24 hours and dilute the resulting solution to the color of weak tea. In the 11 years since I started raising indoor seedlings in a big way, I've only once had aphids on my indoor plants. The pests disappeared when I set the plants outdoors where natural predators apparently took over.

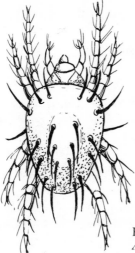

Red spider mite.
Actual size, about 1/16 inch.

Red spider mites are contradictory creatures. These tiny leaf-sucking pests can live in hot, dry air or in excessively damp, stagnant air. So your best method of prevention is to maintain good circulation and adequate but not excessive humidity in your indoor plant nursery. Spider mites damage leaves by puncturing the tissue with their sharp mouthparts, causing mottled, blotchy, discolored leaves. Sometimes you'll see tiny webs on the plants. Repeated forcible spraying with a stream of water, taking care to include the undersides and axils of the leaves, is the safest way of dealing with these pests. Spray every three or four days for about two weeks. Chances are your rapidly growing young seedlings will never see a spider mite. To the best of my knowledge, they haven't found my seedlings yet.

Damping-off doesn't give you much warning. Your first sign that the problem has hit your new plants is the total collapse of a few seedlings; the green leaves are still intact, but the stem has characteristically withered away right at soil level. Young seedlings are the most vulnerable. Once a seedling has been attacked by the damping-off fungus (actually there is a complex of microorganisms,

79

any one of which may cause the trouble) it can't be revived. The lifeline between root and stem has been cut off. So we must concentrate on prevention, and that involves:

- Maintaining good air circulation around seedlings. Keep soil level high in flats and other growing containers. Thin seedlings to avoid overcrowding.
- Avoiding overwatering.
- Sowing seed in a sterile medium such as finely milled sphagnum moss or vermiculite.

It is often possible, however, to save the remainder of a flat of seedlings if only a few have died off. Immediately remove the flat

Healthy broccoli seedling next to one that has "damped off."
Much enlarged.

to a more open area, make sure that it is well drained, and remove the affected seedlings. No sense transplanting the others—you'd just transfer the disease to new soil. But do dry out and ventilate the flat you want to save. I've salvaged several such flats which have gone on to produce early crops after all.

Failure of seeds to sprout may be due to any one or more of the following factors:

- Temperature too low, or too high.
- Soil was allowed to dry out.
- Seeds were planted too deeply.
- Top watering floated seeds off.
- Old seed, poorly stored.
- Insufficient contact between seed and soil.
- Toxic substances in soil.
- Damping-off disease.

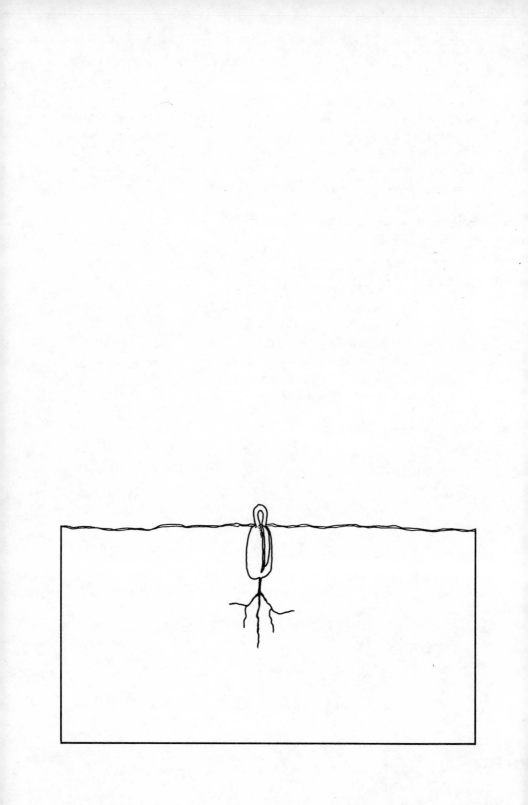

Section Two

It is surprising in how many fields one can step over the frontiers of science beside one's garden path.

Lawrence Hills

12
Soil Preparation

Gradually the late-winter sun rises higher in the sky each day, and its rays are warmer, more intense, even through the brisk March wind. Soon we're able to eat our evening dinner by daylight. As the last winter snow melts into the earth, I begin to shuffle seed packets and round up the garden tools. I know it's still too early to dig, but there's no harm in being ready, is there?

Working the soil too early is a mistake. When the earth is still saturated with melting snow or spring rain, it is easily compacted by treading across it, or even worse, driving heavy equipment on it. In addition, large clumps of wet soil turned over at this time will only bake into impervious clods which will be very difficult to break up later. And, as you remember, plant roots grow best when there are some air spaces between soil particles. Heavy, wet soil doesn't break up into the loose, air-retaining texture that is best for plants. Its clumpy texture is also likely to trap *pockets* of air around plant roots, and that is just as bad as *no* air.

How can you tell whether your garden has dried out enough to be worked? The truest test of soil condition is that age-old gesture of the gardener—fingering a handful of soil.

Pick up about a half cup of earth in your hand. Now squeeze the soil together so that it forms a ball. If the ball of earth can readily be shattered by pressing with your fingers or dropping it from a height of three feet or so, it is dry enough to dig. But if the ball keeps its shape, or breaks only with difficulty into solid sections rather than loose soil, then it still contains too much water. Clay soil that is too wet will feel slick when rubbed between thumb and forefinger. If it is very wet (75- to 100-percent moisture), the mass will be pliable and a ribbon of earth can be drawn out and pressed with your finger. Working soil that wet can spoil its texture for the whole season. Heavy clay soil will form a ball even when moisture content is less than 50 percent.

Soil that is somewhat coarser, a sandy loam or silt loam, tends to crumble when moisture content is low but will probably form a ball at about 50 percent. At 75- to 100-percent moisture it will be dark, pliable, and may feel slick between the fingers. Coarse-

Testing soil for friability and dryness.

textured sandy soil will not form a ball if moisture content is below 50 percent. At 75- to 100-percent moisture it can be pressed into a weak ball, but even then it shatters easily. Coarser soil, of course, may be worked at a higher moisture content than fine-particled clay.

Fall Tillage

By preparing our garden in the fall, we've been able to move our spring digging date up by at least two weeks. Here's what we do : in November, when black frost has laid low all but the wintering-over root vegetables that we've purposely planted at one edge of the garden, Mike plows up both the kitchen garden and the larger

85

back garden. As the one-bottom plow carves up thick slices of earth, the rest of the family stands ready with hayforks to stuff the coarse mulch on the adjoining unplowed land into the newly opened trench. Where mulch has worn thin, we toss in all the leaves we've been able to collect. The next pass of the plow blade roughly covers the mulch-filled trench and opens up a new furrow into which we rake another humus-building line of hay and leaves.

The patch remains rough all winter, catching all the poor-man's fertilizer (snow) that falls. By spring, frost action has mellowed and pulverized the rows of raised soil. The garden dries out a good two weeks earlier than it did when left flat under a season's end accumulation of mulch and weeds. While it is true that exposed loose soil can be eroded by wind or heavy rain, we have not had that problem here.

Preparing the Garden in Spring

With this treatment, our kitchen garden does not need spring plowing, just a going-over with the rotary cultivator. I often hand dig an extra-early row for peas. The larger back garden, which is slower to dry and therefore used for the later crops like squash and tomatoes, is disked, then rototilled in spring.

We do our manure spreading in spring. Fall cleaning of the animals' pens is fine for the garden, but leaves a thin layer of bedding for winter. A heavy layer of bedding, with its natural warmth from deep composting, helps to keep the critters warm. Chicken manure, which the hens have finely pulverized and mixed with their well-shredded bedding, goes on the kitchen garden because it is loose and fine enough to blend in easily with just a few passes of the tiller. (Since we've hung a tire in the pen for him to play with, our buck does enough pawing and prancing to break up his bedding pretty well too.) The heavy sheep, with their fine sharp hooves, do the next best job of chopping up their bedding. Manure from the large loafing pen of milking goats tends to be coarser because it has a lot of waste hay in it and is less worked over than that of the other animals, so we use it on the larger, less finely manicured back garden and the hill garden, where it will be first disked or plowed and then rototilled, and where rows and plants will usually be spaced two to three feet apart.

When we farmed an acre of ground, on our first homestead, we rototilled our vegetable garden. Two or three passes with the rotary cultivator, each slightly overlapping the previous path of the tines, fines the soil up quite well. It's a good idea to till in both directions (north–south and east–west). Depending on the size and shape of the patch we're working, we'll sometimes till in a grid pattern, making the furrows at right angles to each other as in the diagram above; at other times, we'll till in a spiral, perhaps finishing off with a pass across the garden. Watch out for balling up of coarse bedding and weed stalks, especially if using pointed-pick tiller tines. Stop the machine and untangle the accumulated shreds periodically.

Earlier, in city and small-town gardens, we practiced hand-digging entirely. In a small, closely worked garden it is possible to dig a few rows at a time as higher land drains or as time becomes available. Dig as deeply as possible so that the soil is loose to a depth of 8 to 10 inches. As each shovelful of earth is turned over, shatter it with your fork or spade. If it doesn't fall apart readily, you're probably digging too early.

It's a good idea to let the soil settle for a day or two after tilling or digging and raking, especially before planting fine seeds like carrots and parsley that might get washed too deeply into the furrow if a heavy rain follows planting. I seldom wait, though, to plant large seeds like peas and beans.

Spreading Rock Powders

In addition to manure, we routinely add rock minerals to each of our three garden areas. We apply the stuff just before spreading the manure, so that it is all tilled in together. Acids produced by the decaying manure help to release important nutrients in the ground rock. Later, when crops have been planted, the growing roots produce carbon dioxide, which also aids in breaking down the powdered minerals.

The more finely ground a rock powder is, the more quickly it will become available to growing plants. All natural rock minerals work slowly in the soil, breaking down gradually over a period of several years. We dig in limestone and small amounts of granite dust every two or three years.

Soil Deficiency
Symptoms and Treatments

Primary Nutrients	Signs of Deficiency	Natural Sources of Elements
Nitrogen (N)	Pale leaves, turning to yellow, especially lower leaves. Stunted growth.	Manure tea Bloodmeal Manure Feathers
Phosphorus (P)	Reddish purple color on leaves, especially undersides, veins, and stems. Thin stems.	Rock phosphate Bone meal Fish scrap Waste wool
Potassium (K)	Bronze coloring, curling and drying of leaf margins. Slow growth. Low vigor. Poor resistance to disease, heat, and cold.	Wood ashes Greensand Tobacco stems Granite dust

Secondary Nutrients

Boron (B)	Slow growth. Specific symptoms vary according to vegetable. Celery—cracking. Cauliflower—hollow stem, brown curl. Beets and turnips—brown corky spots on roots. Broccoli—browning of buds. Chard—dark stripe with cracking. Tomatoes—stunted stems. Curling, yellowing, and drying of terminal shoots.	Granite dust Vetch or clover
Calcium (Ca)	Curling of young leaf tips. Wavy, irregular leaf margins. Weak stems. Poor growth. Yellow spots on upper leaves.	Limestone
Copper (Cu)	Slow growth, faded color, flabby leaves and stems. Lettuce—shows leaf elongation.	Agricultural frit

	Tomatoes—may have curled leaves and blue green foliage. Onions—thin, pale outer skin.	
Iron (Fe)	Spotted, pale areas on new leaves. Yellow leaves. Yellow leaves on upper part of plant. (Iron is more often unavailable because of insolubility rather than actual soil lack.)	Manure Dried blood Tankage Humus helps make iron more available
Magnesium (Mg)	Plant may be brittle. Older leaves show yellow mottling. Margins and tips may be brown. Corn shows yellow stripes on older leaves. Deficiencies ordinarily show up late, near seeding time, when the element is most needed.	Dolomite Limestone
Manganese (Mn)	Slow growth. Spinach—pale growing tips. Beets—leaf turns deep red, then yellow and brown. Spots develop between veins. Onions and corn—narrow yellow stripes on leaves.	Manure Compost
Sulfur (S)	Lower leaves turn yellow, stems are slender and hard.	Compost
Molybdenum (Mo)	Drying of leaf margins, stunting. Yellow leaf tissue between veins.	Agricultural frit Rock phosphate
Zinc (Zn)	Leaves may be unusually long and narrow, also yellow and spotted with dead tissue. Beans—cotyledon leaves have reddish brown spots. Corn—wide stripes at leaf bases. Beets—dry margins, yellow areas between veins.	Manure

Sources for the above information:
Handbook for Vegetable Growers by J. E. Knott
Soil, the Yearbook of Agriculture, 1957 by the U.S. Department of Agriculture
The Encyclopedia of Organic Gardening by J. I. Rodale and Staff

Rock phosphate contains a good many trace elements in addition to the phosphorus which is in the form of calcium phosphate. Superphosphate has been chemically treated to make it highly soluble and therefore quickly available. The gain in rapid absorption, though, is more than offset by damage to the population of cellulose-digesting fungi in the soil; repeated use of this hyped-up product has been shown to impair the soil's natural ability to build humus out of buried organic matter. Although no general prescription can be given for application rates of rock phosphate since soils differ in their needs, the usual practice is to spread a pound of the powder on each 10 square feet of garden surface, every three to five years.

Lime not only tempers soil acidity, it also helps to minimize toxic effects of such plant-inhibiting elements as aluminum, iron, manganese, and others. Its effect on the soil is physical as well as chemical; by encouraging flocculation, or clumping, of soil granules it counteracts the tendency of clay soils to form a solid mass of fine sticky particles.

The generally recommended rate of application is 50 pounds for 1,000 square feet (or one ton to the acre) every three or four years, although here again less may be needed in areas of limestone soil, and heavier applications may be indicated where soil is strongly acid. Consider your crop, too: blueberries, potatoes, flax, and watermelon, for example, do not like lime. Most other garden vegetables are benefited, or at least not harmed, by soil that is closer to the neutral line (pH 7).

Greensand, an ocean mineral, is an excellent source of potash and many trace elements. It not only enriches the soil but also improves tilth and water retention. The usual rate of application is about two pounds to each 10 square feet of garden surface. We often sprinkle it in the furrow when planting, especially for potatoes.

Granite dust is another excellent source of potash, along with small quantities of trace minerals. It should be spread at the rate of about a pound to each 10 square feet of garden (two tons to the acre) every three to five years. If your garden is large and you intend to spread a lot of granite dust, use a dust mask; long exposure to the fine dust can be damaging to the lungs.

Relative Tolerance of Vegetable Crops
to Soil Acidity

The vegetables in the slightly tolerant group can be grown successfully on soils that are on the alkaline side of neutrality. They do well up to pH 7.6 if there is no deficiency of essential nutrients. Calcium, phosphorus, and magnesium are the nutrients most likely to be deficient in soils more acid than pH 6.

Slightly Tolerant (pH 6.8 to 6.0)	Moderately Tolrant (pH 6.8 to 5.5)	Very Tolerant (pH 6.8 to 5.0)
Asparagus	Beans, lima	Chicory
Beets	Beans, snap	Dandelion
Broccoli	Brussels sprouts	Endive
Cabbage	Carrots	Fennel
Cauliflower	Collards	Potatoes
Celery	Corn	Rhubarb
Chinese cabbage	Cucumbers	Shallot
Cress, garden and	Eggplant	Sorrel
upland	Garlic	Sweet potatoes
Leeks	Gherkins	Watermelon
Lettuce	Horseradish	
Muskmelon	Kale	
New Zealand spinach	Kohlrabi	
Okra	Mustard	
Onions	Parsley	
Orach	Peas	
Parsnips	Peppers	
Salsify	Pumpkins	
Soybeans	Radish	
Spinach	Rutabaga	
Swiss chard	Squash	
Watercress	Tomatoes	
	Turnips	

From *Vegetable Growing,* J. E. Knott, Philadelphia, PA: Lea and Febiger, 1955.

Breaking New Ground

When turning a sodded area into a garden, get a head start, if you can. Dig the patch in the fall and turn it grass side down so that all that green manure can break down over winter. Or, if digging is impossible, cover the area with a layer of some impervious stuff—old boards or plastic—to kill the grass over winter.

Often, though, you'll be digging in the spring. That's when expansion fever seems to hit most of us gardeners. To avoid having all that grass come back at you all summer long, I would shake out each clump of sod as you dig it up and toss the grass, roots and all, on the compost heap. Then you'll be able to rake the ground into a fairly smooth seedbed. If the size of the sod plot you're digging up makes this kind of operation impractical, then I'd let the plot weather for a few weeks after digging, smooth it as well as you can, and use it either for large-seeded crops like corn and beans or for set-out plants. Mulch heavily to suppress the grass that still thinks "lawn." Next year it will be more ready to say "vegetables."

With all I've said about the importance of letting the soil dry before digging, I'm fully aware that the very best way to develop a soil-respecting sense of the right timing is to have the experience of forking up a section of loose, crumbly soil that rakes out so fine you can practically comb it. You know, then, that you've chosen the right time, and you'll find when the next growing season starts, that your impatience to begin is tempered by your memory of that moment of perfection. You won't want to lose it by starting too soon.

Quick Compost

I'd like to give you my recipe for quick compost. I worked this out last year when, at the beginning of the spring gardening season, I had nothing but coarse, partly decomposed stuff in my two compost bins. I needed some fine, crumbly compost to put in the hole with my spring seedings of squash, cucumbers, and cantaloupes, as well as for tomato transplants and other special seedlings.

Lacking a shredder, and not really wanting one either, I needed to find ingredients that were already in small pieces or well chewed-up. A little scavenging around the farm produced the following ingredients:

- Sawdust, well-aged, into which I had poured manure tea several times during the previous year.
- Locust tree leaves—tiny, fine, curled-up, and crisp-

dry, these legume products broke down quickly. It was an easy, pleasant task to scrape up bags of the leaves from the ground in the locust grove.

- Wood ashes.
- Goat manure and hay bedding, both finely shredded —the pelletized droppings actually dried and pulverized by the prancing of our buck as he played with a chain-hung tire.
- Manure tea, which I poured into the pile several times a week for the first two weeks after building it.

To enclose the pile I simply stacked cement blocks in two parallel lines, using the solid block wall of my large compost pile as the back end. Total volume of the pile was not large—about one cubic yard—but it made enough to get my greedy feeders off to a good start.

To build the pile, I layered the ingredients, roughly equal parts

Quick compost can be made without a shredder if all ingredients are naturally finely divided, like the sawdust, locust leaves, and almost-powdery barn bedding I'm mixing here.

of sawdust and leaves, with a three-gallon bucket of manure sifted over each bushel or so of leaves and sawdust. A handful of wood ashes and a heaping shovelful of soil salted each layer. Sawdust, even old sawdust, contains a high proportion of slow-to-rot carbon, but the addition of nitrogen in both manure and manure tea and the legume leaves helped to hasten its breakdown.

When all the ingredients were piled up, I moistened the pile thoroughly so that it was wet without being soggy. Then, over the next 14 days, I poured about 10 gallons of manure tea into it. The weather was cold in March, when I built the pile, and microorganisms sleepy. It took a good two weeks to heat. After four weeks, I turned the pile, and it heated again. Eight weeks after I'd made it, it was ready to use—dark brown, crumbly, spongy, and rich. It was so easy and so satisfying that I started another pile right away.

13
Mapping Out the Garden

Once the soil has been prepared, it's time to find the planting plan we doodled over by the late-winter fire. Already much erased and revised, it will no doubt be changed once again as we confront the reality of freshly raked soil and extra last-minute seed purchases. Subject to revision though it may be, the planting plan is a valuable gardening tool.

Although I wouldn't presume to prescribe what form your plan should take, I *would* like to suggest several considerations to keep in mind while poring over the graph paper with seed orders and pencil in hand.

Orientation of rows. Your first decision, as you face that blank piece of paper, will be to determine which direction your rows will run. If possible, choose a north–south direction so that sun striking the garden from the east and west will cast a plant's shadow onto the space between the rows rather than onto the next plant. This is a fine point, though, and if your land slopes so as to make it impossible for you to run the rows from the north to south, you'll see little if any difference in your east–west (or northeast–southwest) rows.

Tall plants like corn or sunflowers should be planted on the north side of the garden so they don't shade adjacent vegetables— or, if necessary to put them on the south end of the garden, plant parsley, lettuce, or other midsummer shade-tolerant plants next to the corn.

On a sloping plot, where rain tends to carry loose soil downhill, contouring the rows so that they run parallel to the hill (and at right angles to the direction of the slope) will help to conserve much valuable topsoil. Mulching will help too, as will terracing on a very steep slope.

Row spacing will be determined by the kind of plants you grow, the amount of mulch you can get, and the sort of equipment you plan to use for cultivating. Rows must be separated far enough to give the plant sufficient growing room and the gardener at least walking space, often tiller or hoeing space. Single-file rows of nonspreading

Plant and Row Spacing for Vegetables

Crop	Spacing in Inches between Plants in Row	Spacing in Inches between Rows
Artichokes	72	96
Asparagus	12–18	36–84
Beans, broad	8–10	20–48
Beans, bush	2–4	18–36
Beans, lima, bush	6–8	18–36
Beans, lima, pole	8–12	36–48
Beans, pole	6–9	36–48
Beets	2–4	18–36
Broccoli, sprouting	12–24	20–40
Broccoli raab	3–4	24–36
Brussels sprouts	18–24	24–40
Cabbage, early	12–18	24–36
Cabbage, late	16–30	24–40
Cardoon	12–18	36–48
Carrots	1–3	16–36
Cauliflower	14–24	24–48
Celeriac	4–6	24–36
Celery	6–12	18–40
Chervil	6–10	12–18
Chicory	4–10	18–24
Chinese cabbage	10–18	18–36
Chives	12–18	24–36
Collards	12–24	24–36
Corn	9–15	36–48
Corn-salad	2–4	12–18
Cowpea (southern pea)	5–6	36–48
Cress, garden and upland	2–4	12–18
Cucumbers	12, single plants 24–36, hills	36–72
Dandelion	3–6	14–24
Dasheen (taro)	24–30	42–48
Eggplant	18–36	24–54
Endive	8–12	18–24
Florence fennel	4–12	24–48
Garlic	2–3	18–24
Horseradish	12–18	30–36
Jerusalem artichokes	15–18	42–48

Kale	18–24	24–36
Kohlrabi	3–6	12–36
Leek	2–6	12–36
Lettuce, cos	10–14	18–24
Lettuce, head	10–15	18–24
Lettuce, leaf	10–12	18–24
Muskmelon and other melons	12, single plants 24–48, hills	60–96
Mustard	5–10	12–36
New Zealand spinach	10–20	36–60
Okra	12–24	24–60
Onions	2–4	18–36
Parsley	4–12	12–36
Parsnips	3–6	18–36
Peas	1–3	24–48
Peppers	12–24	18–36
Potatoes	9–12 (30 on dry land)	30–42
Pumpkin	36–60	96–144
Radish	½–1	12–18
Radish, storage type	4–6	18–36
Rhubarb	24–48	36–84
Roselle	24–46	60–72
Rutabaga	5–8	18–36
Salsify	2–4	18–36
Scolymus	2–4	18–36
Scorzonera	2–4	18–36
Shallot	6–10	42–72
Sorrel	½–1	12–18, or double rows at 8 on 26 centers
Southern pea (see Cowpea)	. . .	. . .
Spinach	2–6	12–36
Squash, bush	24–48	36–48
Squash, vining	36–120	72–120
Sweet potatoes	10–18	36–48
Swiss chard	12–15	24–36
Tomatoes, flat	18–48	36–72
Tomatoes, staked	12–24	36–48
Turnips	2–6	12–36
Turnip greens	Broadcast	
Watercress	Broadcast	
Watermelon	24–36, single plants 72–96, hills	72–96

From *Handbook for Vegetable Growers,* by J. E. Knott, New York: John Wiley & Sons, Inc., 1957.

plants like beets, lettuce, peas, carrots, and such are giving way, in more and more gardens, to 4- to 36-inch-wide bands of these vegetables. We've had good results with garlic, lettuce, carrots, peas, herbs, and beans planted in wide rows. Careful hand-weeding between the vegetables is necessary in the early stages, but later the plants help to take care of each other by shading out weeds and keeping soil moist. Wide rows use space more efficiently than narrow drills.

Row middles that will be rototilled should be about six to eight inches wider than the tine-to-tine measurement of the tiller. (You can adapt some front-end tillers to work row spaces as narrow as eight inches by removing the two outer tines and reversing the center tines so that their blades face inward rather than outward.)

Mulched rows may be closely spaced, but if you have a lot of coarse mulch, as we do, you will want to plan your garden so that the loose, shaggy stuff will be used to mulch wide rows like tomatoes, and the finer mulches like sawdust or old leaves, or neat bundles like hay, can be saved for narrow rows.

Rambling vine crops like squash, pumpkins, melons, and cucumbers may be planted in rows or hills. There's a certain amount of confusion surrounding the term "hill." Generally, a hill is simply a small designated area, not necessarily raised, in which a group of seeds, usually those of spreading plants, is sown. Except in very small gardens, where vines can be trained to climb fences, hills use space more efficiently than rows when growing rambling plants. The advantages of planting vining plants in a hill rather than in rows include easier placement of compost and manure and simpler, quicker early-season insect control.

Some gardeners DO make hills which are actually small elevated mounds an inch or two above the normal soil level. These small raised beds drain well and warm quickly. Their disadvantage becomes apparent in a dry season when it becomes important to channel all possible moisture to the roots of the vines. Unmulched raised hills dry quickly.

Overwintering crops like parsnips, salsify, and carrots, and late-fall bearers like Brussels sprouts, escarole, parsley, and collards should be planted at the edge of the garden where they will not be disturbed if you intend to till or plow the rest of the garden in the fall.

Perennial vegetables like asparagus, rhubarb, comfrey, and Jerusalem artichokes should, of course, be planted either at the edge of the garden where they will not be plowed up or in a separate bed.

Crop rotation makes sense for two reasons. One, insect predation may be reduced by growing vulnerable plants in a different location each year. The bean beetles and squash bugs will probably still find the plants, but at least won't have a ready feast waiting for them the moment they hatch.

Two, vegetables of different kinds use varying amounts of soil nutrients. Root vegetables need a good supply of phosphorus and potash, but take little nitrogen from the soil. Heavy feeders like corn, cucumbers, lettuce, and other leafy plants require larger doses of nitrogen. Peas, beans, soybeans, and other legumes, with the help of nitrogen-fixing bacteria on their roots, add nitrogen to the soil. A good rotation for one row, then, would be to follow a crop of cabbage with a planting of beans, and then a planting of carrots. Better yet, follow the carrots with a fourth rotation of a soil-building cover crop before returning to another heavy feeder like cabbage or corn. I like to rotate marigolds throughout the garden to discourage nematodes. Let the flowers grow in the same spot for two or three years before changing to different places to get the full benefits of their nematode-threatening power.

Warm-climate gardens may have a succession of three or even four rotations in a season. In most mid-Atlantic, New England, Midwest, and Rocky Mountain gardens, the complete rotation will carry over from one year to the next—another good reason for saving each year's mud-splattered planting plan.

Green manure. With careful planning, you can end the season with a section of garden free of crops, a perfect chance to put in a soil-building crop of winter rye. Or start in spring with oats to be plowed under before they head. Either way, you'll add humus and nutrients to your garden. In order to have a solid block of land ready for a fall cover crop, it's necessary to group a bunch of early-maturing spring plantings together so that when they are harvested in August or September, the rye can be planted right away. (Be sure to get coarse-seeded winter rye, not the fine-seeded grass which may repeat on you in next year's garden.)

Succession crops can be dovetailed in a very intricate way. All kinds of variations are possible. Here are a few examples, from my garden:

- An early planting of peas followed by a late corn planting (but use a fairly early-maturing kind of corn).
- Early cabbage followed by late beans.
- Spring lettuce giving way to fall beets.
- Early onions succeeded by fall lettuce.

Once I planted bean seeds along the row as I harvested leaf lettuce. By the time the lettuce row was used up, all the beans were up and growing.

Interplanting saves space too. It's seldom necessary, for example, to devote a whole row to spring radishes. Plant them, instead, along with your lettuce and carrots and use them as thinnings when they're ready. Last year I grew a long row of bush beans between the widely spaced, just-planted rows of tomatoes and squash. By the time the vines closed over the gap, I'd harvested several bushels of good green beans. Pumpkins do well at the edge of the corn patch where they have space to ramble.

Companion planting, the pairing of plants that benefit each other in close proximity, adds yet another dimension to the juggling of rows and beds. Although reports vary widely—some authorities say that onions and beans do well together, and others warn that beans don't like onions—there *is* a firm scientific basis for the study of plant relationships. Plants are known to produce root exudates that do, in many cases, affect soil life and roots of other plants around them. On vases and grave furniture unearthed in Ecuador and Peru, archaeologists have noted depictions of the marigold *Tagetes minuta* painted right next to pictures of crops on which the people depended for food. Farmers in these pre-Inca civilizations were, in fact, able to grow corn, tomatoes, beans and potatoes on the same land, without any crop rotation, for more than 1,000 years by fertilizing with bird guano and fish waste and interplanting their crops with marigolds. Much study remains to be done in this area. Close observation by gardeners continues to be a valid source of information.

If you want to try companion planting, and I recommend it as a worthwhile gardening practice, take this list and any others that you see as a suggestion rather than a final word. Some reports, even from experienced gardeners, are contradictory. Others recur so often in gardening lore from different parts of the country that their helpfulness is unquestioned. One thing is certain: growing things relate and interact in amazingly complicated and subtle ways. Just as I find it difficult to be dogmatically in favor of all the companion-planting combinations I've heard, it would be equally impossible for me to dismiss the idea as myth. Something, I'm sure, is going on here. We might as well follow the practices that do seem to work, even though we don't know why.

Allelopathy, the inhibition of seed germination and growth by certain plant-produced natural compounds, is sometimes responsible for otherwise-unexplained poor plant growth. Walnut trees, for example, release juglone which retards many plants. I found that out the hard way in my own garden when I planted a row of beets—which are, I have since discovered, particularly sensitive to toxins in the soil—near an English walnut tree at the edge of the garden. The beet seeds didn't even germinate. Other plants—onions and marigolds—have grown fairly well in the same spot, but most things I plant near that tree produce rather half-heartedly. Shade and competing tree roots could also be a factor.

Other notorious allelopathic plants are ailanthus, artemisia absinthium, eucalyptus, and sometimes sycamore. Some crops too are more vulnerable to the effect of toxins. Not only beets but also soybeans, according to one study, were seriously inhibited by juglone in the soil.

Laboratory tests may differ from experience in the field, though. Amounts of a toxin that would be injurious to a plant growing under laboratory conditions may be washed away by heavy rains. In practice, then, plants that would be antagonistic under lab conditions may be able to grow together in the garden.

So the only final word that can safely be said about companion planting is this: Try it! Experiment, keep your eyes open, and jot down what you did and what you observed.

Pollination. When laying out rows and beds, remember that corn is wind-pollinated and should therefore be planted at least four rows

Companion Planting

Herb	Companions and Effects
Basil	Companion to tomatoes; dislikes rue intensely. Improves growth and flavor. Repels flies and mosquitoes.
Bee balm	Companion to tomatoes; improves growth and flavor.
Borage	Companion to tomatoes, squash, and strawberries; deters tomato worm; improves growth and flavor.
Caraway	Plant here and there; loosens soil.
Catnip	Plant in borders; deters flea beetle.
Chamomile	Companion to cabbages and onions; improves growth and flavor.
Chervil	Companion to radishes; improves growth and flavor.
Chives	Companion to carrots; improves growth and flavor.
Dead nettle	Companion to potatoes; deters potato bug; improves growth and flavor.
Dill	Companion to cabbage; dislikes carrots; improves growth and health of cabbage.
Fennel	Plant away from gardens. Most plants dislike it.
Garlic	Plant near roses and raspberries; deters Japanese beetle; improves growth and health.
Horseradish	Plant at corners of potato patch to deter potato bug.
Hyssop	Deters cabbage moth; companion to cabbage and grapes. Keep away from radishes.
Lamb's-quarters	This edible weed should be allowed to grow in moderate amounts in the garden, especially in corn.
Lovage	Improves flavor and health of plants if planted here and there.
Marigold	The workhorse of the pest deterrents. Plant throughout garden; it discourages Mexican bean beetles, nematodes, and other insects.
Marjoram	Here and there in garden; improves flavors.
Mint	Companion to cabbage and tomatoes; improves health and flavor; deters white cabbage moth.

deep, preferably six to eight. If you plant only a small amount of corn, make a block of four or more short rows rather than planting a single long row.

If you are planning to save seed of wind-pollinated garden vegetables like corn and spinach (see Section Three) you will want to follow recommended spacing requirements to avoid crossing.

Climbers like cucumbers, pole beans, certain melons, Malabar

Nasturtium	Companion to radishes, cabbage, and cucurbits; plant under fruit trees. Deters aphids, squash bugs, striped pumpkin beetles. Improves growth and flavor.
Peppermint	Planted among cabbages, it repels the white cabbage butterfly.
Pigweed	One of the best weeds for pumping nutrients from the subsoil, it is especially beneficial to potatoes, onions, and corn. Keep weeds thinned.
Pot marigold	Companion to tomatoes, but plant elsewhere in garden, too. Deters asparagus beetle, tomato worm, and general garden pests.
Purslane	This edible weed makes good ground cover in the corn.
Rosemary	Companion to cabbage, beans, carrots, and sage; deters cabbage moth, bean beetles, and carrot fly.
Rue	Keep it far away from sweet basil; plant near roses and raspberries; deters Japanese beetle.
Sage	Plant with rosemary, cabbage, and carrots; keep away from cucumbers. Deters cabbage moth, carrot fly.
Southernwood	Plant here and there in garden; companion to cabbage; improves growth and flavor; deters cabbage moth.
Sowthistle	This weed in moderate amounts can help tomatoes, onions, and corn.
Summer Savory	Plant with beans and onions; improves growth and flavor. Deters bean beetles.
Tansy	Plant under fruit trees; companion to roses and raspberries. Deters flying insects, Japanese beetles, striped cucumber beetles, squash bugs, ants.
Tarragon	Good throughout garden.
Thyme	Here and there in garden. It deters cabbage worm.
Wormwood	As a border, it keeps animals from the garden.
Yarrow	Plant along borders, paths, near aromatic herbs; enhances essential oil production.

This information was collected from many sources, most notably the Bio-Dynamic Association and the Herb Society of America.

---

spinach, and others can save you space in the garden if you plant them at the edge next to a fence or trellis, so save an end row for some of these space-takers.

Special problems. Perhaps you have a spot in your garden that is poorly drained, a corner that is shady, a section with hardpan, a rocky area. Each of these special situations may be met and sometimes even partially solved by your choice of plants.

Partial shade? Plant summer lettuce, parsley, raspberries, rhubarb.

Hardpan? Treat the problem by planting deep-rooted vegetables like comfrey or Swiss chard to break up the impervious layer of subsoil.

Poor drainage? Avoid planting globe artichokes, sweet potatoes, or other lovers of warm, loose soil in that spot, until you've corrected the problem by trenching to divert and/or digging in more humus.

Rocky? Potatoes will do well, especially under mulch, but any crop that needs frequent hoeing and cultivating will be a challenge. If you use a tiller, get pointed tines for working around rocks. When your whole garden is rocky, you accept it and work around it (and often have as fringe benefits a lovely rock garden and several fine rock walls). But when only one part is rocky, as is the case with us, you might as well minimize the wear and tear on your hoe by selecting crops to plant there that can be mulched early.

Garden beds. Rows are customary, but not necessarily traditional. There are many good arguments for planting vegetables, closely spaced, in small plots or blocks. Soil may be intensively improved. The beds may be raised to improve drainage. Weeding and harvesting are convenient. When well cared for, small garden beds are delightfully attractive. Many arrangements are possible. You can divide your garden area into blocks, separated by paths. Each block will be solidly planted to a single vegetable or an especially chosen combination of vegetables. Or you might want to keep a grassy path between a double row of narrow vegetable beds. Vegetable beds may be spotted on the lawn, next to a house, or along a walkway. One practical problem with garden beds bordered by grass is the encroachment of the grass into the bed. This may often be solved by sinking a thin metal edging strip between vegetable bed and grass or by building a raised vegetable bed and supporting the deeper soil with wooden boards or railroad ties.

14
Hardening Off

Hardening off plants that you'll be putting outside is a two-part process. The first step is to toughen the plants, quite literally to harden them, so that they will be less vulnerable to outside weather extremes. Sappy, succulent growth is easily damaged by wind, sun, and cold temperatures. What you want to do, then, is to hold back your plants for about a week before you introduce them to the

Blocking out broccoli seedlings to encourage the compact root-ball development that's good for transplanting.

105

larger weather. In order to slow down their growth, water them less often and give them no fertilizer during that final week indoors. Keep temperatures on the cool side, if possible a few degrees lower than the temperature that prevailed up until now. The result will be a shorter, more fibrous plant that will suffer less from the transition to the outdoors.

At about the same time you begin hardening off plants indoors, block out any plants that are growing in flats. To do this, cut between the seedlings, across the flat from left to right and from top to bottom, so that each plant will be centered in a cube of soil. Blocking out severs roots that would be broken in transplanting anyway, and stimulates the plant roots within its block of soil. Thus the roots can, in effect, begin their recovery before transplanting.

When your seedlings have been toughened by enduring a cool, dry week without fertilizer, they are ready to begin to become accustomed to outdoor conditions. Even the best-prepared seedlings will fold up if subjected immediately to a full day of direct sun and even gentle breeze, though, so continue to proceed gradually, eager as you may be to get those flats planted out in the row. Begin with a few hours' exposure to filtered sun—in the shade

Flats of onion seedlings hardening off on the front porch (eastern exposure).

Give plants just enough water to prevent wilting during the hardening-off process.

of a bush, porch railing, or improvised shelter. Gradually increase the amount of direct sun the plant receives until, at the end of a week or 10 days, the seedling is able to take a full day of sunlight. Sun dries the plant and the soil, and in shallow flats it is important to keep the soil moist enough to avoid wilting. Most flats will need watering daily, or at least every other day. In addition, the ultraviolet light given off by the sun, formerly filtered out by window glass or not present in significant amounts in fluorescent light, constitutes a stress for the plant. Only by gradual exposure can the seedling acclimate itself to new higher levels of ultraviolet light.

At the same time, wind, which is often strong and gusty in early spring, can damage plants in three ways. Its drying effect can increase transpiration in the plant to the wilting point. A badly wilted plant is often permanently impaired. Wind also breaks stems of taller, unstaked seedlings. And it may whip even small seedlings about to the extent that their roots are loosened or torn from the growing medium. It is important, then, to choose a sheltered corner for the plant's first week outdoors, one where you either have, or can arrange, protection from prevailing winds.

Cold outdoor temperatures pose a less serious threat to your earliest seedlings—the cabbage, lettuce, endive, etc.—than to the later tomatoes and peppers, but celery, eggplant, and melons are especially sensitive to cold temperatures. Have cartons ready to put over outdoor flats when frost threatens.

The use of cold frames and hotbeds can make possible an even earlier transition to the outdoors. For more information on building and using these devices see chapter 16.

Some gardeners like to soak the planting flat with liquid fertilizer just before removing the plants to set them in the garden. It is true that this one-step treatment saves the trouble of individual plant feeding to a certain extent. I prefer to leave the plant a bit on the hungry side, reasoning that the roots will then be more likely to put out extensive new growth in search of nourishment, but I don't believe the first method is wrong. It works, obviously, for those who do it.

15
The Art of Planting Out

Your vegetable plants have come a long way in only a few weeks, from seeds to tiny seedlings to hopeful transplants to flourishing leafy green promises of early good eating. With every stage you've managed successfully—germination, transplanting, maintaining fertility and water balance, hardening off—your young plants have become more valuable to you. With each week that passes, they become more difficult to replace.

All the attention given to choosing the best seeds and starting the plants off right, then, has built up an investment in your plants. It's important now, at planting-out time, to keep that care consistent when setting seedlings out in the garden. It is easy to lose the work of months overnight, from overeagerness, poor timing, or insufficient protection.

Judging the Signs of Spring

Setting out plants at the right time, in the right way, is the mark of a seasoned gardener. I've made plenty of mistakes in putting out my plants. That's how I've learned what's important. Not that I've arrived at any completed state of gardening expertise. Far from it. There are too many variables in gardening—weather, soil, plant vigor, insects, house guests, wind, timing—for any of us ever to claim complete enlightenment or certainty about the whole process. All I can really say is that I'm learning as I go. It's a path, not a destination. And there's lots of ground yet to be covered.

There are, it seems to me, three skills involved in helping young plants to make the transition between pampered confinement inside and life on their own in the big garden outside. The first is the exercise of good judgment. And this began way back in late winter when you decided when and how to start your plants. If you've been able to resist the winter-weary impulse to start your seedlings too early, you'll now have strong, compact plants to set outside, rather than spindly retarded ones that have been kept on "hold" for too long. If the plants aren't overgrown, you won't be so tempted to put them out before conditions are favorable.

Judgment of outdoor conditions doesn't come overnight. It's the result, rather, of patient observation, experimentation, and record keeping. If you're new to gardening, or to the particular piece of soil you're working with this year, allow yourself a few years to develop a sense of earth and weather signs and how they interact.

Record the last (spring) and first (fall) frosts each year. Take note of the prevailing wind direction. Find several favored, lightly shaded, and sun-dappled corners for hardening plants. Discover which areas in your garden thaw first, which drain more rapidly. In many gardens there is a small corner or strip where, with a little hand-digging after early warming, an early chance planting can be made. If it takes, you start eating fresh from the garden a few weeks early. If it doesn't, there's still time and space to make the sure-thing main-crop plantings that must wait a bit for better odds.

What this means, you see, is that you must study your micro-climate. It helps to know average frost dates for your area, but it helps even more to know how cold air moves on your terrain and which patches of ground become workable first. Cold air sinks. Warm air rises. Land in a valley, where there is no lower point to which frosty air may drain, can be a frost pocket. Even here on our farm, on the south side of a mountain (well, *we* call it a mountain, though residents of Vermont or Colorado may snicker), our open land lies on a long gradual slope running from north to southwest. The upper gardens may escape frost damage that hits the lower patch, even though there is still lower land below this spot, to which the cold air can continue to move.

City buildings hold heat and block wind. Large trees shelter plants from wind, but not from frost. Large bodies of water and even small ones, to a lesser extent, can moderate temperature of the surrounding land.

Observe and experiment, then, and keep notes on what happens. When did you set out the first tomatoes? Where? Did frost hit after you planted them out? How did you protect them? When did they start bearing?

After a few years of gardening in Philadelphia, we found that it was generally safe to set out tomatoes by May 9, in the sheltered block of old houses where we lived. When we moved to Wisconsin, we soon discovered that it was foolish to plant tender plants out before Memorial Day. Now, on our south central Pennsylvania farm, we count on a setting-out date around the middle of May, up to a week later than the prevailing safe time in the southern part of our county.

You can run into trouble, though, if you plan strictly by the calendar. Not every year is alike. Keep the calendar at hand, certainly; it will help you to know what to expect. But try to listen and look too for the actual spring signs—the return of certain birds, the budding of key trees, the blooming of flowers—that let you know how the situation actually is, right around you. In trying to learn this approach myself, I've found that much of the traditional country lore, like the advice to plant soybeans when oak leaves are mouse-ear sized, is surprisingly accurate. (For more information on specific signs to watch for, see Section Three on favorite vegetables and their needs.)

Spring peepers, although a cheering early sound of spring, don't tell you much about planting-out safely. Those little tree frogs get spring fever early, and country wisdom has it that they'll see through glass (ice) three times before spring weather settles in. For me, the cheeping peepers are a reminder, though, to start look-

Spring peeper.
Actual size about one inch.

ing for the first wild greens of the season. Sometimes I can rototill
the garden within a week after they start their trilling. But I don't
rely on them for planting information.

The more you become attuned to what is going on around you
outdoors, the sharper will be your sixth sense about the weather.
Soon you will find it possible to sniff the air, watch the moon, feel
the breeze, and make at least an educated guess about the possibility
of frost at night.

When we notice any of the following signs, we get ready to
protect our tender seedlings:

- A calm air, no breeze blowing, and a clear sky often
  indicate imminent spring or fall frost.

*For straight rows,
stretch a string!*

- An early evening drop in temperature to around 40°F. (5°C.) can be a frost warning. I've learned to round up the plant protectors if the thermometer reads 40°F. on my way back from the barn after evening milking.
- The last week before a full moon is traditionally a time of frost danger. Although I don't know why this should be so, I've noticed that it often *is* so, and so I take the saying seriously.

Take a cue too from your experienced neighbors and relatives. In most neighborhoods, there's a certain amount of friendly rivalry to see who can plant the first peas and onions and harvest the earliest tomato. There's also a large store of gardening expertise and often a little plant trading. Your neighbors may have much to teach you. It is also possible that, after a few years of learning and experimenting, you'll have a lot to share with them. I'm thinking of the farm-raised professional man who hesitated to plant zucchini for fear they'd cross-pollinate and affect this year's watermelon harvest. (See Section Four to find out why he needn't have worried.) Or the neighbor who liked hot peppers but didn't know you could raise them from seed. Or another acquaintance who planted spring radishes but never tried winter radishes or planted a fall garden.

Developing a Good Planting Technique

Judgment, important as it is, may sound elusive, up in the air. The next skill you need is quite down-to-earth: develop a good planting technique. First, choose a good day for setting out your transplants. Not a clear, sunny breezy day, but preferably a damp, drizzly, warmish day. You may not always be able to wait for such a day, but if one does come along at the time when other conditions are favorable, then drop everything and devote the day to planting.

Sun and wind, you see, remove large quantities of water from the plant, by transpiration, and the disturbed roots are hard put to make up this water loss. You can get an idea of the extent of water loss, even under ideal conditions, from the following figures published in *Botany for Gardeners* by Harold Rickett: In one season, a tomato plant loses 35 gallons of water by transpiration; a potato

*Setting out young
transplants in May.*

plant, 25; a giant ragweed, 140 gallons.

The less setback a plant suffers in being put out in the garden, the sooner it will be off and growing and putting on melons or tomatoes or good green leaves.

Use a shovel or an extra-large trowel to dig a generous hole, one that will provide ample space for the plant's root ball. If you possibly can, put a handful of compost into each planting hole, especially for melons, cukes, and squash. When adding compost, dig the hole a few inches deeper, mix in the compost, and toss on a handful of fine loose soil before setting the plant in place.

Tomatoes and pepper plants may be set deeply in the hole—in fact, a tomato plant placed flat on the ground in a shallow trench with just the top one or two sets of leaves showing above ground will form roots at each leaf node and escape drying winds. It will also be easier to cover when frost threatens. Cabbage and lettuce plants may be set more deeply than they grew in the flat if they have developed a one- to two-inch stem; otherwise, cover them with soil only up to the bottom leaves. Soil in the crown of the plant will encourage rot.

Plants that have been blocked off in advance will often have a sufficiently dense network of roots to hold the soil around them until you settle them in the hole. A bare root plant suffers more. Try dipping bare roots in a slurry of thick, muddy water to coat the roots, especially if the day is dry and sunny. Water each plant *as you plant it,* rather than setting a group of plants and returning later to water the whole row. As you position the plant in the hole, try to arrange the roots so that they do not double back on each other or fold back toward the top of the hole. Then pour at least a quart of water on each plant to settle it in the hole. Next, fill in the hole with loose soil—never with clods, which would leave root-drying air spaces. Finally, press the loose soil gently but firmly around the plant so that no air pockets are left. At the same time, form the soil around the stem into a shallow, saucerlike depression

Seedlings should be well watered-in.

which will catch rain and funnel it toward the roots.

Peat pots that stick out above soil level are amazingly effective wicks, drawing moisture away from the plant's roots. For that reason, it is important to tear off at least the top inch or so of the fiber pot so that only the stem and leaves are above ground. Since I have less faith than I once did in the permeability of peat pots to plant roots, I sometimes peel off the whole pot—gently, to avoid tearing roots—when setting out a potted seedling. (If the roots have already penetrated the pot, I don't remove it.) The plastic netting surrounding those compressed peat-pellet seedling containers is also suspect, in my eyes, but I've noticed that roots usually seem to penetrate it more readily than they do the peat pots. The netting is easy to tear off, though, in any case where root penetration might be doubtful.

It's often a good idea, if you're making an early planting in hopes of moving your harvest day up a week or two, to save out a few seedlings of each kind of vegetable you're gambling on, as insurance in case anything would happen to the first planting.

Protecting the Plants

The final trick you need for weathering your seedlings successfully through their big move to the outdoors is protection. Protection from frost, wind, and sun. Leaving new transplants to their own devices usually leads to disappointment. Wind and sun work against their survival for the first week they have their roots in earth, and even after that, sneak frosts can wither down a whole planting in just an hour or so of early-morning chill.

I've had to learn not to be vain about the garden in early spring, but rather to stand ready to cover the young plants with all the odd things I can muster if frost seems likely. I use half-bushel baskets, flowerpots, coffee cans, cottage cheese cartons, berry baskets, and gallon plastic cider jugs with one end cut off. The lightweight plastic protectors were sometimes blown off by the wind until we started the practice of routinely topping them with a small stone or clod of earth to hold them down. Two more precautions:

1. Leaves that touch the inside of a metal can protector can get zapped by the frost, conducted right through the metal. I use the cans over the smaller, lower plants.

116

Keep protective covers handy in case a late-spring frost threatens tender seedlings.

2.   An up-ended flowerpot has a hole through which cold air can drain, and in a severe frost that can be enough to kill the plant. It's happened in my garden, so I now put a little stone or plug of moss over the pot's drainage hole. Berry baskets have side holes, but since they permit air circulation this problem doesn't seem to arise.

117

There's usually about a month between the setting out of lettuce and cabbage in April and tomatoes and peppers in May, when I keep the garden cart loaded with my motley plant caps, ready to wheel out to the field when needed. Heavier protectors such as flowerpots, pans, or cans may be left right beside the plant, but the lightweight plastic stuff tends to blow away and so I usually collect and then redistribute it.

There are other ways to ward off early frost damage.

1.   Glass cloches, which can be made by cutting off the bottom of glass jugs, will not only keep out frost but also act as miniature greenhouses for chancy early plantings. Ventilate the top during the day (remove the cap) or the plant may cook in the sun's heat.

2.   Tents of plastic sheeting, supported by wire U-forms and weighted down at the edges with soil or stones, let in sun and keep out frost and wind. Be sure to ventilate them at the ends and at the bottom, rather than the top, to prevent the escape of the rising warm air.

3.   Kelp (see chapter 19) has been shown to confer frost resistance on plants that were sprayed with a dilute solution of the seaweed. In one study, treated tomato plants survived 29°F. (-2°C.) temperatures.

4.   Mulch of loose straw or hay drawn closely around plants and lightly over their crowns provides enough trapped-air insulation to ward off a light frost.

Covering tender plants with old sheets to prevent frost damage.

5. Water can insulate too. In experiments reported by Professor Fredrick Fay of the University of Toronto, plants continued to grow in a cold frame topped by water-filled plastic bags (set right on the glass), even though air temperatures outside averaged 20°F. A space of at least four inches must be kept between the plant and the outside air.

6. You can even take advantage of the warming effect of freezing water. That's right—water gives off heat when frost hits it. One pound of water releases 144 Btu's when it freezes. In an enclosed space like a cold frame or a plastic tent, several wide, shallow pans of water will help to take the edge off the frost as they freeze. It's important to use shallow containers that will chill rapidly. Deep bowls or pans will not cool fast enough to do your plants any good.

Letting the sprinkler run on vulnerable plants also protects against frost kill.

7. Then there's the morning-after rescue. If, despite your best efforts, or because of an extra-sneaky frost, you wake up to see the characteristic darkening of frost-touched leaves in your brave new vegetable rows, keep calm and reach for the hose.

Frost damages plants by forming sharp-edged ice crystals which puncture cell walls. If you can hose the plants with a fine spray of water *before the sun hits them,* you can often prevent the cell damage that kills the plant. No hose handy? Then use the watering can with the sprinkling head on, as I've done more than once. Or use your trombone sprayer. If the sun's coming up fast and you have many plants to spray, toss an old sheet or blanket over the plants that must wait to prevent their thawing—and consequently collapsing—before you can get to them.

Frost watch must sometimes continue for as long as two weeks after you put tender plants outside. Even head lettuce and endive must be defended from severe frosts.

Wind and sun damage to a newly set-out plant is mostly confined to its first three or four days in the ground, up to a week for tomatoes and eggplants or bare-root seedlings. Pale leaves on newly set-out plants indicate sunscald. Cover them promptly and increase exposure gradually over a week or two. I often leave frost-type covers over these plants for most of the first two or three days. No longer than that, though: they need ventilation and light.

Sometimes I use the pint plastic, open-grid berry boxes to filter out some sun on early lettuce and broccoli transplants. When I must set out young plants in sunny weather, I scatter a light covering of dry hay stems, borrowed from the mulch pile, over their crowns. Just a handful for each plant. The hay shades the plants while admitting some air and sun, and by the time the leaves grow above it they are strong enough to make good use of full sun.

Many country gardeners push an old shingle into the ground on the north or west side of their early cabbage to shield it from strong winds. (To determine the direction of prevailing winds in your garden, tie cloth strips to several stakes or poles and note which direction they blow.) An opened, bottomless half-gallon milk carton set around the plant makes a good wind and sun shield. Even brush and twigs pushed into the soft earth around the plant will serve to cast dappled shade and deflect wind.

Last year, when I put out an early planting of head lettuce in a sheltered corner near the back step, I covered the young plants lightly with brush left from the pea patch. For the first few days, I draped feed bags over the brush to cast dappled shade on the tender plants. It looked perfectly awful, but the combination of varying shade and plenty of air, followed by the lighter shade from the twiggy branches after I'd removed the burlap, brought the plants on gradually without any sunscald or windburn.

That first week in the ground is a critical time. The exuberance of early-spring weather can prove overwhelming to a tender young plant. A bit of hovering and preventive protection at this time can make the difference between a setback and a head start.

16
Cold Frames and Hotbeds

Once you have a cold frame, you'll wonder how you ever got along without one. My own simple cold frame adds several weeks to the productivity of my garden, both spring and fall. Here's how I use it:

- For starting seeds in early spring.
- For hardening of spring transplants.
- For late-summer plantings (or transplants) of easy-to-cover fall vegetables like endive and lettuce —and even to winter-over parsley.
- For late-fall sowings of vegetable seeds, such as asparagus, sorrel, or corn-salad that will come up in early spring but would get plowed over in the big garden.

My small three by six-foot frame can't serve all those functions at once, of course. I really need several more cold frames (Are you reading this, Mike?). But by careful planning and prompt rotation of plant populations, I keep the frame busy from March to December.

Location and Design

Your first consideration in planning a cold frame should be location. A southern exposure is a must, and some protection from cold winds will help to maintain the sun-generated warmth in the frame. If the site slopes slightly to the south, so much the better. The spot should be well-drained too, not a hollow where water will collect.

Your aim should be to build the frame so that the sun's rays will strike the glass at a 90-degree angle. Since the sun's position in the sky changes with the seasons, from its low, weak point in winter to its commanding summer position high in the sky, you obviously can't insure a 90-degree angle at all times. Since March and April are the critical

*Flats of seedlings
hardening off in
the cold frame.*

months for seedling protection for many gardeners, the greatest
good for the most plants can probably be obtained by making the
angle of the cold frame cover in such a way that early-spring sun
will hit it head-on, perpendicularly.

Plants that are in the cold frame over summer are often being
protected from strong sun, as in the case of summer lettuce, so the
summer angle isn't important. Fall plants need frost protection and
intensification of the gradually waning sun, which is somewhat lower
in the sky than it was in early spring.

You can build a cold frame that will be a remarkably effective
sun-catcher, both spring and fall, if you make it in sections which

can be bolted together, with a special fall insert to concentrate the pale, weak, late-year sun. In a *Farmstead* magazine article, Rocky Roughgarden describes the modular cold frame he built for his Massachusetts garden. The glass side of the basic spring section slopes at a 35-degree angle from the earth. A wedge-shaped fall insert, bolted on in early autumn, raises the angle of the glass to 55 degrees from the earth. The Roughgarden cold frame boasts, in addition, an extra cover insulated with scrap Styrofoam. The exact angle of the sun will vary, of course, in different latitudes. If you decide to build such a finely tuned cold frame, you'd be wise to observe and record the sun's angle as it strikes your own site both spring and fall before making final plans.

Dimensions of the cold frame can be suited to your site and the materials at hand, but in most cases a maximum width (front to back) of three feet is ideal. A frame that is too wide—over four feet—will be difficult to reach into when you tend the plants. Length of the frame is not critical, but make it as long as possible; soon after it's built, you'll wish it were longer.

Construction

Construction of the cold frame is simple. Dig a hole about a foot deep and three to four inches larger in all dimensions than your projected frame. Build the topless, bottomless box of sturdy wood, reinforced at the corners with metal braces or short two-by-fours, and position it in the hole, taking care to level it well. The two short side pieces of the frame should taper from front to back to give you the desired angle. And the long backboard, of course, will be higher than the long front board. Check to determine whether your rectangle is true by measuring from corner-to-corner in an X. Both lines should be the same length.

In making our cold frame, we used locust lumber cut from our own logs by a neighboring sawyer. We learned too late that locust cannot be cut into even boards until it has aged for a year. The varying thickness of our locust boards doesn't impair their effectiveness in our cold frame, though. Locust, a very heavy wood, has the advantage of lasting a long time in the ground. If you use more rot-prone wood, treat it first with a coat or two of linseed oil to retard rotting. I wouldn't use creosote for fear it would be too strong for young seedlings.

Wood is a good insulator, far better than metal, and so the boards should be a good inch thick if possible. If you have two-inch thick lumber, that will protect your plants even more, although it will be more cumbersome to handle.

Most people use secondhand windows or storm sashes, hinged to the backboard, for the sun-catching top of the frame. Here again, wood-framed windows will retain much more warmth than those that are metal-rimmed. You can even tack on an extra layer of plastic sheeting for more protection in bitter cold weather. When night temperatures fall far below freezing, place burlap bags stuffed with pine needles, batts of hay, old blankets or boards, or other improvised frost protectors over the glass.

Accessories

On good days, when winds aren't high, you will want to swing back the lid of the cold frame to expose the plants directly to the sun. Sudden wind gusts, though, can be surprisingly forceful, so you will want to devise a way to anchor the glass lid so that the wind won't bang it and break it. Our cold frame is built on the south side of the cement-block-enclosed compost pile. When I raise the lid, it leans back and rests on the block wall, but a strong wind can blow it down, with disastrous results. (If you think I'm warning you about this because I slipped up on it the first time around, you're right!) After Mike replaced the broken glass, he put a screw hook into each of the two top windows and fastened wire around and through a block on each end of the compost-pile wall. Now when I open the glassed top I catch the wire loop in each hook so the wind can't blow it down.

Another gadget you'll need to operate your cold frame efficiently is a prop of some kind to elevate the top a few inches when intense sun warms up the interior. This can be as simple as a handy stick or stone, but an adjustable stop, made of a notched two-by-four, will give you more leeway in arranging ventilation to suit conditions. Set the prop stick on the ground and rest the lid of the cold frame on one of the three steps cut into the prop.

In early spring, I use the cold frame to bring on the early lettuce and cabbage under glass. By the end of April it's usually safe to start hardening off the peppers and tomatoes I'll plant in the garden in mid-May. When I put out flats of these vegetables, I leave the glass windows open during the day, unless the wind is strong, and close them at night when temperatures dip. For the first week or so, I use improvised slatted covers to shade out about 60 percent of the sun's rays, so the plants don't suffer from sunscald as they would if suddenly exposed to the full impact of direct sunlight. My shades happen to be the metal grid from the back of a dead refrigerator, and an old wooden gate. A section of snow fencing would work well too. It would certainly look neater.

Plants in the open cold frame dry more quickly than those kept under lights. For some, daily watering is necessary when the sun is intense. Most flats, unless shallow and lacking moisture-retaining moss, do well for me when watered about every other day. Plants that are being hardened off, you'll recall, should be kept on the dry side but not allowed to wilt.

A Cold Frame but a Hotbed

A hotbed is simply a cold frame that is supplied with extra warmth. The heat, usually from the bottom, helps to promote seed germination and steady growth of seedlings that are cold sensitive.

An electric soil-heating cable, laid on a firm two-inch bed of vermiculite (for insulation) and covered with an inch of soil or sand, a layer of wire screening to prevent accidental digging up of the cable, and a final four inches or so of good fine soil, will give steady bottom heat.

If you already have your cold frame set up and don't want to install a permanent heating arrangement, you could warm the frame temporarily with a chicken brooder lamp. Or, for very gentle warmth, take a tip from one of our neighboring master gardeners and tack a string of outdoor Christmas tree lights around the inside of the frame.

Conservation-conscious gardeners are turning increasingly to the manure-heated hotbed, since it's possible to achieve the same end without drawing on electric power. In addition, you improve your soil and eliminate equipment purchase and care. Most old gardening books offer elaborate plans for the construction of hotbeds of heroic proportions. Our grandfathers, who farmed with horsepower, had an abundance of this quick-heating manure at their disposal. Even today, though, the common keeping of pleasure horses by people who don't always have a use for the by-products puts horse manure within the reach of city and suburban as well as country gardeners.

To make a manure-heated hotbed, dig a rectangular hole three to four inches larger all around than the dimensions of your frame and 1½- to 2-feet deep. A week or 10 days before planting, pack horse or chicken manure into the excavation, up to six inches from soil level. Hose this layer down to start decompostion, then spread six inches of fine soil on top of it. The manure will reach its peak of heat within three to six days. Wait to plant, though, until the soil temperature falls to 85°F. (29°C.), or you'll cook your seedlings. Ventilate the bed as necessary to keep the temperature below 90°F. (32°C).

Improvisations

If you like to improvise, perhaps some of the following ideas, used successfully by other experienced gardeners, will work for you.

1. Mini-hotbed—a discarded refrigerator crisper drawer, topped with its original glass, set in a hole over packed, moistened manure as described above.

2. A portable cold frame backed up to a cellar window, which can be opened to admit heat from the house.

3. A long, low tent made of two screen doors covered on each side with a layer of tacked-on plastic sheeting, attached to triangular end frames of outdoor plywood in which ventilation holes have been drilled. Use this as a cold frame, or bury manure in the garden to make it a hotbed.

4. Frames made of scrap wood covered with poultry netting and topped by tacked-on plastic make inexpensive portable cold frames.

As you've no doubt noticed by now, part of the satisfaction of rigging up a cold frame—for me at least—lies in using materials at hand to make a useful thing. See what *you* can come up with!

17
Early Care of the Young Transplant

Extra measures of support given to new plantings—mulching, watering, fertilizing, staking, and thinning—should be carried out with regard for variations in weather, plant growing habits, and row spacing. While differences in climates and individual gardens make rigid prescriptions unworkable, perhaps a few loosely scheduled suggestions would help you to time these practices correctly to encourage rather than impede the plant's growth.

Overview of the garden during the first week in May.

Mulching

Wait until the soil warms up before mulching heat-loving crops like tomatoes, peppers, eggplant, cucumbers, and melons. Begin mulching the cool-weather crops—lettuce, peas, cabbage, beets, carrots—as soon as their seedlings look as though they might amount to something. My mulching program progresses gradually as the season wears on, as each day, starting in May, I spread a few more armloads of discarded barn hay around the lettuce and peas. By mid or late June the soil has warmed, and my husband has cut several wagonloads of weeds for me to use in mulching the large spaces between the tomatoes, squash, and other heat lovers. By early July the garden is completely mulched, except for the sweet potatoes and corn.

Use any fine mulch you may have for narrow rows and save the coarse stuff for wider aisles.

If you use black plastic to mulch melons, as I do when I accumulate enough black leaf-holding bags, put it around the plants soon after they've germinated, to help warm the soil.

How much mulch is enough to keep weeds down?

- Discarded carpet: a single layer.
- Sawdust: two to three inches.
- Leaves: 8 to 10 inches.
- Hay: baled, about a five- to six-inch thickness flaked off from the packed bale; loose, 8 to 10 inches.
- Newspaper: three to six sheets, held down by stones or other mulch.
- Grass clippings: about four inches when first spread. They'll pack down.
- Wood chips: at least six inches unless a layer of newspaper or other light-impervious material is put down first.

When spreading mulch, start at the edge of the patch or row rather than working back from the middle, in order to prevent undue compacting of the soil by repeated treading on the bare ground.

Fertilizing

Newly transplanted seedlings have little need for extra plant food. They're busy forming more feeder roots and adjusting to their new environment. If you've spread fertilizer before digging the garden and have put some compost in the holes at planting time, most of your plants should be well supplied for the season.

Pulling mulch around newly set-out transplants.

Some heavy feeders like cauliflower, cabbage, melons, and rhubarb often produce better if given extra feedings, starting a week or 10 days after setting out. Some gardeners give their tomato plants extra fertilizer to keep them producing well through a long growing season. Corn too may appreciate an extra side-dressing if you can manage it. In a large garden, it's usually difficult to get around to doing these extra things. We put extra manure on our corn plot one year when we had not been able to plow in enough fertilizer when preparing the land, but for the most part we depend on preplanting manuring to carry most plants through the growing season. Exceptions, in our garden, are lettuce, cabbage, cauliflower, and melons, to which we try to give several booster feedings of

Manure tea.
Bag of manure in barrel of water.

either diluted fish emulsion or manure tea. These nitrogenous boosters, since they promote leafy growth, should not be given to your root vegetables, or you may have great leafy spindly-rooted carrots.

Recipe for manure tea. Fill a burlap sack with manure and place it in a barrel or trash can. Fill the can with water. Cover (to keep out flies) and let the brew steep for several days. Dip off some of the enriched water into a bucket or watering can, dilute it to the color of tea, and pour it around the base of the plant. Optional system for easy-to-handle amounts: Put manure directly in old tar buckets, fill with water, and dip off as needed. Refill several times, using original manure. After three to four batches have been made from the same manure, pour the slurry on the garden and start again with fresh manure.

Thinning

Most plants you've direct-seeded right in the ground will need to be thinned, unless you have better control of your planting hand than many gardeners do. Squash, cucumbers, and pole beans are usually intentionally overplanted so that the strongest plants can then be chosen and retained. Thinning should begin early, as soon as the seedlings can be easily grasped, to minimize damage to roots of neighboring plants. You'll soon notice that the remaining plants are growing better with more space around them.

Some edible-leaved plants like Swiss chard, lettuce, spinach, and turnips may be thinned gradually, with the ever-larger thinnings contributing to the soup pot or the salad bowl. Rather than thin only part of the row of these plants thoroughly, thin the whole row somewhat sparingly and then return in a few days to pick thinnings again for the supper table. Firm the soil back around the plants if pulling out thinnings has loosened it.

When I first started growing vegetables, thinning seemed wasteful to me. I even tried to transplant the radish seedlings I had pulled out. But when I found out that unthinned lettuce rarely makes a decent rosette of leaves, carrots entwine and stay small, and fennel shoots to seed with thin stalks, I began to accept what I'd read, that each vegetable needs a certain amount of space in order to grow to its genetic potential. Thinning may be painful, but growing crowded, second-rate plants is wasteful.

Spacing varies according to the plant, of course. Check Section Three to find out how many inches or feet each vegetable needs, and then gradually thin your way to that ideal spacing as the seedlings grow.

Staking

Stakes for plants that need support—tomatoes, pole beans, peas, and others—should be driven into the ground while the plants are still too small to need the stakes in order to avoid damage to the more extensive root system of the older plant. It's also a good idea to take note of the prevailing winds that blow over your garden, and position the stake so that the plant will lean *toward* it, rather than straining away from it when the wind blows.

It is not necessary to stake tomatoes. The trade-off here is the

131

gardener's time in exchange for cleaner, easier to pick fruit and less spoilage. Once you start tying the plant to the stake, you must continue, or the main stem may break. I admire well-staked tomato plants but find it easier, in my garden, to plant a few more plants to make up for the slightly higher fruit loss. I can usually manage to get that first plant-to-stake tie made, but by the time the plants are ready for a second tying, I'm knee-deep in canning, freezing, planting for fall, and helping with haymaking to do more than give them a guilty glance. If I only grew a few tomato plants, instead of the four dozen I usually put in, I'd give each one a circle of strong open-mesh wire fencing to climb on, and let it go its own way.

Weed Control

The old adage "one year's seeding makes seven years' weeding" has its basis in fact. Although few of them have impermeable seed coats, weed seeds have an incredibly long life span, often 10 years and even more. In one experiment, in which 11 species of wild seeds buried in 1902 were still viable 20 years later, eight of these were alive after 40 years, and two still germinated 60 years later. Moral: Try to avoid letting weeds go to seed. Mulch, hoe, or pull weeds when plants are small. Later, when plants are bearing, weed competition may be less damaging, and in some cases it even helps the plant by shading, keeping roots cool, or bringing up trace minerals.

Watering

Well-mulched gardens can endure a drought that would parch unprotected vegetable patches, but even a mulched garden will begin to suffer if two or three weeks pass without rain, especially in August when the sun is extra hot. (For some Western gardeners, of course, irrigation is a necessity.)

If you must water, follow these guidelines:

1. Water as infrequently as possible. Constant moistening of the upper layer of soil encourages plant roots to remain close to the surface where they are vulnerable to prolonged drought, and also to hoeing, if the ground is bare.

2. Water thoroughly when you *do* water. Give the plants a

Watering transplants

steady soaking, enough to make the soil wet four to six inches down. (Three inches may be enough for lettuce, which is quite shallow-rooted.)

   3.   Get the water to the roots. A soil-soaking hose or system

Sunken can for deep watering special plants, eggplant here.

of irrigation trenches is far more efficient than a revolving sprinkler, which evaporates a good bit of the water before it even reaches the soil. In a small garden, pour buckets and sprinkling cans of water directly on the base of the plant. Not on the leaves. For special plants, you can sink a large can with nail holes punched in the bottom (or an old leaky bucket) next to the vegetable or hill, and fill it with water from the hose. The water will seep into the soil and be available to the plant at root level.

There's seldom enough soil-soaking hose to go around in the large garden. If I must water my garden during a hot, dry spell, I leave the sprinkler head on the hose but turn it upside down and tuck it under the thick mulch. In that way, hardly any water is lost to evaporation and yet the sprinkler gives off a more gentle spray than the hose nozzle would, so that soil at the point of water impact is less likely to erode.

I've found, too, that if I begin by placing the hose with sprinkler head at the farthest end of the row, I can then simply pull the hose toward me to reposition it, without getting drenched or turning it off. (If it's hot and dry enough to irrigate, though, the cool sprinkling is sometimes welcome.)

4. Increasing the humus content of your soil will improve its water-retaining capacity.

18
Direct Seeding

Planting seed right in the ground is a ritual that links us with people of generations past, who sowed the ancestors of these same seeds in even more precarious times, as well as with other land-based people around the globe, many of whom depend desperately and directly on the fruit of the seeds they sow. For the gardener, seed sowing is essentially a hand operation. True, there are mechanical seed-sowing devices, and preplanted tapes of seed may be had for a price, but somehow these have never tempted me. At a sacrifice, perhaps, of some precision and seed economy, I prefer the immediate contact between hand, seed, and soil.

So it is every spring. We gardeners are usually ready with our seed packets long before the soil is in condition to work. After we've started the early cool-weather crops indoors and planted flats of the later tropicals like tomatoes and peppers, we go over the seeds for outdoor planting and divide them into groups:

- First-thing plantings—peas, dill, leaf lettuce, radishes, turnips, onion sets.
- Second-early plantings—carrots, beets, cabbage, fennel.
- Mid-season earlies—parsnips, salsify, celeriac, later carrot and radish and lettuce plantings, early corn, New Zealand spinach, purple green beans, leeks, sweet onions.
- After-frost plantings—cucumbers, tampala, soybeans, green beans, corn, summer lettuce.
- Warm-weather plantings—melons, limas, squash, pumpkin, more corn.
- Early-summer plantings—kale, rutabaga, Brussels sprouts, cauliflower, endive, head lettuce, Chinese cabbage, winter radishes.

Then, when we've dug or plowed or rototilled the garden, and the soil has settled for a day or two, we start with the earliest, hardiest seeds on our list. The soil should be in good tilth, as finely worked and raked as possible. It may be cold, but it should not be wet and lumpy.

As the soil warms and the weather moderates, we work our way through the increasingly tender vegetables, all the while watching the signs in the world around us as well as our schedules and records from previous years. Some old herbals, in fact, advise the gardener to go out naked to sow his spring crops. At first hoot, this suggestion seems ridiculous as well as impractical. For most of us, it remains impractical, but surely we must admit that the gardener who goes out unclothed (without even an overall pocket for his planting plan and extra seed packets!) will surely be sensitive to air and soil temperature, and therefore less likely to plant seeds recklessly early.

Years ago, and even today in cultures that acknowledge our absolute dependence on plants, the planting of seed would be a ritual, carried out with a sober and hopeful sense of its significance. In his book *Indian Corn in Old America,* for example, Paul Weatherwax describes the many ceremonies and taboos associated with the planting of corn, including a period of abstinence from sexual activity preceding the time of planting, culminating in ritual intercourse at or just before seed sowing.

Planting by the Moon

Planting by the moon is another example of applied folklore that is still widely practiced. Now that the moon's influence over bodies of water is universally accepted, the assumption that living

Bean seed sprouting.
Dark area is seed case splitting off.
Length of seed, one inch.

things are also affected by changes in the moon's relationship to the earth seems reasonable, even probable. If the moon really does exert a force that raises groundwater as it does the ocean tides, perhaps the rising of nutrient-carrying water from the roots through the stem to the leaves of the plant is stimulated too.

Research studies at Tulane University have shown that seeds absorb water and germinate on a regular cycle that coincides with the lunar month. This solid evidence from impartial observers would seem to add credence to what has until now been considered a superstition or, at best, a harmless but silly country folkway.

I have not experimented in any serious way with moon planting. Not that I think the practice is foolish—I don't. It makes sense, in many ways, even though details are sometimes fuzzy and occasionally contradictory. I'd really like to plan more of my plantings by the phases of the moon. So far, though, I've had entirely enough variables to dovetail at spring planting time—condition of soil, wind delaying lime spreading, rain delaying manure spreading (the tractor shouldn't go on wet ground and, being something of an antique, won't start in freezing weather when ground is hard), book deadlines, spring guests, goat kidding and other barn happenings, that to work around one more schedule demand—planting in tune with the moon—might only confuse the already delicate balance between weather, seed planting, and other work.

Don't let me discourage you. Let's just say that I'm not well enough organized yet to give the system a fair trial. Actually, some experienced practitioners of the art of moon-phase planting maintain that the method *helps* them to organize their garden chores by establishing a schedule for planting, weeding, and harvesting chores. You even get a period of rest. The influence of the moon, by the way, is thought by many people to affect not only plants but also animals (and people!) and so you can find directions in some country almanacs for propitious times to castrate, dehorn, and wean livestock.

The lunar month is divided into four quarters. During the first two quarters, beginning with the appearance of the new moon, the moon is waxing, or growing. This is the time to plant or transplant aboveground crops—leafy vegetables, grains, the cole family, parsley, peppers, and cucumbers in the first quarter.

The third quarter, when the moon has begun to wane, is the time to plant root crops.

"Don't plant anything during the last quarter," advise the moon-planting sages. That's a barren time, best reserved for weeding and cultivating. Furthermore, the day the moon changes quarters, and the four days when the moon is almost full and just past full are not propitious for important projects, according to some moon-sign authorities.

Consult your almanac or feed store calendar for exact timing of the moon's phases, and one of the books on the "Recommended Reading List" for more information on using this practice to guide your garden work. Your calendar may provide extra information that could be confusing, unless you realize that in each lunar month, according to those who map out such things, the 12 signs of the zodiac rule in the same succession they follow in the yearly calendar (Pisces, Aquarius, Capricorn, etc.). If you *really* get into moon planting, you'll avoid the barren signs too (Leo, Gemini, Virgo) and plan important plant work during the fruitful signs (Cancer, Scorpio, Pisces). Personally, I have enough to contend with in just getting the ground prepared between snow melt and spring rains, but perhaps I'm missing something by not making a consistent effort to plant by the moon.

Bean sprout with one cotyledon removed.

Presoaking Seeds

Presoaking the seed before planting may hasten germination of some kinds of seeds. Parsley and carrot and other slow-germinating seeds, or seeds with hard coats like morning glory or New Zealand spinach, are often soaked in warm water overnight before planting. When ready to plant, drain the seeds and mix tiny seeds with a dry substance like sand or coffee grounds so they don't clump together.

I often presoak pea and snap bean seeds for a few hours before planting. Lima beans and soybeans contain so much protein that they may swell too much and then split, if soaked too long. When I do presoak these seeds I drain them after they've been submerged for an hour.

Inoculating Seeds

Inoculation improves plant vigor and yield by coating the seed with helpful bacteria at the time of planting. Most inoculants come in powdered form, and the seed should be moistened to help the powder to adhere.

The kinds of inoculants available to home gardeners will no doubt be more numerous in the near future. At present, specific strains are available for garden legumes, potatoes, and various grains, and there is a special mixture for use on a variety of garden vegetables.

An inoculant containing the nitrogen-fixing bacteria in the rhizobium group, commercially available as Nitragin, is familiar to most gardeners. It is applied to pea and bean seed at planting time to ensure that a good supply of soil and crop-improving rhizobia are present in the soil. If you are planting seed in a spot where rhizobium-inoculated crops have grown before, you may not need to reinoculate. I usually treat the seed anyway, just to be sure. In the days before inoculants were commercially available, farmers would mix soil from a previous stand of high-yielding peas or beans into the row for the next crop.

Specific strains of the bacterium are available for different field crops like alfalfa or clover, as well as for soybeans. If you are planting soybeans in your garden, either the field variety or a kind bred especially for table use, you need a special soybean inoculant.

(See "Sources for Some Items Mentioned in the Book," page 355.)

A new inoculant has recently come on the scene. Azotobacter differ from rhizobia in that they live in the soil, not on plant roots. Studies by Russian, British, and American microbiologists have shown that azotobacter benefit plants in five ways:

- They capture atmospheric nitrogen for their own growth, subsequently releasing this nitrogen to the soil when they die. (Each bacterium lives about 24 hours.)
- They produce hormones, notably gibberellic and indoleacetic acids, which stimulate plant growth.
- They also produce antibiotics which can kill some pathogenic soil fungi and bacteria.
- They produce vitamins which nourish both the rhizobia that live on legume roots and the mycorrhizal fungi that make soil nutrients more readily available to the plants on whose roots they live.
- The phosphate used by azotobacter in its life processes is taken from soil phosphate which occurs in a form that plants can't absorb and is transformed by the bacteria into a different kind of phosphate compound, which becomes immedi-

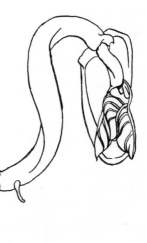

Bean sprout with one cotyledon removed.

ately available to nearby plants when the bacterium dies.

If this sounds like something you'd want to have going on in your garden soil, you might like to know that azotobacter inoculant is newly available commercially. You can order it by mail and apply it at planting time, just as you would the legume inoculants you may already be using.

Like all soil life, azotobacter may be inhibited or encouraged by the conditions surrounding it. For example:

- It thrives in well-aerated soil. Cultivate and keep humus content high.
- Acid soil (below 6.5 pH) is not to its liking. Keep soil well limed.
- Fungicides and other chemicals used to treat seeds discourage the growth of azotobacter.
- Manure in the soil helps to increase the bacteria's ability to use atmospheric nitrogen.

Sowing

Now to plant those seeds. First, you'll want to mark the row so that you have a guide for sowing seeds in a straight line. An old farmer of our acquaintance maintains, with a twinkle in his eye, that you can grow more plants in a crooked than a straight row. But since the placement of each row affects the one next to it, straight rows (unless you are contouring around a hillside) use space more efficiently and prevent a lot of headaches if you rototill. Nothing like getting to the middle of a row with the tiller and finding you can't get through without destroying some plants. I know—I've done it. The good old stake-and-string row marker is old stuff to most gardeners. What is not so generally recognized, though, is that your row will be marked more accurately if you tie the string near the bottom of the stakes, rather than at the top, so that it doesn't waver around in the wind. Then hoe or rake to one side of the string.

When making a furrow, common practice is to use the pointed edge of a hoe to form a V-shaped trough ──∨── . This is all right for large, sparsely planted seed. But a wider, shallower depression in the soil allows seeds to spread out rather than tumble together in a clump. ⌐__⌐

Some gardeners like to make what they call "spot plantings"—placing groups of two to six seeds in the row with a few inches left bare between groups, which are later thinned.

Depth of planting affects both aeration and temperature surrounding the seed. Soil at lower levels is cooler and more tightly

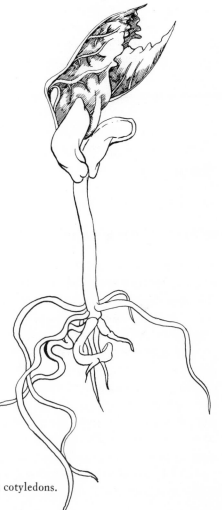

First bean leaves emerging from between cotyledons.

packed. In most cases, shallow planting is to be preferred in spring. Cover the seed with no more than three times its size in soil. Firming of the seedbed is important, to ensure close contact between seed and soil. Ground moisture in spring is usually sufficient for germination. Occasionally I'll water carrot and parsley seeds into the row to get them well settled.

Vegetable specialist Victor Tiedjens recommends a method of eliminating early weed competition that should work well if the soil is finely raked. Rake an inch of fine soil over the row where you've just sown and covered seed. Then, in about 10 days, go along the row with the flat edge of your rake, knocking off the small ridge of soil, and with it thousands of potential weeds.

To help avoid overcrowding, fine seed may be mixed with three or four parts of sand, fine dry soil, or coffee grounds. Too much sand or other diluent, though, will cause an uneven distribution of the seeds.

A last reminder from an absentminded gardener: Mark the row you've just planted, with a stake at each end. Seed packets pulled over the stakes look cheerful and hopeful, but the wind usually blows them off. Some gardeners staple the packets to the stakes. Record, indoors, what you've planted and where. After a few rains, the evidence of your having worked the ground will be erased, and it's embarrassingly easy to find yourself replanting the same row.

When Conditions Are Less than Ideal

You know, and I know, that there'll occasionally be times when we'll be putting seed in the ground when by rights we probably shouldn't. If the soil is still rough and full of clods, but you *must* plant corn, sow it thickly—six seeds to the foot—and try to rake away the clods before pulling dry soil over the seed.

If the soil is still colder than it ought to be, but you want to gamble an early planting, sow thickly then too. If it is not a large planting, and you have some compost, spread a layer of compost in the furrow before placing the seed. Cold soil, according to University of Minnesota soils specialist Curtis Overdahl, slows down the uptake of nutrients by the plant. Studies have shown, though, that putting fertilizer right in the row when spring was cold (as opposed to broadcasting it) boosted the eventual yield of corn, the plant under consideration. Thus, making organic nutrients immediately available to the plant may well help to counteract unfavorable conditions. In addition, if the compost is nearly but not quite finished, its continued decomposition might release enough heat to boost seed germination. These last two conjectures, while unproven, cost little time and effort to try.

Bean plant after first leaves are making food, cotyledons are shrinking, roots growing rapidly.
Actual above-ground height, 5½ inches.

145

19
Kelp

Some remarkable results have been obtained both in the laboratory and in the field by researchers using a spray of diluted liquified seaweed extract to treat plants. Gardeners are beginning to apply the results of these studies in their backyard patches, often with surprisingly noticeable benefits.

Let's take a look at some of the beneficial results that have been obtained under controlled conditions. The following results have been measured and recorded by different scientists working with various crops in several nations:

- Increased crop yields.
- Longer storage life of fruits and vegetables.
- Improved seed germination.
- Frost resistance in growing plants.
- Resistance to attack by insects and fungi.

Studies, beginning in 1959 and continuing today, have repeatedly demonstrated that *something* does indeed happen when plants are sprayed with a seaweed extract solution. Why have we gardeners been so slow to apply these findings to our family food crops? The stuff is nontoxic, easy to use, and moderate in cost. But the idea is new to us; skepticism has too often squelched curiosity.

The *practice* of using seaweed to improve plant growth, though, is very old. All along the shores of northern Europe, since at least the twelfth century, tillers of the land have collected seaweed for cattle fodder and soil improvement. Portuguese fishermen who kept their catches fresh by piling wet seaweed over the fish tossed the slimy stuff aside, often on their gardens, when it had served its primary purpose. Gradually, as people recognized that plants grew better in seaweed-treated plots, they gathered and spread the weed intentionally. Even earlier, centuries earlier, in fact, coastal Oriental gardeners had discovered the value of seaweed as a soil improver and systematically used it to help maintain the fertility of their soils.

During the seventeenth, eighteenth, and nineteenth centuries, the ash of burnt seaweed, known then as kelp, was used as a fertilizer. In 1912, a patent on a liquid preparation of dried seaweed was issued in England. A few studies on the use of liquid seaweed preparations were done during the 1930's, but by far the bulk of the scientific evidence that tends to bear out the effectiveness of this plant treatment has been printed since 1960.

The Benefits of Kelp

You're still shaking your head, perhaps, wondering whether any one substance can affect a plant from seed germination through flower formation, maturity, and fruit production.

Perhaps you'd like to hear about some of the measured effects that have been reported. Hundreds of studies have been done. The following are representative:

Crop yields. Celery plants sprayed at 20 days of age with a 1:100 solution of seaweed extract yielded larger stalks than the untreated control plants. Snap beans treated one week before bloom showed a 10-percent increase in yield on the first picking. Weekly spray applied to cucumber plants during the fruiting season resulted in a yield increase of 41.8 percent in a three-year study. Dr. T. L. Senn observed earlier fruiting of pepper plants to which medium and low concentrations of the solution had been applied. In one test, corn yield (number of ears) was actually lower in the treated plants, but the ears were 15 to 20 percent larger than the controls.

Longer storage life. In studies reported by Kingman and Senn at Clemson University, peaches from seaweed-sprayed trees had a longer than usual shelf life, and the growth of decay organisms seemed to be inhibited. Those cucumbers that were more prolific after seaweed treatment also kept longer than cucumbers from control plants.

Improved seed germination. Seeds of some species of plants germinate more rapidly and completely when treated with seaweed extract, according to Dr. Senn, who also noted that the treatment caused accelerated respiratory activity in the seed. (See chapter 6, "Germination.") Too strong a solution inhibited germination, though. In an experiment exploring the effect of seaweed extract on the germination of seeds of creeping red fescue grass, Button and Noyes reported improved germination of seeds treated with concentrations of 0.5 percent and one percent. A five percent solution reduced germination sharply. Seeds that were allowed to dry between soaking and planting did not perform dependably.

Frost resistance. Seaweed-treated tomato plants studied at Clemson University were able to survive temperatures as low as 29°F. (−2°C.). Untreated control plants were killed by this frost. Eskimos have long used seaweed to protect vegetables from frost damage, although the first recorded instance of this practice occurred during the 1940s.

Resistance to insect and fungus damage. Studies done at the Virginia truck experiment station demonstrated that a seaweed preparation protected tomatoes from fungus damage as effectively as a fungicide. Some early work done in France and England suggests that nematodes tend to avoid fields that have been treated with seaweed.

Dr. Byrley Diggers of Rutgers University recorded an appreciable drop in the red spider mite population of seaweed-sprayed apple trees. While studies done by another researcher did not corroborate this evidence under greenhouse conditions, this whole area is still largely unexplored, and it is possible that controlled experiments will suggest further applications. Since, as E. Booth of the Institute of Seaweed Research has reported, the reproductive rate of the red spider is known to fall when carbohydrate and phosphorus content of the leaf increases, it would seem that the field is wide open for more studies on the ways in which seaweed extract spray affects the plant tissues.

While it is too soon to say with any certainty that seaweed extract sprays will definitely protect a plant from insect and fungus attack, it is not a bit too soon for gardeners to try the method for themselves. It can't hurt, as long as low concentrations (about 1:100) are used, and it might very well help.

The Secrets of Kelp's Effectiveness

Test results have given us an inkling of what can be done in fortifying plants with seaweed extract solutions, all the way from improving germination to lengthening fruit storage life. Although some results are not yet conclusive, evidence continues to mount. The more curious among us are probably wondering "How does it work? What does seaweed contain that would account for its effectiveness in boosting plant yield, vigor, and resistance?"

Some definite facts are known about the properties of seaweeds and their effect on plant tissues. New theories are being tested right now. And speculation continues about the many facts of this interaction that are still not understood. Even what we know is often best expressed as what we know doesn't happen. The nutritional value of the spray, which has been established by test results, seems to be unrelated to the seaweed's content of the major elements—nitrogen, phosphorus, and potassium.

Studies have shown that treated plants made better use of boron, copper, iron, manganese, and zinc. In fact, tomatoes that had been sprayed were found to have more manganese than the seaweed itself had contained. The conclusion seems logical that some active agent in the seaweed helped to release previously unavailable manganese from the soil. Dr. Senn has shown that pineapple seedlings can absorb enough trace elements—magnesium, zinc, and boron—from the foliar-sprayed extract to stimulate almost normal plant respiration. One assumption is that the alginic acid the seaweed contains helps to bind these trace elements in a more soluble and therefore more available form.

In trying to account for the peculiarly wide-ranging effectiveness of seaweed, earlier speculation centered around the trace minerals. A plant subjected to cold temperatures, for example, has been found to lack the ability to synthesize certain vital components of metabolism. The theory that trace elements in the seaweed make up for this deficiency (and thus confer a degree of frost protection) has not yet been discredited.

But other substances have entered the picture. Auxins, plant-produced chemicals which control growth, have been thought to be responsible for the growth-promoting effect of the seaweed, and yet tests have so far not borne out this theory. Solutions of auxins are known to be unstable. Although auxins were detected in fresh, whole seaweed, none could be identified in the solution of dried, powdered seaweed. Seaweed samples have shown gibberellin-like activity, but only when the solution was freshly prepared; after four months the gibberellin content of the solution was not large enough to be effective.

Kelp, *Laminaria digitata.*

Most recent theories center around the cytokinins, growth-promoting hormones which have been discovered in seaweed. Cytokinins have been reported in the seaweed *Laminaria digitata;* as far as I can determine, studies have not been completed on other species of seaweed. According to Dr. Gerald Blunden of the Portsmouth Polytechnic College in England (speaking at an *Acres, U.S.A.* conference), cytokinins are powerful, safe, and not toxic to people. They are quickly absorbed by the leaf and they remain there. Their beneficial effect on the plant's ability to make carbohydrates and chlorophyll helps to stimulate longer plant life, increases production, and makes for higher protein content. In Dr. Blunden's opinion, it is the cytokinins that account for the special effects credited to seaweed.

Cytokinins are apparently easily lost when seaweed solutions are applied to the soil. They are known to be readily absorbed by leaves, though, especially young leaves, so foliar spraying has come to be the recommended method of treating plants.

Commercial seaweed preparations may differ in the level of their cytokinin activity, depending on the method of extraction (high or low heat or hydrolysis), the species of seaweed used, the time of year it was collected, and conditions affecting the storage life of either the unprocessed weed or the extract. A seaweed solution with standardized cytokinin content is available. Other so far unstandardized brands have, nevertheless, been shown to give good results in university and experiment station tests.

Regardless of the brand of commercially available seaweed extract used in the experiments, researchers agree that the treatment is effective in very low concentrations, concentrations so low that the amount of trace minerals being applied must surely be very small. Heavy concentrations, above five percent, seem to have a negative effect.

Using Kelp

What does all this mean for you, the seed-starter? Just this, that kelp might well be useful to you:

- In germinating seeds.
- In protecting plants from frost, both early and late.
- In increasing blossom set and yields.

- In rooting cuttings.
- In protecting your plants from insects and destructive microorganisms.

If you remember nothing else from this chapter, make note of the following:

1. Low concentrations of seaweed extracts are effective. High concentrations are toxic.

2. The spray is most effective when applied while the leaf is still young.

3. For vegetable plants, one application per season is often enough. Use no more than three (remember that cytokinin stays right there in the leaf).

4. Use the solution to:

- Presoak seeds before planting.
- Soak fiber pots before planting—not a proven technique, but one you might like to experiment with.
- Apply to tomatoes, beans, and cucumbers in flower stage, just before bloom.
- Root cuttings.
- Protect plants before frost.

Proper concentrations for different uses are as follows:

For soaking seeds and bulbs before planting, or for presoaking peat pots: four teaspoons of seaweed concentrate to one quart of water, or for larger quantities one-half pint seaweed to five gallons of water. (That's a 1:80 dilution.)

To spray vegetable plants: one tablespoon of seaweed concentrate to one gallon of water every one to two weeks, or for larger quantities one-half pint to 25 gallons. (That's a 1:400 dilution.)

For watering seedbeds and rooting cuttings: one tablespoon of seaweed concentrate to one quart of water, or for larger quantities one-half pint to 7½ gallons. (That's approximately a 1:120 dilution.)

For potted plants and house plants: four teaspoons of seaweed concentrate to two quarts of water every 7 to 10 days, or for larger amounts one-half pint to 10 gallons (approximately a 1:160 dilution).

We are just beginning to get a more complete picture of what kelp can do for seeds and garden and farm plants. Many questions remain unanswered. But the message I get from the studies that have been done is this: Seaweed extract looks like good stuff. Let's use it, and take careful note of our results. We have just begun to use kelp spray for frost protection, watering seedlings, and presoaking seeds. This year we're doing more spraying of young vegetable plants. Although it is too soon for us to draw any definite conclusions, we are sufficiently convinced of the merit of the method to recommend that other gardeners try it too.

20

Raising Seedlings for the Fall Garden

One of the surest signs of gardening expertise, to my way of thinking, is the fall garden, still producing good food all the way to the first frost and even beyond. Something about fall gardens pleases me so much, in fact, that my husband and I have begun to collect colored slides of fall gardens when we see a good one. Some of my favorite pictures show short rows of silvery cabbage, red tomatoes, blue green Brussels sprouts, ribbony leeks, fat complacent rutabagas, ruffly green escarole, all edged by a row of marigolds, blooming with the deep, rich, almost-glowing oranges and golds of those last few weeks before frost.

Such a garden doesn't just happen. It is very easy to let the rows peter out and the hills grow scraggly when the first planting of beans finishes and tomato picking takes over. Keeping a productive garden right up to the edge of winter takes a little planning, and sometimes a little shoe-horning, but the slight extra trouble will repay you well. Succession planting can double your garden's yield.

The trick is to remember, in late spring and early summer, how good it was to have fresh young beets and turnips, crisp new greens, and delicate Chinese cabbage to put on the table near the turn of the year. After the spring rush, when both the early lettuce and cabbage and the later tomatoes and peppers have graduated from growlight to cold frame to garden, and the heat-loving melons have just been set out, I turn my attention to starting the fall take-over crops.

Some, like carrots, Chinese cabbage, winter radishes, and turnips, are planted right in the garden row, usually where an earlier crop—peas, early cabbage, lettuce, or radishes—has finished. For summer seed plantings, when weather is likely to be dry, I hoe out a slightly deeper furrow than I did in spring. And I take the watering can and run a stream of water all along the furrow *before* planting the seed. Then I rake and firm dry, loose soil over the seed. Often, especially for carrots, I scatter fine dry grass clippings over the planted row, an additional ounce of soil-crust prevention.

For most other mid-summer plantings, I start plants in flats, and transplant them to the row after a week of hardening off.

Brussels sprouts, escarole, cabbage, lettuce, broccoli, and cauliflower *can* be seeded right in the row, of course, but I find I can raise better plants and make more efficient use of garden space if I start the plants indoors or in flats in the open cold frame and set them out in their appointed rows or odd corners when they're three to four inches high and flourishing.

Later, in the fall, you can plant peas for spring in well-prepared furrows and sow seed of corn-salad for early spring eating. In the south and parts of the west, fall sowings of turnips, parsnips, lettuce, beets, and other vegetables that flourish in cool weather will live over winter.

There aren't many months, in fact, when you can't be planting *something,* either indoors or out.

21

The Competition: Insects and Animals

Although most of us are prepared to accept a certain amount of insect damage and even animal predation later in the season, when young plants are struck they may never have a chance to reach harvest size or to produce their fruits. If you've ever lost a plant to a cutworm or rabbit I'm sure you can remember how indignant you felt, and how helpless to reverse the damage. It's one thing to be willing to share the harvest with other life forms that may have come on the scene first; it's quite another to lose seedlings before they have a chance to get off the ground.

Insect Pests

Protecting young plants from insect attack is largely a matter of prevention, plus a few defensive strategies you can use if bug trouble is serious. Here's a list of insect pests that commonly feed on young plants, along with some suggestions for saving your crop from the marauders.

1. Extended.

3. Pupa case, as often found in ground in summer.

2. Rolled, as often found.

Cutworm.

Cutworm. This pest is one to 1½ inches long, grayish, and coils up when exposed. The damage they do is large compared to the amount of plant tissue they eat. The trouble is that they operate at soil level, and so when they cut through a stem the top of the

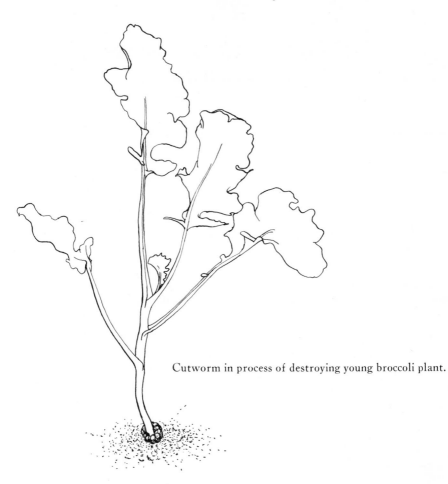

Cutworm in process of destroying young broccoli plant.

plant dies. Well-rooted tomato plants that have been decapitated by cutworms will sometimes sprout again, but since you can't be sure that they will, you must still replant. The cutworm must wrap itself around the stem of a plant in order to "bite" through it. Consequently, any device that will make this encircling maneuver difficult or impossible for the cutworm will protect the plant. We have used each of the following methods successfully:

    1. Cut slits in an index card or any stiff paper, as illustrated, and wrap the card snugly around each plant stem. Half the card should be above soil level and half below. This works, but it's a nuisance to do when cold spring winds are stiffening your fingers.

2. Small tin juice or tomato paste cans confer the same sort of protection, but must be placed with care to avoid damaging roots and top growth, and it is difficult to firm plants correctly into the ground when they're growing through a can.

3. Much simpler, and in my experience completely effective, is the use of small woody twigs, stuck into the ground three inches below soil level and protruding two to three inches above the soil. The twig should be right next to the plant stem, touching it, so that

Tomato plant set in garden with can to protect from cutworms.

Tomato plant set in with twigs to protect from cutworms and with stem bent to promote root growth.

it forms a tough barrier that foils the soft-bodied, bristly-mouthed worm. If you've dug wood chips into your garden soil, you'll probably have plenty of twigs within reach as you work your way down the row with the flats and trowel. Otherwise, collect a supply in advance. Dry asparagus stalks are often handy and work quite well.

4. Easier yet, and unlikely to chafe the plant's tender stem, is the method I used last year. Tear scrap aluminum foil into pieces about three inches by two inches. Wrap the foil around the plant stem as you get the seedlings in the ground, again making certain that half will extend below ground level and half above.

Be sure to protect your plants from cutworms when you set them out. The very next day may be too late.

We've had less trouble with cutworms here on our farm garden than in other gardens we've had. We spread all our chicken manure on the kitchen garden, and when I heard some time ago that hen-fertilized gardens have fewer cutworms, I thought, "That must be it!" But the next year I lost several young head lettuce transplants to cutworms. So the only conclusion I've been able to draw is: You never can tell. Meanwhile, expect cutworm damage and take one of these simple steps to prevent it.

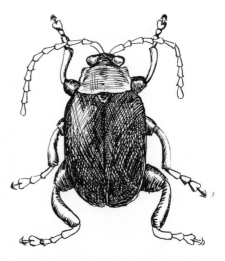

Flea beetle.
Actual size approximately ¹⁄₁₆ to ¼ inch.

Flea beetles. These tiny, very active, pinhead-sized black bugs appear early and riddle certain plant leaves with small round holes. Eggplant, tomato, broccoli, and other small cabbage-family seedlings are especially vulnerable. Last year I lost a flat of cabbage seedlings to flea beetles who devoured them in just a day. I had made the mistake of putting the flat out at the edge of the garden near some flea-beetle-infested weeds.

Flea beetles thrive in hot, dry places. They dislike moisture and shade. In small gardens they can be washed off the plants with a stream of water from the hose. The best defense I've found is to dust the plants with diatomaceous earth. This nontoxic insect control kills by mechanical rather than chemical action. Its many fine, ultrasharp particles puncture the insect's body covering (exoskeleton), causing death by dehydration.

Slugs.

Slugs. Soft-bodied, snaillike creatures with shells, these are on the prowl during the damp, early days of spring. They seem to be especially fond of lettuce and peas. If you know what they like (beer or yeast solution in saucers or halves of citrus fruit) you can trap them. Or consider what they don't like: powdery, sharp, dry, or abrasive surfaces, and guard your garden accordingly by spreading lime, wood ashes, or salvaged insulating materials around your plants, or ashes, sand, or cinders along garden paths.

Wireworm.
Length approximately one to 1½ inches.

Wireworms. These inch-long, brown, hard-shelled, segmented larvae of the click beetle eat the juicy interior tissue of roots and seeds. The damage they do to young seedlings can be severe in a badly infested plot. They often persist in gardens recently dug from sod. Baiting them with potatoes or other food is a short-term remedy. The best plan is to correct the conditions that favor wireworm population growth: poor drainage and lack of aeration. Dig up the former sod patch early in the season and disk or till it. At the same time, incorporate as much compost, old mulch, rotted manure, or other organic material as possible into the soil to increase aeration deep down.

Sowbug.
Length approximately ½ inch.

Sowbugs. These are half-inch long, gray crustaceans that roll up into balls (hence their other common name, pillbugs) when disturbed. They feed on tender roots and shoots of young plants and can be a real problem in garden beds next to buildings, for they lurk in crevices and under boards and debris. I've never had any luck in getting rid of them once they were established. The best defense is prevention: clear away all boards, boxes, piles of plant refuse, etc., from the garden area, and try moving your vegetable patch to an open space in the yard if plantings next to your house are bitten hard by these pests. Woody and mature plants are not as attractive to sowbugs as young, tender seedlings. Watch out for sowbugs under the protective covers you put over new transplants, especially opaque covers.

Nematodes. Nematodes exist everywhere, even in polar tundra. Most of the thousands of different nematodes that have been identified are smaller than a printed period. The majority of nematodes are helpful, or at least innocuous, but the minority (one-tenth or so) that do damage plants are responsible for a vast amount of plant destruction. Tiny as they are, their sharp mouthparts, formed like a hollow spear, are capable of penetrating tough roots. Then a suction-forming bulb behind the nematode's esophagus draws out plant juices. All this violence goes on underground, unseen. Symptoms of nematode infestation are, in fact, vague and nonspecific. The plant may simply go into a slow decline. Often the nematode-weakened plant succumbs to a secondary bacterial or fungal invasion.

But help lives in the soil too. Predacious fungi, which thrive on organic matter in the soil, are capable of trapping and engulfing, even of hunting damaging nematodes. At least 50 different nematode-attacking fungi have been identified so far, and more are being found as studies continue.

Once again, then, we find that good soil-building practices like composting, green manuring, and digging in mulch will defend our plants on many levels.

Marigolds produce a root exudate that makes the soil around their roots inhospitable to nematodes. It is sometimes necessary to plant the flowers in the same spot several years in a row to get the full benefit of their nematode-spooking activity, but then you can rotate a "cutting garden" row of marigolds around the vegetable patch year by year.

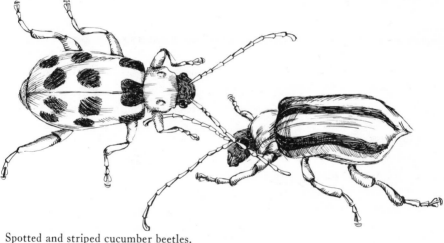

Spotted and striped cucumber beetles.
Actual length, ¼ inch and ⅕ inch.

Cucumber beetles. Small yellow bugs just under one-fourth inch long, with black stripes down their backs, these beetles prey on the whole cucurbit family (melons, cukes, squash, and pumpkins). There are spotted cucumber beetles too, with black spots on a yellow body. You don't want them in your garden either.

The cucumber beetle threatens seedlings in three ways. Its small white larvae, about one-third inch long, feed on the underground parts of plants. The adult beetle eats the delicate young stems and cotyledons of newly emerged seedlings, and later the blossoms and tender leaves. Even worse is the disease-carrying habit of both the striped and spotted cucumber beetle. They spread bacterial wilt and mosaic, two murderous diseases that affect all cucurbits. When a planting is badly infested, it may never bear a single fruit.

Every measure you take to defend your seedlings against this small but powerful pest will increase your chances of a good picking when summer comes. The suggestions that follow will not eradicate every beetle from your patch. That kind of supercontrol would be likely to upset other delicate life balances in your garden. But the use of one or several of these practices should at least add the makings of a few more jars of dill pickles or frozen melon balls to your winter larder.

Prevention of cucumber beetle damage starts early. The following measures should be taken before planting:

- Order disease-resistant varieties of the affected plants. A good seed catalog will give you this information.
- Try starting some seedlings indoors so they will be tougher and larger when you set them out—a defense against the direct action of the beetles, but not, unfortunately, against the diseases they carry.

Then, at planting time, try the following:

- Plant a ring of radishes around each hill of cukes, squash, or pumpkins. This can be done up to a week before planting the main crop in the hills, or the radish seed can be scattered as you plant. I've done it both ways. Advance planting of radishes ensures a ready and waiting beetle deterrent when the cuke seeds sprout, a ploy that is especially useful when you plant presoaked cuke (or squash, etc.) seeds. Radish plantings have made a noticeable difference in the number of cucumber beetles attacking my patch. The beetles still come, but we get to pick some produce too.
- Bury onion skins in the hole when you plant your

cucurbits. According to an experienced gardener who reported her success in following this advice that she had read in an early issue of *Organic Gardening and Farming* ®, the method really works. I'm trying it for the first time this year, armed with a bag of onion skins I've been saving since last fall.

- Marigolds planted next to the cucurbit plants will often deter beetles to some extent. I'd rate them on a par with radishes as a deterrent. Here again, prestarted marigold seedlings set out at planting time will give you more protection than planting the flowers at the same time as the vegetables.

And here are some things you can do after planting:

- Mulching around the plant apparently impedes progress of the larvae from underground to their adult feeding stations above ground, in some cases. You'll need to do more than mulch, though, if your cucumber beetles are as numerous as mine!
- To trap the beetles, set out saucers of water with a thin film of oil on top.
- Dust with rotenone early in the season, before the first generation of beetles has a chance to reproduce. This nonpersistent insect control is not toxic to people and warm-blooded animals, but it should be used cautiously near ponds since it is toxic to fish even when greatly diluted by rain and pond water. I apply rotenone when the seedlings are quite small. It has saved me many a crop.

Carrot rust fly larvae. Responsible for eating those unsightly tunnels in carrot roots, they may be foiled by timing and rotating your plantings. The first generation of larvae hits plantings made before early June, and the second generation is not usually active before September. Planting carrots in different areas and harvesting with an eye on the calendar can prevent a damaging buildup of these garden pests.

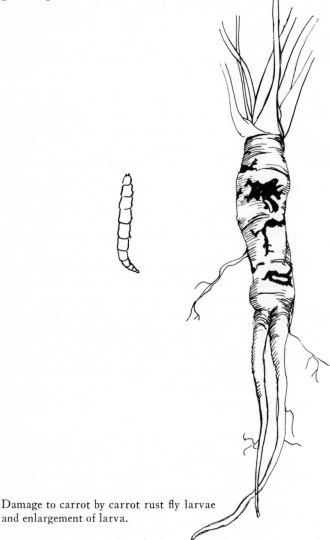

Damage to carrot by carrot rust fly larvae and enlargement of larva.

Bean beetles. Bean beetles also may often be circumvented by making both an extra-early planting of a cold-resistant bean like Royalty and a late planting of a quick-maturing kind like Bountiful Stringless (47 days). The early beans will usually yield one good picking before the beetles have a chance to multiply, and late plantings, even

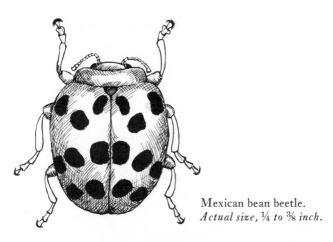

Mexican bean beetle.
Actual size, ¼ to ⅜ inch.

though cold nights may slow them down a bit, often thrive in the absence of the heat-loving beetles during early fall.

A new insect-control method, that of spraying affected plants with a diluted solution of the ground-up unwanted insects, has been gaining favor among adventurous gardeners and experimenters. While it's been suggested that the effectiveness of the spray is due to its ability to infect healthy bugs with contagious diseases from infected bugs, the whole idea is still very much in the experimental stage. The nice thing about it, though, is that it doesn't cost much to try.

Animal Predators

Fending off raids by seedling-destroying wildlife has brought out the creative ingenuity of many a gardener. The following devices have worked for a good many gardeners. Perhaps one of them will help you. Ask elderly neighbors and relatives too. Folklore is particularly strong and often effective in this department.

Deer. Spread wire-mesh fencing *flat on the ground* where they must cross it to get to the garden. Or scatter lion manure around the garden. The essence of fierce predator that this conveys to non-carnivorous animals makes them uneasy. Sprinkle blood meal around the edge of the garden. Or water around the plants with water in which you've soaked the liver of a butchered animal. In extreme cases, fence in the garden with six- to eight-foot fence.

167

Rabbits. Either the lion manure or the blood meal treatment will scare them off until the stuff gets rained into the ground. Then it must be repeated. I've read that a few dead fish spotted around will deter rabbits, but I haven't tried it.

Mole tunneling after a white grub.

Moles. Although their tunnels are unsightly on the lawn, the moles may not really be damaging your vegetable seedlings. They're after grubs, not your plant roots, when they burrow underground. If their search for food does disrupt your young plants, though, try one of the following:

- Plant scilla bulbs over the runways.
- Flood the runways with water.
- Use a windmill or pinwheel on a stick or any other device that will send vibrations into the tunnel.
- Plant castor beans near the runs. (Be aware, though, that the seeds of this plant are poisonous.)

Once you start to ask around, you'll hear all kinds of mole cures. Some of them even work—sometimes.

Crows. Crows eating your young corn? The crow is no dummy; any scare device you use to drive him off must be changed frequently.

- Crisscross the patch with string about five inches above ground. This makes takeoff difficult for the birds.
- Hang fur pieces—pelts and trimming from old coats —around the patch.
- Suspend shiny pie plates or other reflectors that blow in the wind and catch the light.
- Make a scarecrow, though this will be more picturesque than effective.
- String several kernels of corn on a long piece of horsehair and leave in the field. Crows that get the hair stuck in their throats are said to give out alarm cries, warning other crows away.
- Plant thickly.
- If things are really bad, replant.

Red-wing blackbirds. Red-wing blackbirds also eat corn. Try applying one teaspoon of turpentine to each pound of corn seed several hours before planting.

22
The Young Seed-Planter

Tending a small plot, or a garden row of a certain crop, can be a fine activity for the child, provided he or she *really* wants to have a garden. It is the garden assignment imposed from above, as a Worthwhile Experience, that may lead to trouble because the expectations of parent and child differ. (I'm not talking here about the necessary and normal help that a child is expected to give in the main garden with weeding, picking, and shelling, but about the special plots that are sometimes unrealistically given to the child for his or her own use.)

Above all, you want the child's first gardening efforts to be successful, satisfying. A child who experiences repeated gardening failures such as poor germination or weed takeover would be better off not having had a gardening experience, but rather waiting until motivation and capability were better matched.

Sooner or later, though, most children want to plant something. How will you guide them in their first seed planting efforts? Whole books have been written on this subject (see "Recommended Reading," page 349).

I'll just sketch here a few things we learned when helping our own children with their small gardens, which enjoyed varying degrees of success.

Give the child something besides radishes to plant. I don't care what the gardening books say, radishes can be tricky. Yes, they're fast and bright-colored, but they can be strong tasting and maggot-tunnelled just as easy as not. Beans take only a few weeks longer, and the large seed is easy for a child to handle. Nasturtiums are good, and you can eat the leaves. A small plot of corn attains spectacular growth, but be sure to protect it well from animal raiders. Cherry tomatoes come on fast and make good snacks. Sugar peas bear before the weeds get bad. They were one of our children's most dependable garden vegetables. Sunflowers are a natural for kids— fast growing and good snack fodder. Onion sets shoot up fast, but need pretty thorough weeding. Save the carrots and eggplants for later.

Choose a patch of good soil, not a rubble of builder's fill or hard clay ground where *you* wouldn't want a garden. Give the child every chance to succeed by providing the best possible conditions.

Begin simply and keep the plot small. Nothing is more discouraging than feeling overwhelmed by the garden, and no child needs the guilt feelings engendered by a weedy, unmanageable patch.

Help the child to plant late enough in the spring so that germination will be prompt and frost is unlikely to damage his planting. Children like fast results; it's better to delay planting for a week or two to help ensure steady growth.

Decide on the method of weed control before mapping out the child's garden. Rows should be spaced widely enough to permit easy hoeing or mulch placement. Children under 12 shouldn't operate a rotary cultivator without direct supervision. Plant a solid bed of something only if you are convinced that the child can handle the intensive hand-weeding that will be necessary during the early weeks.

Whatever the child grows, use it respectfully and appreciatively. Even a few peas can make pea-potato soup. Zucchini may be picked young so as to use more of it. One pepper may be stretched by cutting it into the tossed salad. Or perhaps the young gardener would like to eat it himself, stuffed with rice and meat and topped with cheese.

Accept the child's need to explore, which may take the form of pulling up half-grown beets or dismembering a flower to see what's inside. And if he eats the beans when harvesting from his five plants, be glad. What else is a garden for?

Section Three

The world is so full of a number of things, I'm sure we should all be as happy as kings.

Robert Louis Stevenson

23

Growing Vegetables from Seed

In this section, you'll find hints for handling the seed planting and early seedling care of the full range of popular garden vegetables. For cultural directions spanning the entire season, refer to one of the excellent general vegetable books listed on page 349, "Recommended Reading." Time from planting to maturity, indicated after each vegetable heading, varies according to variety chosen and local conditions.

Artichokes, Globe (Bear a year after planting, sometimes the first summer.) Although very sensitive to cold weather, this perennial has been successfully grown in the mid-Atlantic and New England states, far from its center of commercial production in California. Chilling during early growth in some cases stimulates bud formation the first year. Sow seed indoors about three months before the last frost, and set the plants out, preferably in a protected place with a southern exposure, when weather has settled thoroughly

Globe artichoke seedlings.

Globe artichoke.

—late May in the mid-Atlantic region. Space plants about two feet apart in fertile, humus-rich, well-limed, well-drained soil. Keep soil out of the plant's crown when setting it out. Plants need careful protection where winters are cold, and even then some may die from crown rot. Achieving a bud (edible artichoke) the first year makes all the effort worthwhile, though.

Asparagus (Harvest begins three years after planting.) Seed may be started indoors, but is most commonly sown in the garden, often in a special nursery row, either in the fall or in the spring, about the time apple blossom petals begin to fall. Soak the seed in water overnight before planting.

The tiny, feathery seedlings look delicate, but they transplant well. Thin them to stand three inches apart and transplant them out of the nursery row no later than the second year, because older plants grow deep roots which must be sacrificed in digging up. The permanent asparagus bed can be well prepared while the seedlings are growing. Dig in plenty of limestone and well-rotted manure and make certain the ground is well drained and well aerated. Deep planting is not necessary; just dig a hole adequate for the roots.

Basil (about 80 days) An herb, yes, but a necessity for many who plant tomatoes. Plant seeds of this aromatic annual outdoors after frost danger is past, or indoors in flats about six weeks before the

Botanical Classification of Vegetables

Monocotyledoneae

    Gramineae—Grass Family

Zea mays	var. *rugosa*	Sweet corn

    Araceae—Arum Family

Colocasia esculenta	Taro or dasheen

    Liliaceae—Lily Family

Asparagus officinalis	Asparagus

    Amaryllidaceae—Amaryllis Family

Allium sativum		Garlic
Allium Porrum		Leek
Allium fistulosum		Welsh onion
Allium ascalonicum		Shallot
Allium Schoenoprasum		Chive
Allium Cepa		Onion
Allium Cepa	var. *aggregatum*	Potato onion
Allium Cepa	var. *viviparum*	Top onion

Dicotyledoneae

    Polygonaceae—Buckwheat or Knotweed Family

Rheum Rhaponticum	Rhubarb
Rumex Acetosa	Sorrel
Rumex Patientia	Spinach dock

    Chenopodiaceae—Goosefoot Family

Beta vulgaris		Beet
Beta vulgaris	var. *Cicla*	Swiss chard
Atriplex hortensis		Orach
Spinacia oleracea		Prickly-seeded spinach
Spinacia oleracea	var. *inermis*	Round-seeded spinach

    Aizoaceae—Carpetweed Family

Tetragoniaceae expansa	New Zealand spinach

    Cruciferae—Mustard Family

Brassica oleracea	var. *acephala*	Kale, borecole, collard
Brassica oleracea	var. *gemmifera*	Brussels sprouts
Brassica oleracea	var. *capitata*	Cabbage

Brassica oleracea	var. *botrytis*	Cauliflower
Brassica oleracea	var. *italica*	Sprouting broccoli
Brassica oleracea	var. *gongylodes*	Kohlrabi
Brassica oleracea	var. *alboglabra*	Chinese kale
Brassica Napus	var. *napobrassica*	Rutabaga
Brassica Napus	var. *pabularia*	Siberian kale
Brassica campestris	var. *Rapa*	Turnip
Brassica Ruvo		Broccoli raab
Brassica juncea		Leaf mustard
Brassica juncea	var. *crispifolia*	Southern curled mustard
Brassica hirta		White mustard
Brassica perviridis		Spinach mustard
Brassica pekinensis		Pe-tsai, Chinese cabbage
Brassica chinensis		Pak-choi, Chinese mustard
Barbarea verna		Upland cress
Nasturtium officinale		Watercress
Armoracia rusticana		Horseradish
Lepidium sativum		Garden cress
Raphanus sativus		Radish
Crambe maritima		Sea kale

Leguminosae—Pea or Pulse Family

Pisum sativum		Garden pea
Pisum sativum	var. *macrocarpon*	Edible-podded pea
Vicia Faba		Broad bean
Phaseolus vulgaris		Kidney or common bean
Phaseolus vulgaris	var. *humilis*	Bush bean
Phaseolus coccineus		Multiflora or scarlet runner bean
Phaseolus coccineus	*Albus*	White Dutch runner
Phaseolus lunatus		Lima bean
Vigna sinensis	var. *unguiculata*	Cowpea (Southern pea)
Vigna sinensis	var. *sesquipedalis*	Asparagus or yard-long bean
Glycine Max		Soybean

Malvaceae—Mallow Family

Hibiscus Abelmoschus esculentus	Okra
Hibiscus Sabdariffa	Roselle

Continued

Umbelliferae—Parsley Family

Daucus Carota	var. *sativa*	Carrot
Foeniculum vulgare		Fennel
Foeniculum vulgare	var. *dulce*	Florence fennel
Petroselinum crispum		Parsley
Petroselinum crispum	var. *tuberosum*	Turnip-rooted or Hamburg parsley
Apium graveolens	var. *dulce*	Celery
Apium graveolens	var. *rapaceum*	Celeriac
Pastinaca sativa		Parsnip
Anthriscus Cerefolium		Salad chervil

Convolvulaceae—Morning Glory Family

Ipomoea Batatas	Sweet potato

Solanaceae—Nightshade Family

Solanum tuberosum	Potato
Solanum Melongena	Eggplant
Lycopersicon lycopersicum esculentum	Tomato
Physalis pruinosa	Husk tomato
Capsicum annum	Bell or sweet pepper
Capsicum frutescens	Tabasco pepper

Martyniaceae—Martynia Family

Proboscidea Jussieui	Martynia

Valerianaceae—Valerian Family

Valerianella olitoria	Corn-salad

Cucurbitaceae—Gourd Family

Cucurbita Pepo		Pumpkin and winter squash
Cucurbita Pepo	var. *Melopepo*	Bush summer squash
Cucurbita Pepo	zucchini	Zucchini and marrow squash
Cucurbita moschata		Pumpkin and winter squash
Cucurbita maxima		Winter squash
Cucurbita mixta		Pumpkin
Citrullus vulgaris		Watermelon
Cucumis Anguria		West India gherkin
Cucumis sativus		Cucumber

Cucumis Melo	var. *reticulatus*	Netted muskmelon or cantaloupe
Cucumis Melo	var. *inodorus*	Winter or casaba melon
Sechium edule		Chayote

Compositae—Composite Family

Cichorium Intybus		Chicory
Cichorium Endivia		Endive
Scolymus hispanicus		Spanish oyster plant or scolymus
Scorzonera hispanica		Black salsify or scorzonera
Tragopogon porrifolius		Salsify
Taraxacum officinale		Dandelion
Lactuca sativa	var. *crispa*	Leaf lettuce
Lactura sativa	var. *capitata*	Head lettuce
Lactura sativa	var. *longifolia*	Cos or romaine
Cynara cardunculus		Cardoon
Cynara Scolymus		Globe artichoke
Helianthus tuberosus		Girasole or Jerusalem artichoke

References on Botanical Nomenclature

Bailey, L. H., *Manual of Cultivated Plants,* New York: The Macmillan Co., 1949.

Hedrick, U. P., *The Vegetables of New York.* Vol. I, Part II, *Beans.* Geneva, NY: Agricultural Experiment Station, Rept., 1931.

Musil, A. F., *Distinguishing the Species of Brassica by Their Seed.* U.S.D.A. Misc. Publ. 643, 1948.

Smith, P. G., and Heiser, C. B., Jr., "Taxonomic and Genetic Studies on the Cultivated Peppers, *Capsicum Annum, L.* and *C. frutescens, L."* *American Journal of Botany.* 38:362–68, 1951.

Whitaker, T. W., and Bohn, G. W., "The Taxonomy, Genetics, Production and Uses of the Cultivated Species of Cucurbita," *Economic Botany* 4:52–81, 1950.

From *Handbook for Vegetable Growers,* by James Edward Knott, Professor of Vegetable Crops, University of California at Davis. New York: John Wiley & Sons, 1957.

last frost date. It transplants well. Space plants six to eight inches apart. Use thinnings to flavor soup.

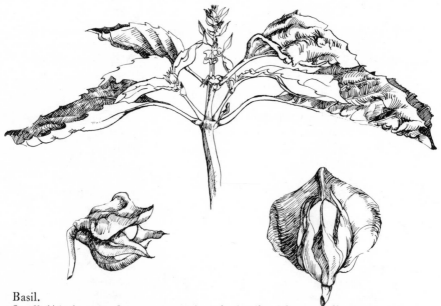

Basil.
Small, ¼ inch, green flowers emerge from leaf axils of flower stalk.
Side and bottom view of flower, *enlarged*.

Beans, Lima (60–85 days) Real tenderfeet. Wait to plant the seed until the soil is thoroughly warm—late May for us in south central Pennsylvania, when peonies are in full bloom. The seed rots quickly in cold soil. It is especially vulnerable to damage from low temperatures in the early stages of germination when it is absorbing moisture.

Presoak seeds in water for an hour or so if you wish, but not too long, or they'll split. Inoculate them with garden pea/bean inoculant. Plant them *eye side down* so that the root and cotyledons that emerge on germination will be headed in the right direction. Space seeds every five inches in rows three feet apart, with one inch of soil drawn over them. Thin to at least eight inches apart. Don't transplant. Germination is sometimes slow in acid soils.

If seedlings decay at the soil surface, excess surface moisture may be to blame, especially in heavy soil. In *The Vegetable Encyclopedia*, Tiedjens recommends filling in over the planted seed with a small amount of sand in such cases. Pods may drop off if plants are cultivated deeply, so get weeds under control by blossoming time. Limas require more warmth and more calcium in the soil than snap beans.

Beans, Snap (40–56 days) More of a snap to grow too than their delicious but more temperamental cousins. Plant briefly presoaked (for an hour or two), inoculated bush bean seed two to three inches apart, an inch deep, when all danger of frost is past. An exception, the Royalty purple bean, can be planted as early as three weeks before the last expected frost, since it is less prone to rot in cold soil. The chance planting of Royalty we generally make in late April usually pays off in beans by the end of June.

Make succession plantings of bush beans, which bear heavily but for a short period of time. Neither the bush nor the pole beans transplant well. I always put in a late planting at the end of July to bear in early fall when cool nights have sent the bean beetles on their way.

Beans are sensitive to an excess of potash in the soil, a fact I learned the hard way one year when I planted pole beans in a spot where a big, heavy, wet bag of wood ashes had burst and spilled the previous year.

Pole beans, which begin to bear somewhat later but continue longer than bush beans, should be planted in a circle around each pole, about 8 to 10 seeds per pole, thinning to four or five plants. These taller-growing vines should be planted on the north side of the garden to avoid shading other plants.

When setting the poles, some gardeners dig a hole, push in the pole, and fill in the hole with compost topped off by an inch of soil—a good starting bed for the bean seeds.

Beets (55–80 days) Plant seed in the garden about a month before you expect your last frost. Earlier plantings sometimes suffer from freezing. Presoaking seed will hasten germination, but the wet seeds are more difficult to handle. The beet seed that you plant is actually a seedball, an aggregate of two to six individual seeds. Consequently, even when you follow the recommended spacing of two inches apart, the seedlings will need to be thinned.

Beet seed, for some reason, needs to be well tucked in. It often fails to germinate if not in sufficiently close contact with the soil. An accomplished gardener of our acquaintance says "Cover the seed

with one-half inch of soil and then *stamp* on it!" He's used to working sandy soil. Here, on our heavier clay, I walk toe-to-heel over
the row after planting the seed. Beets are also very sensitive to toxic
substances in the soil and may fail to germinate if planted too close
to walnut trees or in soil with herbicide residues.

Thin plants to stand four to six inches apart. Thinnings may
be transplanted, giving you, in effect, a succession crop since the root
insult sets them back about two weeks. Some gardeners nip off the
long thready tip of the beet root when transplanting. When I do
this, I cut off the outer leaves too, to balance root and top growth.

Broccoli (55–98 days) An early start on this cool-weather annual
will give you fine-quality green sprout-heads before uniformly hot
weather reigns. Plant seeds thinly in flats about five to six weeks
before planting-out time, which can be up to a month before your
last expected frost. Transplant the seedlings at least once into
larger flats and set out young plants 18 to 24 inches apart. I like
Green Comet for spring plantings. Waltham 29 is still a good fall
broccoli. Make an early-summer planting—directly in the row if
you wish—to produce fresh new plants for fall eating. Cutworms,

Broccoli seedlings.

Head of broccoli.

flea beetles, and larvae of the cabbage moth are common enemies of the broccoli seedling.

Brussels Sprouts (92–120 days) A cool-season crop which does best planted in late spring either in the garden row or in flats in the cold frame, and transplanted to its permanent spot when three to five inches high. Space transplants two feet apart. May or early June seedlings grow into mature, harvest-size plants by fall. Don't bother to plant Brussels sprouts in early spring for a summer crop. The tiny leafy heads that are so delicious after frost taste pretty murky before being nipped by cold. Brussels sprouts aren't extra particular about soil type, but shortages of potash, phosphorus, or magnesium will hold them back. For good solid sprouts, firm the transplants well into the soil. Loose, leafy sprouts often result from drying or insufficient soil-root contact at transplanting time.

183

Cabbage Your earliest plantings may be seeded thinly in flats indoors about four to six weeks before planting-out time, which can be a good month before the frost-safe date. Since cabbage seed seems to germinate at least 100 percent, keeping a rein on your seed-sowing hand will ensure sturdier seedlings. If you do get carried away, transplant those crowded seedlings to a roomy flat before they develop their true leaves, or they'll get hopelessly leggy. For an exercise in self-discipline—and a fine stand of seedlings—use tweezers to place seeds in the flat at two-inch intervals. If your seed is fresh, plenty of them will come up, believe me!

Red cabbage in the making.

Although it lives through a fairly severe frost, cabbage that is subjected to a considerable period of very cold weather when the plant is young sometimes becomes fibrous, a stage on the way to developing an early seed stalk. Cabbage started indoors, on the other hand, shouldn't be subjected to night temperatures above 60°F. (16°C.). Those are fine points, though. Cabbage is easy to raise. Easier than radishes, I think.

Make repeated plantings every month or so for fresh tender cabbage for the table. The large-headed kraut types requiring a long growing season should be planted in mid or late spring.

Enlargements of Chinese cabbage flowers.
Actual size, ¾ inch across.

185

Cabbage, Chinese This cool-weather vegetable is extremely prone to bolting when weather turns warm. It does not transplant well, either. Although it is occasionally possible to get away with moving the seedlings when they are very young, they are usually severely checked, or sent into bolt. It's better to seed early plantings in peat pots. There are several new varieties, Spring A-1 and Takii's Spring, which can be grown in the spring, but for most people the best plan is probably to consider Chinese cabbage solely a fall crop. Sow seed in July right in the row, perhaps where the early peas have

Flower stalk of Chinese cabbage.

just been yanked out, and thin to 18-inch spacing. Good, fertile, humus-rich soil will encourage rapid growth of tender leaves. Flea beetles can be hard on young seedlings, but rotenone or diatomaceous earth will control them.

Cantaloupe (82–90 days) Wait until the soil is thoroughly warm (late May here in Pennsylvania) to direct-seed melons in hills four to six feet apart. Thin to four to five plants to a hill, but not too soon, because some may die of wilt if cucumber beetles strike. Cantaloupes need heat. The seed germinates rather unevenly, especially if the ground turns the least bit cool. Nothing like cabbage! So I've taken to presprouting seed (in a moist paper towel kept at 70° to 80°F. [21° to 27°C.]) and then planting the germinated seed in a peat pot indoors in early May. This gives me a good many more plants than I got when planting the seed directly in the pot, and far more than I got from planting outside. Fertilize the potted seedlings with diluted fish emulsion two or three times a week, using a one-half or three-quarter strength solution.

You can't transplant cantaloupe seedlings, so keep the roots contained by either a degradable pot or a cardboard plant band.

Site, as well as soil, is important for good cantaloupes. A southern slope is excellent. The soil should be rich in humus, not too acid. I plant a ring of radishes around each hill of cantaloupes, often sowing the radish seed 7 to 10 days before melon planting-out time so the leaves will be up and growing when they're needed to fend off the marauding cucumber beetle.

Carrots (60–76 days) Choose seed of a variety that's suitable for your soil type. The half-long carrots like Danvers are far better choices for heavy soil than long thin kinds like Imperator, which can reach full length only in sandy soil. This fine-seeded cool-weather crop is easily overplanted. Dilute seeds by mixing them with sand or dry used coffee grounds. Plant as soon as the ground can be worked fine, but remember that a severe frost can damage germinated carrots. Germination is very slow; a month is not unusual for early plantings in cold soil. You might want to dribble a few radish seeds in the furrow to mark the row. Cover the seed with no more than one-half inch of soil. Second early plantings made in the beginning of May do better for me than extremely early ones. For the best-quality carrots, make several succession plantings up until July, always in deeply worked soil. If the tunnel-boring larvae of the carrot rust fly are a problem in your area, you might find that carrots you plant after June 1 and harvest before mid-September escape both the first and second hatches of larvae. British gardeners plant sage or scorzonera (black salsify) to repel the carrot fly.

Young carrot seedlings are easily overwhelmed by weeds, which often seem to get a head start, especially in wide-row plantings. The best time to thin carrots is when the soil is damp. Plants should stand two to four inches apart, depending on size; the closer spacing is ideal for the smaller Baby-finger carrots, the wide spacing for the Oxheart types.

Cauliflower (50–85 days) A little finicky, but not really difficult. The important thing to remember is that any insult—real or imagined—will send cauliflower into a pout. The result is a thumb-sized buttonhead, or none at all. Just keep the seedlings growing steadily. Don't expose them to severe frost when young, water and shade well immediately after transplanting, firm soil well over seedling roots, and do all necessary transplanting when the plants are young, up to six or seven inches or so. If possible, water the seedlings daily for several days after moving them.

Plan on setting out spring-started cauliflower seedlings about two or three weeks before your last frost date, not a bit earlier. Plants for the fall crop may be started in May. Either way, avoid having plants mature in hot, head-stunting summer weather.

Celeriac This cool-weather biennial does well on heavy soil. Seed can be planted right in the row in early spring, but since germination is slow and weeds are fast, I prefer to raise celeriac seedlings indoors in flats, setting them out two or three weeks before our last expected frost, about when the apple blossoms begin to fall. Earlier planting-out may cause bolting. They transplant well, as long as you remove only one plant at a time from the flat and protect the roots from drying out. Dipping them in a thick slurry of muddy water will help. Set the seedlings six to eight inches apart in well-limed soil, and keep them moist until they catch on, as evidenced by new leaf growth.

Celery (98–130 days) May be planted indoors in February or March and set out about two weeks after the last expected frost, or sown in April or May for a fall crop. Germination is fairly slow

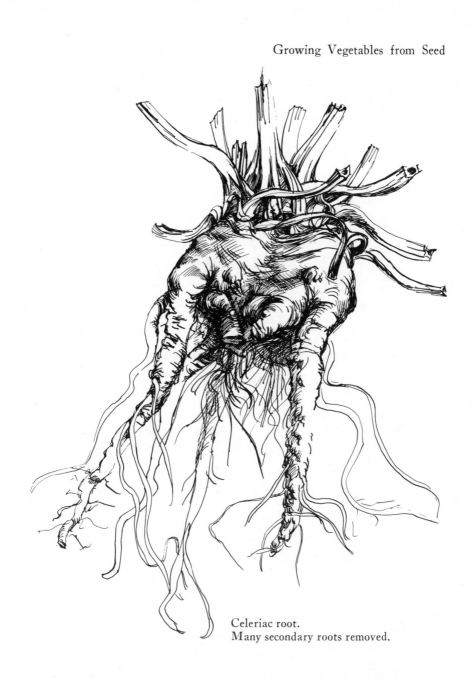

Celeriac root.
Many secondary roots removed.

—about three weeks. Celery does best in cool weather. If temperature at planting time is unfavorably high (celery germinates best at 60° to 70°F. [16° to 21°C.]) exposures to light will help to stimulate germination. Alternating temperatures (warmer by day, cooler at night) also helps. At the preferred lower temperature, light

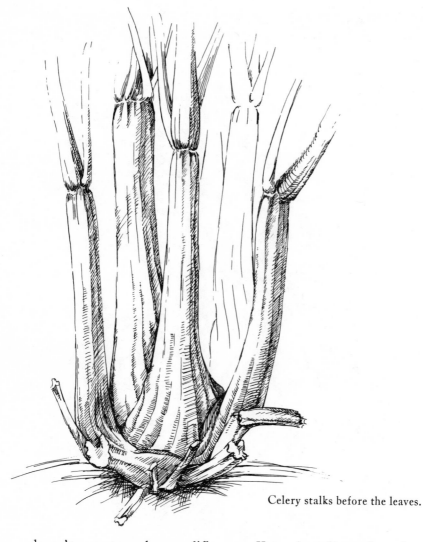

Celery stalks before the leaves.

doesn't seem to make any difference. Keep the soil evenly moist, but never sopping wet, during germination. When hardening off, avoid chilling the plant below 50°F. (10°C.) or it may bolt to seed.

Celery has a skimpy root system and transplants well, as long as the job is done early (three to five inches) before a taproot forms. It needs an excellent supply of moisture, but drainage should be good. Try sinking bottomless cans between plants, which should be planted 8 to 10 inches apart, and fill the cans with water from the hose.

Chives (four to five months to harvest from seed) Easily grown from seed, this perennial may be started indoors in February. Thin or transplant the seedlings to stand one inch apart in the flat, and keep them clipped back to a height of two to three inches. Set the plants out in good, loamy, not-too-acid soil in mid-spring, about a month before your last expected frost. Leave a five-inch space between plants.

Collards (80 days) Treat like cabbage. As with most cabbage family members, germination is profuse, so plant seed thinly, especially in the flat. May be started indoors and transplanted or sown in the garden row in early spring. Unlike most cabbage, it will remain in the garden row all season (it's really best after frost), so plan your rows accordingly. A few plants are usually enough for the average family. Space them two feet apart, or closer if you plan to use the thinnings for soup greens.

Corn (64–94 days) With the exception of the man I once read about who started his small block of early corn in peat pots indoors under lights, gardeners plant corn in the open ground, starting a week or two before the last expected frost for the earliest corn. Early planting should be covered with one inch of soil. The first

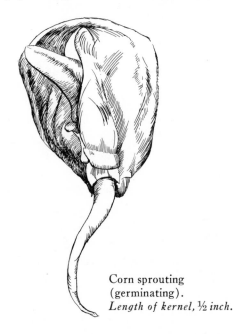

Corn sprouting
(germinating).
Length of kernel, ½ inch.

shoots are fairly frost-resistant, but foot-tall corn will be killed by frost. It does not transplant well.

Even if you're planting only a small amount of corn, arrange your rows in blocks at least three rows wide so that the wind-carried pollen will reach more of the other plants. Four short rows are better than two long ones. Drop two to four seeds in every foot of furrow and thin later to about 10 inches apart for the shorter, early varieties, 12 to 15 inches apart for more robust late corn. That old folk saying about planting corn has it just about right:

> "One for the rook,
> One for the crow,
> One to rot and
> One to grow."

The North American Indians, who had no calendar, went by tree signs in planning their corn plantings, making their first plantings when the white oak leaves were as large as a squirrel's foot.

Make successive plantings 10 to 14 days apart. Towards midsummer, sow earlier-maturing corn (65–70 days) to sneak in another picking before frost. If you've got 90 days to go until your average first fall frost date, don't plant a 90-day corn. The cool fall nights, which can begin early in September, will slow its growth. You may find that these summer plantings of corn will germinate best, especially in a dry season, at a depth of two to three inches.

Although corn thrives in a good many different kinds of soil, it needs plenty of nitrogen and moisture to support its rapid, exuberant growth.

Cucumbers (50–80 days) Cucumber seeds germinate best around 90°F. (32°C.); at temperatures below 60°F. (16°C.) they're likely to rot before they sprout. Yet, once germinated, they can grow well at an average of 65° to 75°F. (18° to 24°C.). You can make an early chance planting of cukes by presprouting the seed and planting the germinated seed in a hill where you've buried a good handful of not-quite-finished compost under an inch of soil. Presprouted seed should be watered in well at planting time. Start this early planting about the time the tall late irises bloom—mid May here in my garden. Be sure to cover plants if frost threatens. Night temperatures below 40°F. (4°C.) will retard cucumber plants. I make a second, main-crop planting in late May and a third planting

Corn.

in July to take over when wilt decimates my early vines. Some gardeners report improved germination when sowing the seeds thin edge down.

Burying the skins from two or three onions in each hill will, I've heard, discourage the insects that prey on young cucumber plants. Although I haven't tried this yet, having read it just last fall in the OGF letters column, it seems well worth doing—simple, free, and nontoxic. I have a large bag of onion skins saved and intend to add the onion-skin maneuver to my regular ritual of planting radishes in a ring around each hill.

Choose seed that is resistant, or at least tolerant, to whatever cucumber plagues prevail in your gardening area. Cucumbers don't transplant well. It *is* possible, as I've mentioned, to presprout the seed, but once set in soil, it shouldn't be moved. To start the seeds indoors in soil, use peat pots or Jiffy pots, and plant them about three to four weeks before the safe settled-weather date.

Outdoors, plant 8 to 10 seeds in a hill, with hills spaced four or five feet apart. Thin later to the best plants (not too soon, though, till you see how much damage the cucumber beetle will do to the young seedlings). It's better to pinch or cut the seedlings. Pulling them might tear the roots of the ones you want to keep.

For row planting, sow seeds about eight inches apart and thin later so plants stand at least a foot apart. Whatever your garden plan, try to provide good air circulation for cucumber plants, and keep at least a few hills within reach of the garden hose so you can water them if a week passes without a good rain.

Don't mulch the young plants until the soil is thoroughly warm. Combat disease-carrying striped cucumber bettles with the natural preventive measures suggested above and, if necessary (and it often is for me), a dusting of rotenone.

Dill (70 days) If you grow cucumbers or tomatoes, you'll most likely need dill for pickling. The young fresh leaves are good snipped on potatoes too. Sow the seeds, one every inch or so, as early in spring as the ground can be worked. Thin the feathery seedlings to four to six inches apart for use as greens, 10 to 12 inches apart for seed production. Late-fall seedings will usually produce good stands of early-spring dill. The seedlings transplant fairly well, with some wilting when small, but they develop a taproot that makes moving the half-grown plant impractical.

Eggplant.

Eggplant (56–76 days) A heat lover—all the way through. Plants must be started early indoors (usually eight to nine weeks before planting-out time, in order to mature before cool fall weather sets in again. Seed germinates best between 75° and 90°F. (24° to 32°C.). I often presprout the seed in damp paper towels tucked into a plastic bag and kept on the stove's pilot light. Even with that boost, germination can take 10 to 14 days. Keep the seedlings growing steadily. Any wilting or exposure to cold weather can prevent their fruiting later.

Since the plants are extremely tender, not only to frost but to cool temperatures in general, they should not be set out until the soil is thoroughly warm and daily temperatures remain in the 65° to 70°F. (18° to 21°C.) range. Eggplant seedlings should not be chilled or deprived of water to harden their tissues for a move to the outdoors, as you would do with tomatoes or lettuce. Such harsh treatment can cause woody stems and poor fruiting. Instead, just set them out for increasingly long periods of exposure to the sun, and shade them lightly for a day or so after planting in the garden row.

Transplanting doesn't do eggplants any good, but you can usually get away with it if you're careful. Block out the flat a week or two beforehand so that new roots will form close to the plant, take a good ball of earth along with each transplant, and water it thoroughly as soon as you set it in the hole. Growing the seedlings in peat pots minimizes root shock when setting out, but I've found that fiber pots dry quickly and need close watching.

Flea beetles like young eggplant seedlings. Diatomaceous earth or rotenone can be used to control them. Watch out for cutworms too.

Endive and Escarole (85–98 days) Although it is possible to grow a spring crop of these delicious pungent greens by planting seeds indoors in March and setting out three to four weeks before the last frost, the plants are best, I think, in the fall. Late-spring plantings bolt to seed when days turn hot. For a fall crop, I sow seed in the cold frame in July and transplant seedlings to gaps in the garden rows. Cover the seed with no more than one-fourth inch of fine soil, and thin the plants to stand about a foot apart, although 10 inches is sufficient if you plan to tie up the leaves to blanch them. Choose a fertile, well-limed, well-drained spot for your endive and escarole. (Escarole is the broad-leaved form; endive, the frilly cut leaf.)

Fennel (60–70 days) The biggest mistake most gardeners make with fennel is to sow a whole row of it at once. Then it all matures at once—and grows woody at once when not used. Make small succession plantings instead, beginning in April and early May, skipping the hot summer months which tend to bring on bolting, and planting a fall crop in July or August. Thin the plants to stand at least six inches apart for best development of the crisp, licorice-flavored bulb. You *could* start fennel indoors ahead of time, but you should get it transplanted before it starts to develop a taproot. A light frost won't hurt it.

Gherkins (60 days) Botanically the gherkin is slightly different from the cucumber, but it is begun and grown in the same way, usually for pickles. The leaf and vine are smaller than those of the average cuke, and the plant can be more closely spaced—about three feet apart for hills, eight inches apart for plants grown in rows.

Grains Although sowing seed in drills three inches apart and covering it with one-half inch of soil will give you the best germination,

Buckwheat flowering.

for a small garden patch of grain you can broadcast seed and rake it in. Oats are planted in early spring. Rye is often fall-planted. Whether you plant your wheat in spring or fall depends on whether you choose winter wheat or spring wheat. Check at your local feed and seed store and buy the kind of wheat that is most commonly planted in your area. In a dry season most grain seedlings can hold

197

their own against weed competition, but in wet weather weeds can overtake a planting if not checked.

Kale (55–65 days) Extra nutritious, fast-growing, pretty much pest-free, kale even tastes good after a frost. To have leafy mature kale plants ready when you need them in the fall and winter, start plants indoors, in the cold frame or in a special nursery row in May, transplanting them in June into their appointed row at 12- to 16-inch intervals. Hanover, a spring kale, develops rapidly during the spring months, but I think it's hard to beat the flavor of well-frosted fall kale. I often interplant fall kale with Butterhead lettuce, which matures before the kale is ready to eat and thrives in the light shade.

Kohlrabi (55–60 days) Early plants for June eating may be started indoors in flats and transplanted to the cold frame when they have their second pair of true leaves. They may be set in the garden row about three to four weeks before the last frost date, spaced four inches apart. Seed may also be planted in the open land, but starting with seedlings will give you better control of plant spacing and in my experience produce a stronger plant.

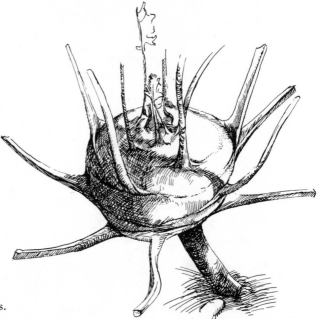

Kohlrabi, minus leaves.

Growth is best during cool weather, so for good results get an early-spring start and replant in early summer for fall bulbs.

Leeks (70–105 days) An easy-to-grow touch of menu luxury. I plant the seeds in flats in February, keep the thready tops clipped back to two or three inches high, and thin the seedlings to stand no closer than one inch apart in the flat. Plant them out in April or May, or direct-seed in the ground in April. Leeks need a long

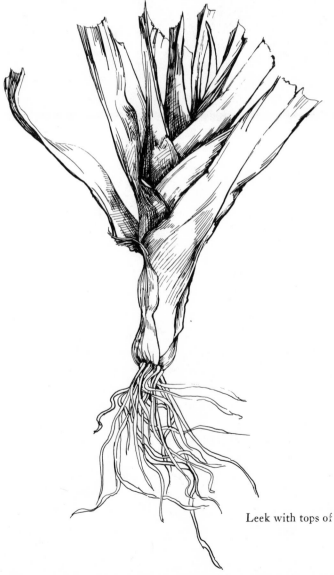

Leek with tops of leaves cut back.

199

Head lettuce seedlings.

growing season (120 to 130 days), but accept a variety of growing conditions. I've read lots of complicated growing directions for planting leeks in a trench and hilling them later, but I've gotten perfectly satisfactory crops by simply setting the delicate little quill-like plants every six inches in the row, slightly deeper than I had them in the flat. They do respond well to deeply dug soil, plenty of humus, and steady moisture.

Lettuce, Head (72–96 days) Must be started indoors to beat the summer heat, since it needs 75 to 85 days to head. Plant seeds in flats six to seven weeks before planting-out time, which can be as much as a month before your frost-free date if you cover plants when the weather forecast predicts a severe freeze. Light frost won't hurt them. Transplant to two-by-two-inch spacing in a larger flat when seedlings have their true leaves. When ready to plant outdoors after hardening off, clip off all outer leaves, leaving a one- to two-inch stub of small new leaves. Those outer leaves, when left on, do the plant more harm than good. They tend to be whipped about by the wind and draw off more moisture from the roots than they are worth in feeding power. The new little leaves that grow up gradually will be sturdy, and they have a chance to acclimate themselves to full sun by the time they have grown big.

Set head lettuce plants a good foot apart in the row. Lettuce has a skimpy root system that does not range far, so it must have a good supply of water and nutrients close to home. The leaves are, in fact, 95 percent water. If April rains are insufficient, you'll have to take water to the plant yourself, by hose or watering can.

For fall head lettuce, plant seed in late July, no later than the first week in August, if you expect killing frost by October. High temperatures send lettuce seed into dormancy, which explains occasional poor germination of summer plantings. Older seed is less responsive to this effect of heat. If you've had trouble getting your summer lettuce plantings to germinate, you might want to save out seed each year to store for the following summer. Chilling the seeds by keeping them in the refrigerator overnight will also help to break this summer dormancy. Lettuce is one of the few vegetables that germinates better when exposed to light. Water the furrow well, then, before planting seed in summer, and barely cover the seed with fine light soil, or just a sprinkling of dry grass clipings.

Lettuce, Leaf (Butterhead 58–64 days, Loose leaf 40–45 days) Loose leaf lettuce grows so quickly in the cool days of early spring

Head lettuce transplants set out in April will be ready for the table in early June.

that few gardeners start it early indoors, although if you have the space to do so, you might beat the season by a week or so. Plant seed of lettuce and the Butterhead types, which take 50 to 60 days, as soon as the ground can be worked, and about one-half inch deep. Although lettuce seed you sow indoors usually germinates within a week, early outdoor plantings in cold soil may not come up for two weeks. I always transplant some of my first thinnings, watering them in well with a kelp solution and leaving the remaining plants about three inches apart. Then, in another two or three weeks, I pull alternate plants for salad, letting the rest grow to soft-head or full-leaf size spaced six inches apart.

Since lettuce doesn't keep and can't be canned, plant short rows or blocks every two or three weeks all season, using one of the slower-bolting kinds for summer plantings. I've read that you can even scatter seed on bare ground during a winter thaw for record-early May lettuce. I haven't tried this yet, but it makes sense. A nice little patch of volunteer Buttercrunch appeared near my asparagus patch this spring, a good two to three weeks ahead of my row plantings.

Summer heat sometimes sends lettuce seeds into dormancy. To get around this, and raise lettuce to go with your tomatoes, you can:

- Expose the germinating seed to light.
- Refrigerate the seed for several days before planting.
- Use old seed, which is less likely to maintain dormancy in hot weather.

Okra (52–56 days) These ornamental pod-forming vegetable plants need plenty of heat, but they grow quickly. Wait to plant seed outdoors until the soil is good and warm: no sooner than the end of May for us here in Pennsylvania, earlier, of course, in the South, and the first week of June for New England and the north central states. Okra doesn't take kindly to transplanting, but you can get a head start by planting the seed inside in peat pots about a month before setting-out time.

For direct seeding, presoak the seed for about 12 hours and plant it no more than an inch deep, about three or four seeds to the foot. Thin later so that mature dwarf plants, the kind usually planted in the North, stand 2½ feet apart. Tall okra needs three to four feet of space between plants. Okra is not particular about soil, but generous fertility will encourage quick growth that will increase your yield.

Onions (92–115 days) Easily grown from seed, provided you get a good early start and keep after sun- and moisture-robbing weeds when the plants are spindly and defenseless. Indoor planting gives you a running start on the weeds, and for me it works best. Sow seed in flats in February or no later than mid-March, and transplant the little spears to 1½-inch spacing when they straighten up. Clip them back to two inches high every few weeks. Although seed germinates best at 65° to 80°F. (18° to 27°C.), young plants should be grown cooler, near 60°F. (16°C.), no higher than 70°F. (21°C.) by day and 50°F. (10°C.) at night. Set them out four inches apart after proper hardening off, a good month or six weeks before your frost-free date. In all but the warmest states, long-season onions like the Sweet Spanish, which can take 120 days to mature, must be prestarted indoors. You can also plant onion seed directly in the ground for summer-bunching or fall-storage onions. Sow the seed in April or May, no more than one-half inch deep

Onion seedlings growing in a cut-down milk carton.

Keep onion seedlings trimmed to a height of two to three inches.

(one-fourth inch in heavy soils) and thin to four inches apart when the top spears have become as thick as a spear of chives. Weeds, again, are your worst enemy when plants are young. They sometimes shoulder ahead of seed planted in mid-spring before the grasslike seedlings can get off the ground.

Perhaps you'd like to try growing your own onion sets, those miniature dry bulbs that grow into eating-sized onions when planted in their second spring. Just set aside a bed a few feet square, or a wide row, and scatter about an ounce of seed for every 25-foot, two-inch-wide row. Don't thin the onions. Crowding and borderline malnutrition keep them small. Pull the plants late in July before they reach a diameter of three-fourth inch. The smaller sets will

Young onion.

give you larger bulbs and are less likely to shoot to seed next year. Any sets larger than one inch diameter should be tossed in the pickle crock. Cure the sets in the sun until the tops are thoroughly dry— a week or 10 days—and then remove the tops at the neck of the small bulb. Store in a dry, airy, cool but not freezing place.

When planting sets in the spring, push them into the soft earth just far enough to hold them in place, if your soil is heavy; in sandy soil a trifle deeper, but never covered. If you have a cat that likes to scratch in the garden, as we do, you might have to do some resetting of bulbs for a week or two until roots grow and the rains beat down the stirred-up soil so it isn't so inviting for puss to dig in.

One of my gardening acquaintances who plants by the moon insists that onions will not remain well-set in the ground if they're planted in the wrong moon sign. "Plant your onion sets when the moon is waning," he maintains, "and they'll stay in the ground." He could be right. I've never really *seen* our cats raking at the onions; it just seemed logical to blame them. Next year I intend to try planting them by the moon. If it works, I'll be a bit surprised, but very pleased.

Parsley (72–85 days) Easy to grow, but exasperating to start. Just when you're ready to reorder seed, you'll notice those perky little scalloped-edge seedlings beginning to emerge. Plant the seed as early in the spring as you can set foot in the garden, about two seeds to the inch and one-fourth to one-half inch deep. Presoaking the seed for a day may knock a day or two off of parsley's L-O-N-G germination time—at least three weeks and more often four or even more, in my experience. I've also gotten relatively prompt germination of late-spring sowings after pouring over the planted seed very hot water, which I've brought to a boil and just then removed from the stove. Many gardeners spot a few radish seeds along the row to mark the spot. Weeds are often the first to appear and must be kept under control. If you can spare the room in your greenhouse or under lights (don't use valuable windowsill space for this) you can start parsley seedlings indoors in midwinter or early spring and set them out in April. I've found this a good way to beat the weeds.

It was an old country custom to hang a parsley seedhead on a tree, grape arbor, or fence adjoining the garden so that the wind-blown seed would be scattered in the garden. Parsley volunteers are easy to plant around. If you try this bit of lore, don't count on it for your whole crop. Put in a sure-thing, in-the-ground planting too.

Parsnips (100–120 days) Be sure to use fresh seed, and sow even that thickly (at least one every inch) because parsnip seed is notoriously low in vitality. I've gotten a decent stand from year-old seed, sown in a practically continuous band, but I wouldn't count on it. Even the seedlings are weak-kneed and easily overwhelmed by a heavy soil cover, so pull no more than one-half inch of fine light soil over the furrow. A light sowing of radish seeds that will emerge early and break the soil crust will make things easier for the young parsnip plants to push through. In a dry spring, sprinkle the row if a week passes without rain before seeds have germinated. Seed should be sown in the open ground, April or May at the latest, but not before the daffodils bloom. Germination is slow; allow three weeks. Thin seedlings to stand three to four inches apart. Deeply worked soil will grow longer, better-shaped parsnips. They do not transplant well. But the sweet-flavored, frost-proof roots make up for their wobbly start by feeding your family faithfully through the coldest days of fall and even winter, as long as the ground can be dug.

Peanuts (110–120 days) Warm soil—loose, well-drained, and generously limed—promotes good peanut growth. Press the nuts, either shelled or unshelled, two inches deep into well-worked soil when you're pretty sure you've had your last frost. Southern gardeners can afford to wait two weeks or so after their last frost to let the soil warm up, since there'll still be plenty of time for the nuts to mature before cool fall weather. Northern gardeners, though, need to rush the season a bit in order to take advantage of every warm day of summer. If you've removed the shell (just be careful not to split the peanut), plant the nuts three to six inches apart in rows three feet apart. Nuts left in the shell may be spaced eight inches apart.

Peanuts don't transplant well, but if you're just growing a few for fun, you can get a head start by preplanting the hulled seeds, two to a peat pot, indoors four to six weeks before your last frost date. (Pinch out the second best plant if both germinate.) You can also grow a trial crop of peanuts in a large tub, crock, or barrel placed in full sun. Be sure it is well drained.

You can make the plant's job of peanut formation easier if you'll hoe up a bank of loose soil on each side of the plant clear down the row, when the plants have grown a foot high. This will provide an easily penetrated bed for the peduncles, which arise from the fertilized flowers and then grow underground, forming peanuts on their tips.

Spanish peanuts—small but more prolific and earlier maturing—are the best choice for northern gardens.

Peas (55–75 days) To put early peas on your table, you must get them in the ground early, and to do that, you often need to prepare the row in the fall. Some gardeners even plant pea seed in late fall, or during a February thaw in a predug furrow. The trouble, you see, is that while it's safe to plant peas in cold soil, it's not wise to work the garden while the earth is still heavily sodden. We get around this, here in our garden, by doing a late-fall plowing, burying all the mulch and leaves and leaving rough mounds. Frost action pulverizes that exposed soil over the winter, and I find that I can usually get out there with a hoe in early March and pull open a furrow of fairly loose soil, going along the top of a ridge left by the plow (*not* in the deeper, colder "valley" between ridges).

Plant peas thickly, about one every inch, and cover the seed with one to 1½ inches of soil. Shake some garden legume inoculant on the moistened seed before planting. Double rows of peas, spaced about four to six inches apart, make more efficient use of soil space than single-file rows. Wide rows of peas, up to three feet or so, are even more efficient. Dwarf varieties should stand two to three inches apart, tall varieties three to four inches apart. They don't transplant well.

Pea sprouting.
Actual size, ½ inch.

In any case, your peas will need some support, even the low-growing ones. Twiggy brush is excellent for all kinds of peas, and the best choice for wide rows. For tall-growing vines like the Mammoth Melting Sugar, grown in single rows, I supplement the brush with binder's twine strung the length of the row between three steel poles. Netting, chicken wire, garden fencing, and string supported by stakes are also successfully used by many gardeners.

Pea roots are weak and small, easily dislodged in weeding, so I usually let some weeds grow, close to the plants, to prevent root damage and also to help shade the pea roots, which prefer cool growing weather.

You can make successive plantings of pea seed throughout the cool weeks of early spring, but there's no point in sowing most kinds of peas later than two or three weeks before the frost-free date, because the yield of peas maturing in warm weather seldom justifies the space they take. An exception is Wando, a good pea for those who must wait in the spring until their community gardens have been plowed.

Peppers (55–80 days) Although the traditional timetable for starting pepper plants is six to eight weeks before outdoor planting, I've had excellent results with much earlier seeding in late January or early February, which for me is a good 12 to 14 weeks before the frost-free safe date.

If you can keep the soil temperature of your planting flat around 80° to 85°F. (27° to 29°C.), the peppers will germinate more rapidly than at 70°F. (21°C.), at which they usually take two or even three weeks. At cooler temperatures, 55° to 60°F. (13° to 16°C.), the seed may rot before it germinates.

Transplant the young seedlings at least once to a roomier flat and harden them off a week or two before your last frost date. If they're in blossom when you set them out, you might find it worthwhile to cover the plants at night until night temperatures are warmer. Cool nights in May and June can cause blossom drop.

Peppers do well without much added nitrogen, but they need a good supply of magnesium. They are also more tolerant of acid soil than many garden vegetables. Hot peppers are less likely than sweet peppers to object to the low level of aeration in heavy clay soils.

When setting out pepper plants, I bury them two to four inches deeper than they were in the flat, but not on their sides in a trench like tomatoes. Protect them from cutworms and avoid soil where related plants—tomatoes, eggplants, potatoes—have recently grown if you've had disease problems.

Don't let tobacco users handle your pepper seedlings without washing their hands first. The virus that causes tobacco mosaic, which affects peppers, survives cigarette manufacturing processes.

Potatoes, Sweet (about four months of frost-free days) You might need to begin your sweet-potato growing career by purchasing plants—actually rooted slips—from a southern grower. Or you might be lucky enough to find them locally, at a farmer's market or neighborhood store. Once you have sweets, though, and learn how to keep them over winter (cure for two weeks in a hot, dry place and store them, wrapped individually in newspaper, in a warm, dry, well-ventilated spot protected from rodents), you can raise all the plants you'll need by rooting your own potatoes. I've gotten 50 slips from one large potato.

Begin by choosing a large, sound potato, or two or three. Find a jar with an opening the right size to admit about two-thirds of the sweet potato. Keep it in a warm place (75° to 90°F. [24° to 32°C.]) day and night if possible, to induce sprouting. Shoots are much slower to form at lower temperatures. I kept my two jars on the pilot light of my gas stove. Although I'll admit it's not always convenient to have two extra jars to shove out of the way when I use all four burners, I know I'd have no sprouts without that warmth.

Some studies done on diluted seaweed concentrate have indicated that it encourages sprouting of sweet potatoes, and I intend to try immersing my sweets in kelp water rather than plain water next year to see whether I can get them to sprout sooner than four weeks, which is what it took this year, even with the booster warmth from the pilot light.

As soon as a leaf cluster forms above the roots on each slip, it may be twisted off the parent potato and planted directly outdoors, if the weather is warm enough, or in a deep flat (I use an old refrigerator crisper) in potting soil to wait for warm weather. A farmer's wife who grows sweet potato plants to sell at the local farmer's market has told me that she grows her slips in a hotbed heated with horse manure. Other gardeners start their slips indoors

*Home-raised sweet
potato slips have
excellent roots.*

by placing the potatoes on their sides in damp sand or vermiculite
and keeping them in a warm place until they sprout.

There's no point in putting sweet potato plants out in the
garden until the soil has become thoroughly warm: 70° to 85°F.
(21° to 29°C.) is ideal. That should be about 10 days after the last
spring frost, late May in my garden. Draw up a ridge of soil by
hoeing inward toward the row from both sides, and poke the slips
into this ridge a foot apart, using the largest plants first so that
inferior leftovers can be discarded when you get to the end of the
row, if you run out of space. Hill the plants again just before they
start to vine out.

Sweet potatoes grow well in slightly acid soil, mainly because
the acidity helps to keep down disease. They don't need much nitro-

gen; in fact, heavy applications foster excessive vine growth and late maturity. Although they should be well watered in when the slips are planted, the growing vines are amazingly drought-resistant.

Potatoes, White (new potatoes are ready 8 to 10 weeks after planting) Since cool weather favors tuber growth, white potatoes should be planted as early as the soil can be worked. A later planting, in mid- or late spring, will produce fall potatoes. Soil for potatoes should be on the acid side, well-supplied with humus and enriched with wood ashes or greensand to supply the potash that makes for a good mealy potato. Only well-rotted manure should be dug into the potato patch, because fresh manure encourages scab.

If you've grown potatoes the previous year, chances are you have some small spuds left over. If they've begun to sprout, that's just fine, although it's better if they don't have long white sprouts. If they do, you can break off extra-long, weak sprouts as long as there are several eyes remaining that can grow. Egg-size potatoes are good for planting whole. Those that are *much* smaller may not have enough stored nourishment to develop a strong plant.

Large potatoes with many eyes should be cut, exposing as little cut surface as possible, into pieces containing one to three eyes apiece. Too many eyes will produce a leafy plant with small pota-

When cutting seed potatoes, aim for two good eyes to each cut piece.

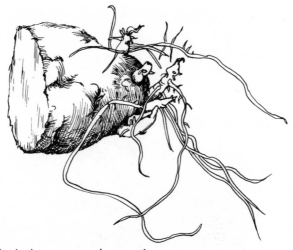

Half potato beginning to sprout shoots and roots.

toes. (The eye is a dormant bud.) Let the cut pieces dry for a day
or two before planting so the surface can heal over. They are less
likely to rot in the ground then. Unsprouted seed potatoes may be
nudged into growth by being exposed to the light for a few weeks in
a cool room.

Place the potatoes, or the pieces cut side down, every 10 to 12
inches in trenches two to three feet apart. Cover them with three
inches of soil and draw up loose soil around the plants when the
tops are nine inches high.

Or you can grow potatoes in mulch. They will be clean and
easy to harvest and should yield at least as well, sometimes better,
than in-the-ground plantings. Scab and potato bug damage are
seldom a problem with mulched potatoes. The one catch is that you
must really pile on the mulch, and keep a good foot of mulch over
the developing tubers, replacing it as it settles, or they'll turn green.
The greened parts of potatoes, and the sprouts, contain an alkaloid
poison, solanine. Except for the greening problem, I've been delighted with the potatoes we've grown under mulch. The only
trouble we have is that it's difficult for us to find enough hay or
leaves that early in the season to cover all the potatoes we want to
grow.

If you're experimenting with planting seeds from that seedball
one of your potato plants might have produced last year, be pre-

These seed-potato sections have been dried for two days to allow the surface to heal over before planting.

pared for a wide variety of plants, most of which will be worthless. Plant the seed in a marked row or seedbed in early or mid-spring. The best temperature for potato seed germination is 68°F. (20°C.). If good tubers do form on any plants, save them and plant them to increase your stock of seed potatoes the following spring.

Pumpkins (100–115 days) Start like squash, with a generous shovelful of compost or well-rotted manure in each hill. When the plant starts to vine out, anticipate the squash borer by firming two or three shovelsful of soil over several vine nodes to encourage auxiliary rooting. Try the new semibush pumpkin, Funny Face, if space limitations have kept pumpkins out of your garden. Other

214

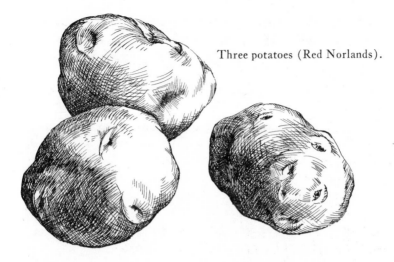

Three potatoes (Red Norlands).

kinds need lots of space; a hill will ramble over an eight-by-eight-foot square of ground by summer's end. Planting at the edge of the corn patch works well. The vines wander among the corn and, not so incidentally, help to discourage freeloading raccoons.

Seeds of naked-seeded pumpkin varieties like Lady Godiva, Streaker, and Triple Treat have a seed coat which is just a thin film. Lacking the thick protective coat which makes regular pumpkin seeds harder to get at, the naked seeds tend to rot more readily in cool, damp soil. You'll get more plants from a packet of seed if you presprout the seeds and then plant them in individual degradable pots, setting them out when warm weather has come to stay. Or if you do plant the seed directly in the ground, make it your last cucurbit planting and wait until settled warm weather to make it. No sense taking early chances on these rot-prone seeds.

Radish, Summer (20–30 days) Start planting as soon as the soil can be worked, but make small weekly or biweekly plantings rather than large infrequent ones, for radishes mature all at once and become fibrous and bitter when old, on their way to going to seed. For best radish quality, promote rapid growth. That means cool weather, ample moisture, sandy or loosely worked soil. Dryness makes radishes tough and strong flavored.

Drop a seed every inch or so in drills a foot apart, cover with one-fourth to one-half inch of soil, and thin to two- to three-inch spacing. Some gardeners plan most of their spring radish plantings

215

as row markers for carrots, parsnips, parsley, and other slow-germinating crops, but I like to have at least a short row of just radishes too. I seldom plant them after early June, for they don't do well in hot weather.

Radish, Winter (50–65 days) Start these good keepers in late July or early August so they'll finish in cool weather. They grow more slowly than spring radishes and are slightly more solid, less delicately crisp than a well-grown early radish. I find, though, that their quality is more consistent. They keep better in the soil without turning bitter or tough, and they don't start going to seed overnight. Plant as for spring radishes, but thin to four to eight inches apart according to variety. Some winter radishes, like Sakurajima, grow to prodigious size. Our favorite is China Rose.

Rhubarb (90–100 days) The most desirable kinds of rhubarb are propagated by root division. Seed is usually available only for the green-stalked Victoria, and plants grown from seed seem to have an unfortunate tendency to bolt right back to seed early in the season. Strawberry rhubarb, for which you might also be able to find seed, is red, as its name implies. Since I have not grown it from seed, I can't say whether it goes to seed as eagerly as Victoria, but my guess is that any seed-grown rhubarb would tend to perpetuate seed-prone stock over that which concentrates on vegetative growth.

Having said all that (and adding, as I feel I must, that a professional rhubarb grower once wrote to me that he'd rather have a field of Johnsongrass than one of seed-grown rhubarb) I still think there's a place for rhubarb grown from seed.

The year I grew it, for example, our perennial homestead plantings were just a year old. Our raspberry bushes bore only handfuls, we'd picked all the blosoms off our new strawberry patch, and our fruit trees were too young to blossom at all. We were hungry for fruit—our own fruit—and so the two rows of rhubarb plants I raised from seed that year were important to us.

I hadn't expected them to act like annuals and reach eating size that first summer, but that's what they did. From a packet of flaky seed, planted two inches apart in a half-inch-deep furrow and well firmed in, we got a whole plantation of rhubarb. Starting with seeds planted a good month before the last frost, and helped by a rainy season, we were able to eat crisp, succulent stalks of rhubarb by midsummer, about the time we'd ordinarily have had to quit picking from the roots. The seedlings transplant well. I spaced them about a foot apart in rich soil and gave them several feedings of manure tea. The stalks were excellent that first season. It wasn't until the second year that they started throwing seed stalks before the end of April. Grown as an annual, then, and generously fed and watered, rhubarb is worth raising from seed if you recognize its limitations. There aren't many other plants that will give you fruit the first season.

Rutabagas (90–100 days) This is primarily a fall crop, unless you usually have cool summers, since the roots grow tough in hot

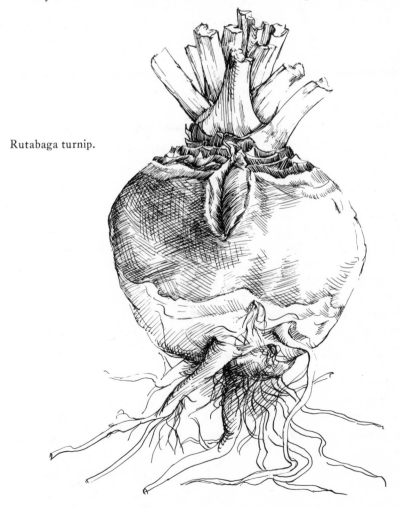

Rutabaga turnip.

weather. Sow seed in the garden, two inches apart in rows 15 to 24 inches apart, in June or early July. Rutabaga is one root vegetable that does well in heavy soil. When the seedlings are three inches high, thin them to stand six to eight inches apart. Flea beetles can be hard on young rutabagas, especially if soil is dry. Control them with diatomaceous earth.

Although I've never tried transplanting rutabagas, and know no one who has, I'd guess that you might get away with it, though perhaps not quite so easily as with turnips, which have a less-extensive root system.

Salsify (115–120 days) You can sow seed of the oyster plant, as this tasty root vegetable is also called, as soon as you can dig the garden in the spring. Ordinarily there's no need to rush, though. Although salsify needs 120 growing days, it's at its best after frost in the fall. If you plant seed around the time of daffodil bloom, or even a week or two later, the roots will have plenty of time to develop by fall. If you're using seed that's more than a year or two old, sow it thickly.

Loose, well-dug, fairly light soil produces good roots. Plant the seed no more than one-half inch deep and thin to stand three inches apart in the row. The foliage, in case you're growing it for the first time, is flat and ribbonlike, resembling that of garlic but larger and bushier.

Sorrel (60 days) Also called sour grass, this tangy-leafed perennial green is easy to grow from seed. Start plants indoors a month before the last frost, or sow seed directly in the row in mid-spring. A late-summer sowing will be ready to eat the following spring. The plants do well spaced six to eight inches apart in rows 15 to 18 inches apart, or in a special perennial bed. Once established, sorrel produces harvest-size leaves quite early in the spring. Somewhat sour alone, they are delicious mixed with other, milder greens.

Soybeans (75–110 days) Choose one of the varieties offered especially for home gardens. Field soybeans, I've been told by one seedsman, have a higher oil content. The flavor of vegetable soybeans is sweet and nutlike in the green stage, more ordinary when they're dried. Soybeans like warm weather, plenty of lime, and reasonably good drainage. Plant the seed when apple blossoms start to fall, no earlier. If spring weather is wild in your area, wait until around the time of your last frost. Drop a seed every two inches in rows three feet apart, cover with one inch of soil, and thin to three or four inches apart. Our goats consider soybean thinnings a special treat.

Spinach (43–50 days) Get it in the ground as early as you possibly can, because warm weather and long days all too soon trigger seed-stalk formation. Plant the seed no more than one-half inch deep, and thin the seeedlings to stand about six inches apart. If your garden is slow to dry for early-spring digging, you can prepare your spinach row in the fall, plant the seed, and mulch the row lightly. Gradually rake off the protective covering the following spring. In many areas, fall-planted spinach that has grown to a height of an inch or so will winter-over under a straw or hay cover.

When making late-summer plantings for fall eating, you may find that the seed is reluctant to germinate in warm weather. You can usually induce it to sprout by spreading it between damp paper towels and keeping it in a plastic bag in your refrigerator for five to seven days.

Spinach is a heavy feeder and needs a well-aerated, well-limed soil. Strongly acid soils often make available substances that are toxic to the plant.

Spinach, New Zealand (70 days) This thick-leaved green produces well all summer and into the fall, unlike conventional early spinach. It thrives in hot weather, but, oddly enough, germinates

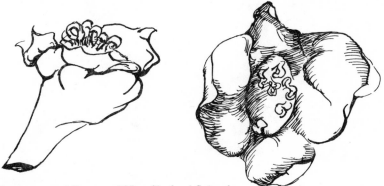

Enlargements of flowers of New Zealand Spinach.
Actual size of flower, 3/16 inch across.

219

readily when it's cool. In fact, it needs exposure to temperatures lower than 55°F. (13°C.) in order to germinate well. You can plant the slow-germinating seed about two or three weeks before your last frost date, either in hills three to four feet apart or every six inches in a row. Soak the seed in tepid water overnight to hasten sprouting. Thin row-planted seedlings to stand at least a foot apart. You might be surprised to see how far they'll sprawl by summer's end. Volunteers from seed ripened by last year's plants often appear in my garden in mid- to late April.

Squash, Summer (zucchini, patty pan, yellow crookneck) (43–75 days) A warm-weather crop, but one on which I always gamble an early- or mid-May planting (a week or ιo before our usual frost-free date) because replanting is easy and germination rapid. Once sprouted, the plants will grow well at a lower temperature than they needed for germination, so presprouting of seeds indoors works well. Plant the seeds, whether presprouted or not, in hills three to four feet apart for vining kinds, or spaced every four to eight inches in rows three to four feet apart. I bury a shovelful of compost in

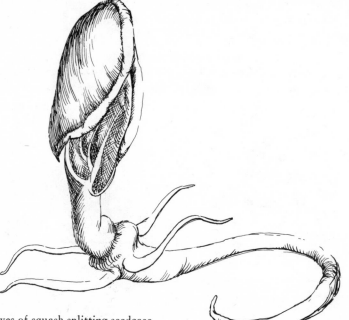

First leaves of squash splitting seedcase.
Length of seedcase, ¾ inch.

each hill, topped by an inch of soil and then the seeds. Hills should be planted with six to eight seeds and thinned to the best three. Squash seedlings do not transplant successfully.

Since the squash borer often attacks my early plantings by midsummer, I make a second planting, especially of zucchini, in mid-June. Radishes planted with the squash help to deter insects. Rotenone is a more aggressive defense if your insect problem is serious.

Pick the fruit when it's young and tender, four or five inches for yellow crookneck, four to eight inches for zucchini, silver-dollar size for patty pan. Do some comparison-shopping in the seed catalogs to find the earliest-bearing zucchini, which—often a hybrid— can beat other kinds by as much as a week. Having too much zucchini is less of a joke around here now that I've found they can be pickled by the same recipe I use to make dilled cucumber pickles, and they are delicious. (See the *Ball Blue Book* put out by the Ball Corporation, Muncie, Indiana, for recipes.)

Squash, Winter (Acorn, Buttercup, Butternut, Hubbard, etc. 85– 110 days) Give them the same good soil and compost, but wait to plant them till the weather's good and warm—about a week after the last frost, when the late iris are in bloom—because you're not after a quick summer crop, but a well-matured fall harvest. Soil temperature should be about 60°F. (16°C.). Hills should be spaced five feet apart, with five or six seeds in each, thinned later to three.

Acorn squash.

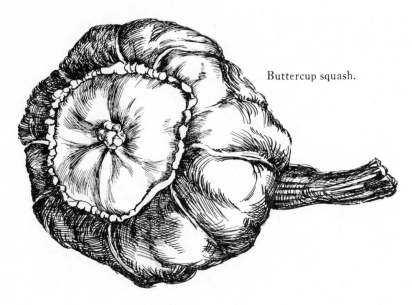

Buttercup squash.

For row planting, sow seed every six inches, no more than an inch deep, in rows eight feet apart. Pull alternate seedlings (not *too* early, though, until you see how much damage the bugs are going to do), leaving plants a foot or 18 inches apart.

Winter squash don't transplant well either, but they may be started indoors in pots if you have an extra-short season.

Strawberries (perennial; fruits year after planting unless started indoors in midwinter) The little alpine strawberry may be easily grown from seed. Plants started indoors seven to eight weeks before the last frost transplant easily to the garden row or rock garden, at or shortly before the frost-free date. Soil well supplied with humus, lightly limed if heavy clay, and close to the hose for irrigation is a good choice for your strawberry transplants. If you put them in a spot where they'll receive lightly dappled shade after bearing, they won't mind. Regular large-fruited garden strawberries are propagated by transplanting runners. Baron Solemacher alpine strawberries, which may be grown from seed, do not produce runners.

Sunflowers (100–120 days) Large plantings should be made in rows three to four feet apart, with plants thinned from a seeding every six inches to stand, finally, a good two to 2½ feet apart. For just a few heads, spot-plant the seeds around your home place, a few by the bird feeder, the mailbox, the backporch, the garage. Remember that they'll grow tall and shade nearby plants, which can sometimes be an advantage, but not always. Plant the seeds around the time of the last frost, since the plants thrive in heat and seedlings are frost-tender. Volunteers, however, which often seem the most vigorous, were obviously planted before that, so if you

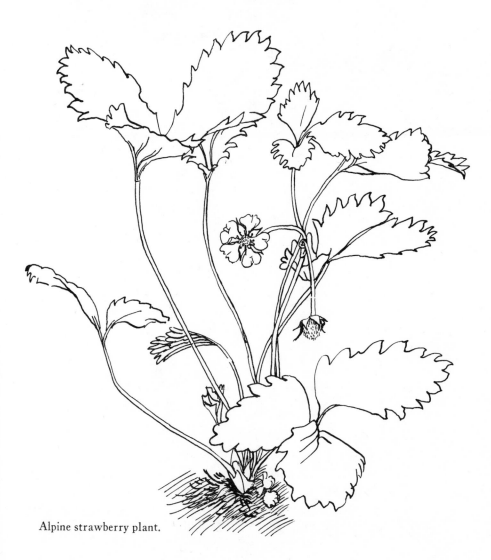

Alpine strawberry plant.

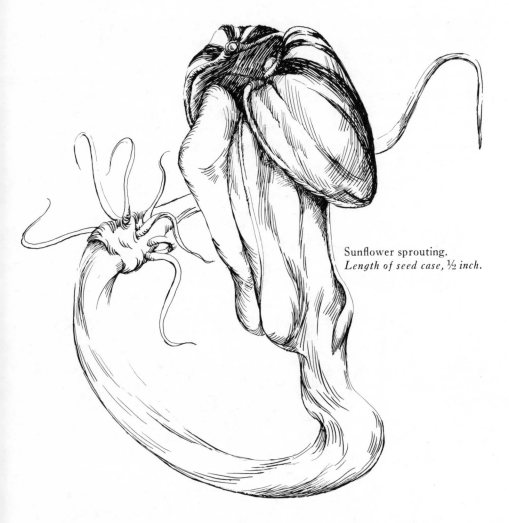

Sunflower sprouting.
Length of seed case, ½ inch.

have plenty of seed you can toss out a few seeds even earlier. Not for row crops, though: Too much work could be wasted.

Swiss Chard (50–60 days) This easy-to-grow, loose-leafed beet relative puts down a long, strong root, so it can make do even on fairly poor soils, although better soil, with plenty of organic matter, will give the best results. Young seedlings, up to two or three inches or so, may be transplanted, but older ones suffer loss of deep root tissue. When maples are in bloom, sow about eight seeds to the foot in rows 18 to 24 inches apart, and cover seed firmly with a half-inch of soil. Thin plants to an eventual spacing of 8 to 10 inches apart, but don't be in a hurry to do so. Let them grow till they crowd each other, then eat the thinnings. Thinning gradually in this way, you can get several early meals from the row while the plants are still growing. With some protection, chard will often winter-over.

Tampala (42–55 days) This nutritious leafy member of the large amaranth family likes warm weather. Plant seed one-fourth-inch

Small section of rhubarb chard; flower stalk very similar to beet.

Enlarged chard flower.
Actual size, ⅜ inch across.

deep when the soil has warmed up, about the time the late irises are in bloom. Thin the young plants gradually, eating them as you go, to an eventual spacing of 18 inches apart.

Tomatoes (45–87 days from setting out plants, including cherry tomatoes. Fruits ripen 45–55 days after blossoming.) We were amused, recently, to hear from friends who live in a proper central Pennsylvania town that the custom there, for quite some years, had been to get free tomato seedlings from the sewage plant. (Tomato seeds are well known for their ability to escape from the digestive tract unscathed, as anyone who has ever fed the fruits to pigs can testify.) These free seedlings were, of course, a grab bag of varieties, and no one knew until they bore fruit whether they had planted 25 cherry tomatoes or 25 different kinds. Now that hybrids are more generally grown, such freebies are less promising, because the second generation from hybrid parentage is unlikely to be as good as the first.

To grow your own seedlings, plant seed indoors in flats six to eight weeks before your frost-free date. Keep them as close as possible to 80°F. (27°C.) for prompt germination. Transplant, at least once, into larger flats with two inches between plants, setting the seedling deeper than it grew before, especially if it has gotten leggy. Tomato seedlings growing indoors should be kept near 60°F. (16°C.) to prevent overly rapid, difficult-to-harden growth.

Vernalization—chilling to induce early bloom—often works well with tomatoes, but it must be done early, when the first true leaves are opening up and the plant is only about 1½ inches tall. Night temperatures of 50° to 55°F. (10° to 13°C.) for two or three weeks are usually effective. Not all vegetable specialists agree that this method makes sense. If you decide to try it, treat only part of your crop so you'll have some unchilled plants for comparison.

Wait to set out your tomato plants until you're reasonably sure you've had your last frost. That's mid-May for us, about the time the barn swallows return. Set the plants three feet apart (two feet for earlies or small-fruited types) in rows three to four feet apart. Remember to protect them from cutworms. Since spring winds can still be punishing during the last two weeks in May, I like to bury my tomato plants, parallel to the soil surface, right up to the top tuft of leaves. Dig a long, shallow trench for this, rather

226

than a deep hole. It's too cold way down there in the ground for the roots of the warmth-loving tomato, which is at its best between 70° and 90°F. (21° and 32°C.).

Avoid planting tomatoes near walnut trees; they are extremely sensitive to the toxin, juglone, which is exuded by walnut tree roots. They are also sensitive to unnatural chemicals in the soil and vulnerable to diseases spread by tobacco users. Indoors, natural gas leaking from cooking stoves or other appliances may retard tomato seedlings.

Good drainage and soil aeration, reasonable fertility, and an ample supply of potash and phosphorus are important. Purple-leaved tomato seedlings are most likely suffering from a phosphorus deficiency. Dig in rock phosphate and bone meal before the final

Tomato cluster.

transplanting. A seedling that develops purple leaves near planting-out time often returns to normal when transplanted to the garden row, if the soil is adequate. Avoid giving too much nitrogen during early growth. It will promote vining at the expense of fruiting. The tomato's nitrogen requirements rise at blossoming time, though, and that's when you can give the plants a boost of manure tea or diluted fish emulsion.

As an alternative to prestarted transplants, you might like to try direct-seeding some kinds of tomatoes. The small early cherry tomatoes and the new cold-resistant subarctics are obvious candidates for this treatment, but any except very late varieties are worth a try. Seed planted at the time the maples bloom will wait out the early cold and germinate when the weather's right, just like all those volunteer tomatoes that grow well without any help from us. Such plants will be a bit later to come into bearing, but they'll often take over at the end of the season when the main planting is on the decline.

Staking of tomatoes seems to be traditional, in small gardens especially, for it looks neat, keeps the fruit clean, and promotes slightly earlier ripening. It isn't necessary, though. Much as we admire a well-staked tomato patch, we let our plants sprawl on a deep mulch, trading a few spoiled fruits and a tangled patch for the time we'd have to spend tying the plants and pruning the suckers that appear in the leaf axils. If you do stake, it's a good idea to sink the support soon after planting so you remember where you've buried the long stem of the tomato plant. Use soft cloth strips of old sheets or knit fabric to tie plants. Encircle the plant stem once, make a loose knot, and then tie a second circle with the same strip of cloth around the stake. This prevents damage to the plant from rubbing.

Many gardeners report excellent results using either wooden frames set over the plants for support or surrounding each plant with a circle of hog wire or concrete reinforcing wire with holes large enough to reach into for fruit picking.

Mulching helps to promote even tomato growth throughout the season, but it should not be done until the soil warms up. It's often mid-June, at least, before I have my tomato patch mulched.

Turnips (30–60 days) Rapid growth in cool weather produces good turnips. Those maturing in hot weather tend to be more fibrous and strong-flavored. Particularly for the early-spring crop, when you're racing the calendar to beat the hot weather, soil should be loose and humus-rich. Sow seeds one-fourth to one-half inch deep, as soon as you can work the soil in spring, and 9 to 10 weeks before your fall frost date for a late crop, which for many gardeners is the main turnip planting. Turnip seeds vary widely in size. For some reason, small seeds tend to produce flat-shaped roots.

Thin early turnips to stand three inches apart, fall-storage turnips to six inches. Check catalog descriptions. Some turnips are better suited to fall than spring production. The Japanese hybrid Just Right, for example, has excellent flavor but tends to bolt to seed when weather warms up, so it often fares best as a fall planting. Turnips, by the way, can be transplanted, with reasonable care, according to an experienced market gardener with whom I've corresponded. If you're short of space, you might like to try the old gardening practice of broadcasting turnip seed between the corn rows.

Watercress seedlings do well in an eight-inch pot set in a pan for bottom watering. Keep them well-supplied with moisture.

Watercress (perennial; reaches picking size in five months but thinnings may be eaten at two or three months) This nutritious peren-

*Watercress,
raised from seed,
growing in a pot
on the front step
(eastern expo-
sure).*

nial likes cool weather, plenty of lime, and a good supply of well-aerated water. You don't need a pond to grow it, though. I've kept an eight-inch clay pot of watercresss growing on a porch that gets some east sun, with the pot set in a pan into which I pour water several times a week.

The seeds are fine and sure to be overplanted. Transplant the seedlings, as soon as they can be handled, to one- to two-inch spacing in flats. Transplant to pots when two or three inches high, and to stream and/or pond banks about a month before the last frost. Once established, watercress is easy to propagate from cuttings, which root quite readily, and if you want a *lot* more, you can gather the seedpods when they ripen in the fall.

Watermelon (74–90 days) A space-grabber unless you plant one of the new bush types or grow small melons on a fence, but lots of fun to grow. The seed needs consistent warmth, 75° to 80°F. (24° to 27°C.), for 5 to 10 days, to germinate well. Seed for the seedless types of watermelon germinates less readily than the regular kind and is even less tolerant of cool temperatures.

Many northern gardeners start watermelon seed indoors in pots for setting out when weather is warm, a good 10 days or so after the last frost. The more warm days the vines experience, the more fruit they'll bear. Southern gardeners have enough time between frosts to plant the seed directly in the ground. Transplanting doesn't work well.

Hills should be six to eight inches apart, with one or two plants to a hill. Thin when the plants have five leaves. The best site for northern gardeners is a southern slope that is well-drained. Watermelons do well in sandy, humus-rich soil that is more acid than cantaloupes need, and they don't require much nitrogen.

One grower recommends preparing a rye cover crop in the watermelon bed, the fall before planting. In spring, then, you can till a three-foot furrow down through the center of the rye, let it settle for a week or two, and plant your watermelon seed (or set out plants). As the plants vine out, continue to till under the rye until the whole cover crop has been turned under. If you mulch, wait until the soil is good and warm, in late June or so, unless you use black plastic.

How Much Seed Do You Need?

Artichokes, globe—¼-ounce yields about 75 plants.

Asparagus—1 ounce yields 10,000 plants if started inside at 80° to 90°F. 1,000 if sown in rows outdoors.

Beans, lima—1 pound will plant 100 to 150 feet of row, depending on size.

Beans, snap—1 pound sows 150 feet.

Beets—1 ounce sows 100 feet, average packet about 25 feet of row.

Broccoli—1 ounce produces 3,000 to 4,000 plants, most packets about 200 plants.

Brussels sprouts—1 ounce produces about 3,000 plants.

Cantaloupe—1 ounce of regular size has about 900 seeds. More in the case of small-seeded melons like Takii's Honey. Most packets will plant about 20 hills.

Carrots—1 ounce sows 250 to 300 feet. Most packets are enough for about 30 feet of row.

Cauliflower—1 ounce produces 2,000 to 3,000 plants, most packets 150.

Celeriac—1 ounce produces about 7,500 plants, most packets about 400.

Celery—1 ounce produces about 10,000 plants, most packets 400 to 500.

Collards—most packets sow 100 feet of row.

Corn—1 pound plants 800 to 1,000 feet of row.

Cucumbers—1 ounce plants 50 hills. Most packets, except for hybrids, contain 100 to 150 seeds.

Dill—An average packet plants 30 feet of row.

Eggplant—1 ounce produces about 2,000 plants. Most nonhybrid packets contain about 60 seeds, hybrids 25 to 30.

Endive and Escarole—1 ounce sows about 200 feet, an average packet 20 to 30 feet.

Fennel—1 ounce sows about 300 feet of row, average packet 30 to 40 feet of row.

Gherkins—1 ounce sows about 80 hills, average packet about 20.

Kale—1 ounce sows 200 feet of row, average packet about 40 feet.

Kohlrabi—1 ounce sows 200 feet of row, average packet about 40 feet.

Leeks—1 ounce sows 200 feet of row, average packet 25 feet.

Lettuce, head—1 ounce sows 400 feet of row. Most packets plant 40 feet.

Lettuce, leaf—same as head lettuce.

Okra—1 ounce sows 50 feet of row, average packet about 15 feet.

Onions—1 ounce sows 200 feet. Most packets plant 20 feet of row.

Parsley—1 ounce sows 200 feet, most packets 20 to 30 feet of row, plenty for several families.

Parsnips—1 ounce sows 200 feet, most packets 15 to 20 feet.

Peanuts—1 pound plants 200 feet of row. Average packet of Spanish (small seeds) plants 45 feet of row; large-seeded Virginia, 15 feet of row.

Peas—1 pound sows 100 feet of row. Most packets plant about 20 feet (single row).

Peppers—1 ounce produces about 1,500 plants. Packets of nonhybrid varieties contain about 150 seeds, most hybrids 50 to 100 seeds.

Potatoes, sweet—100 slips will plant 100 feet of row.

Potatoes, white—about 7 pounds of seed potatoes are needed to plant 100 feet of row.

Pumpkins—1 ounce sows about 25 hills, most packets about 5 hills.

Radish, summer—average packet sows 20 feet of row; 1 ounce sows 100 feet.

Radish, winter—1 ounce sows 150 feet of row.

Rhubarb—1 ounce plants 100 feet of row, a packet 15 to 20 feet.

Rutabagas—1 ounce plants 250 feet of row, a packet about 40 to 50 feet.

Sorrel—1 ounce sows about 100 feet of row.

Soybeans—1 pound will sow about 100 to 150 feet of row.

Spinach, New Zealand—1 ounce sows 75 feet.

Squash, summer—1 ounce plants about 100 feet of row. Average packet is enough for 15 to 20 feet of row.

Squash, winter—1 ounce plants 60 to 100 feet of row or 20 to 30 hills. Average packet plants 6 to 8 hills.

Sunflower—¼-pound plants 500 to 800 feet of row, average packet about 50 feet.

Swiss chard—1 ounce sows 100 feet, most packets 25 feet.

Tampala—Average packet sows about 25 to 30 feet of row.

Tomatoes—1 ounce produces 3,000 to 6,000 plants (seed size varies). Most packets of nonhybrid types contain 100 to 150 seeds, 25 to 75 seeds for hybrids.

Turnips—1 ounce plants 200 feet, average packet about 50 feet.

Watercress—average packet yields about 1,000 plants—seed is very fine.

Watermelon—1 ounce plants about 30 hills, most packets 5 to 6 hills.

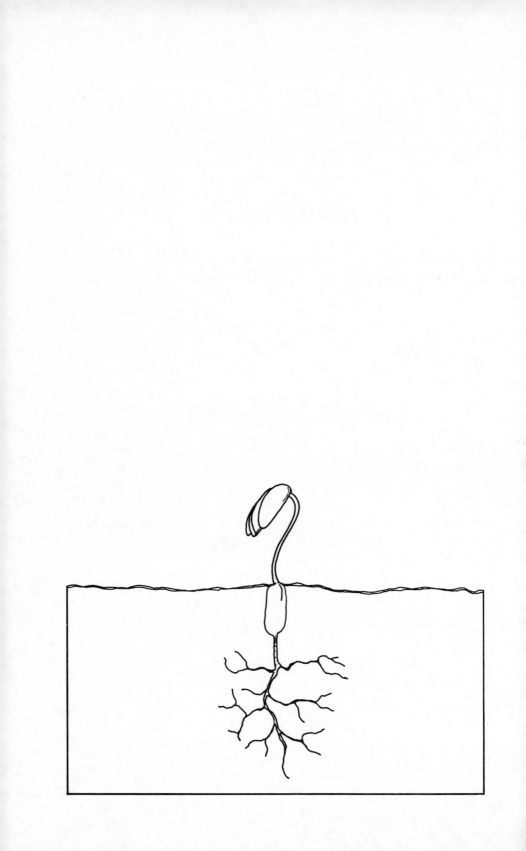

Section Four

No plant is ever a finished product.

Luther Burbank

24
Why Save Seeds?

The gardener who saves seed from this year's crop to plant in next year's garden has, in addition to the assurance that he or she is prepared for the future, the prospect of experiment, discovery, even surprise. Selection of seed-bearing plants, along with deliberate crossing by nurserymen and dedicated amateurs, has made possible most of the improvements that have been developed in our favorite garden vegetable and flower plants.

Improvement of the yield, earliness, disease resistance, or other quality or constellation of qualities in a certain strain of vegetables can often be accomplished simply by selection—saving seed from the best plants. Over a period of years, consistent selection of seed from outstanding plants can give you a superstrain that yields better, earlier, tastier, larger, or whatever you've selected for, than the original seeds.

Economy is important to most of us. And, although commercial seeds are modestly priced in relation to their potential, home-saved seeds cost even less—usually nothing, unless you purchase stakes or storage supplies.

Adjustment to local weather conditions is achieved by many seed-savers after a few years of selecting the most frost-resistant, early-germinating, or drought-proof seeds. Even without deliberate selection, the simple act of saving seed from thriving plants will often condition the plant strain to the peculiarities of the place where it is regularly replanted.

Untreated seed, although increasingly offered by seed companies in response to growing concern among gardeners for the health of their soil, is most certainly yours when you save your own.

Heirloom strains of garden vegetables that are not commercially available can be perpetuated *only* by means of home-saved seed. "The greatest service which can be rendered any country," wrote

Thomas Jefferson, "is to add a useful plant to its culture." It is equally true that the dying out of an irreplaceable variety is a loss, not only to the gardener who depended on it but to other gardeners and eaters, both present and future. Several good vegetables now offered by seed companies, Royalty snap bean and Clemson Spineless okra, for example, were developed from heirloom strains that had been repeatedly grown and saved by isolated families.

Keeping these old strains alive, then, by replanting and saving the seed, is a responsible action that might be greatly appreciated by some future generation. It isn't necessary to plant most kinds of seeds every single year in order to keep the strain alive. Renewal planting every second or third year will keep seed of most vegetables alive and well, provided the seed is well stored.

Preference for open-pollinated varieties of vegetables is increasing, with many gardeners choosing to grow corn and tomato varieties that have not been subject to the rigorous inbreeding program that is part of the hybridizing process. Open-pollinated corn, for example, has been shown to frequently contain higher amounts of protein than hybrid corn. In addition, its genetic heritage is more diverse, so that it is less likely to be totally wiped out by disease that would be more serious in strictly controlled, uniform seed crops. Hybrids bear well and many of us will continue to plant them, but there is new respect now for the genetic diversity of open-pollinated seed.

Experimenting with saving, selection, and possibly even deliberate crossing of certain varieties constitutes a challenge for the experienced gardener. Planting and evaluating the results of each year's careful choices of seed can be an ongoing adventure. There is even the possibility—remote, but nonetheless real—of discovering a worthwhile new strain.

Although most new vegetable introductions within the last 28 years have been produced by purposeful crossing, simple discovery accounts for the appearance of many garden favorites. The Henderson bush lima, for example, was spotted along the roadside in the 1870s by an elderly man who was taking a walk. Golden Bantam corn, still a favorite, was selected and developed by two Massachusetts gardeners. (Two quarts of the seed were sold to the Burpee seed company sometime in the 1890s for $25.)

Beneficial mutations affect about one plant in a million within each generation. Mutation, the sudden altering of plant character caused by a change in the molecular structure of its genes, usually produces undesirable changes in the plant. The fact that mutations are not reversible makes it possible to breed new generations of like plants from the one that has suddenly changed. Burpee's Fluffy Ruffles sweet pea, introduced in 1928, was a mutation.

The gardener who discovers something new is the one who spends time with plants, observing, recording, with a sensitivity attuned to subtle shades of difference. Granted, the odds against a dramatic plant discovery are high, but the search is a lot of fun.

Self-reliance becomes a more realistic goal each time we read headlines about fuel shortages, rising postal costs, unemployment, or drought conditions in seed- or grain-raising parts of the country. A supply of well-chosen, correctly stored garden seeds will feed you next year, no matter what happens to prices of food, fuel, or postage. Saving seed will also yield satisfaction that can't be price-tagged—pride in being able to provide for yourself, and possibly for a few other people as well, and satisfaction in refining and upgrading the crops you grow.

25
Annuals, Perennials, Biennials

The easiest seeds to save, and those you should probably begin with if the process is new to you, are those of the annuals, such garden vegetables as tomatoes, lettuce, corn, and eggplant, which produce seed the same season they're planted.

Perennials are easy too, since the seed appears each year once the plant has reached the proper stage of maturity. Vegetable perennials don't always set seed, though. Those that do are listed in the table that follows. The others, Jerusalem artichoke, comfrey, and horseradish, must be propagated by root cuttings or plant division. The Burpee seed company once offered $1,000 for viable horseradish seed, but had no takers. Comfrey, although it flowers, hardly ever produces viable seed.

Biennials are another story. Vegetables in this group, which includes most of the root vegetables and the cabbage family, produce

Jerusalem artichoke, flowers and edible tuberous roots.

an edible crop the year they're planted, but they do not flower and develop seed until the second year. In most temperate-zone gardens the plants intended for seed production must be protected over the winter, either by a heavy mulch or—if winter cold is severe and persistent—by digging, storing in sand or sawdust, and replanting in spring. When replanted, they should be buried deeply, right up to the crown of the plant.

List of Annual, Biennial, and Perennial Vegetables Which Form Seed

Annuals

Beans snap and lima	Okra
Broccoli (if started early)	Onions
Cucumbers	Peas
Dill	Peppers
Eggplant	Pumpkins
Endive and escarole	Radish (if planted early)
Fennel	Soybeans
Gherkins	Spinach
Lettuce	Squash
Melons	Tomatoes

Biennials

Beets	Kale
Brussels sprouts	Kohlrabi
Cabbage	Mustard
Cabbage, Chinese	Parsley
Caraway	Parsnips
Carrots	Radish, winter
Cauliflower	Rutabagas
Celeriac	Salsify
Celery	Turnips
Collards	

Perennials

Artichokes, globe	Rhubarb
Asparagus	Sorrel
Chives	Watercress

The flower stalk that will grow tall and go to seed in the plant's second spring begins to form in the winter. Biennial vegetables that are at marketing size in the fall, neither immature nor old and woody, will be the best seed producers. A month or two of cold temperatures, no higher than 40° to 50°F. (4° to 10°C.)—promotes seed stalk formation. Hot weather during the short days of winter can interfere with proper development of the flower in beets and cabbage.

26
How Seeds Are Formed

Your seed-saving efforts will be more successful if you have some idea of how the seed is formed.

The Reproduction Cycle of Plants

The process is a cycle, and so we can't say, really, whether it begins with the flower or with the original seed that produced the plant. Since we must start somewhere, let's break into the cycle at the point of flowering.

A flower's reason for being is to produce seed. There are all kinds of flowers—the large, showy yellow trumpets of the squash family, the small white stars of pepper and tomato, the bright yellow florets of broccoli, the inconspicuous petalless blossoms of spinach. Their variations in color and form have evolved as ways

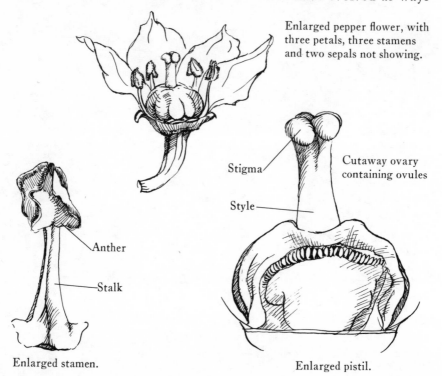

Enlarged pepper flower, with three petals, three stamens and two sepals not showing.

Stigma

Cutaway ovary containing ovules

Style

Anther

Stalk

Enlarged stamen.

Enlarged pistil.

of encouraging pollination. Insect-pollinated flowers need to attract attention, whether by producing nectar, smelling sweet, or assuming an inviting color. Wind-pollinated flowers, since there is no necessity for them to invite insect visitors, are often drab, tiny, or otherwise obscure.

All flowers, though, whatever their outward form or color, have pollen-bearing and pollen-receptive parts.

The pollen-bearing, fertilizing part of the plant is the *stamen*. It is composed of a long, thin stalk, the *filament,* and *anthers,* pollen-containing sacs on the ends of the filaments.

The receptive, seed-nurturing parts of the flower are called the carpels. These include 1) the pollen-receptive region, the *stigma;* 2) the *style,* a long, thin tube that leads from the stigma to the ovary; and 3) the *ovary,* an enclosure containing an *ovule* (egg) or ovules. In flowers containing a cluster of more than one carpel, the whole assembly is called a pistil (after the Latin for pestle). The term pistil is also used for a single carpel. The *calyx,* the cuplike outgrowth of the stem, which may be composed of individual parts called *sepals,* and the *corolla,* or petal cluster, are supportive parts without any reproductive function. A flower can be fertilized in the absence of the corolla; in fact, many people remove the corolla when practicing hand-pollination.

If the flower is to form seed, the ripe ovule must be fertilized by a grain of pollen. The speck of pollen, whether it lands on the stigma by the agency of wind, insects, or gravity, has the same fabulous journey to make. It begins by growing an extension of itself, a long, tenuous thread of tissue, which is somehow potentiated by the arrival of the pollen in the right place, at the right time. This living thread extends, cell by cell, growing down through the style until it reaches the ovary. There it enters an ovule, penetrating the embryo sac.

The two cells, that of the pollen and that of the ovule, unite to form a single living cell, a zygote, which is able to divide repeatedly and multiply into the complex organism that will be the seed embryo. The ovary grows and toughens into the protective seed coat.

The origin of the endosperm, the supply of stored nourishment for the encapsulated plant, is a bit more roundabout. We have a pretty good idea of *what* happens, but we don't know *why.* Mysteries still abound in the plant world. Backtrack for a moment to that grain of pollen. Sometime between the time it is shed from the anther and received by the stigma, the original single grain splits into two cells. One of these cells, as we have just seen, fertilized the ovule. The other cell unites with two polar nuclei in the ovule's embryo sac and gradually grows into the endosperm. (Some seeds, those of the bean, pea, pumpkin, and watermelon, for example, have no endosperm.)

When the developing seed has reached its characteristic size and complexity, it stops growing and begins the drying, ripening process that precedes dormancy. The ripened seed-containing ovary is called a fruit. A bean pod, for example, is a fruit. The seeds it contains are ripened fertilized ovules.

The Vagaries of Pollination

In order to fertilize the ovule, pollen must be of the correct kind and it must arrive at the right time, when the plant has achieved enough vegetative growth to enable it to begin to reproduce. Pollen from unrelated species will not "take." Pea pollen landing on a tomato blossom, for example, won't get anywhere. Even within a species, some plants are not receptive to their own pollen. A flower will sometimes discharge pollen before its stigma is ready to receive it. Other flowers are sterile to their own pollen.

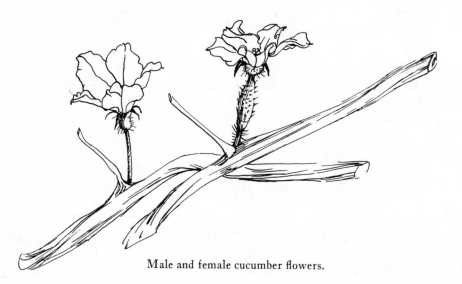

Male and female cucumber flowers.

A whole group of vegetables—the cucurbits—which include melons, cucumbers, pumpkins, and squashes, bear two kinds of incomplete flowers on each plant. The staminate, or male flower, appears first, followed in a few days by the pistillate, or female flower. Spinach plants can occur in a bewildering number of gender variations. Some produce both male and female flowers, others only female; still others are either pollen producers or seed nurturers. Female asparagus plants tend to produce thicker, but fewer stalks. Males are thin but more numerous. Berries are, of course, borne only by the female plants. That's why not every frond in your asparagus patch will go to seed. Some are males.

Most other vegetable plants have complete flowers, containing both stamens and pistils.

Self-pollinating flowers, those in which the flower accepts its own pollen, with or without insect intervention, can be depended on to produce seed that will grow into plants like the parent, since their inheritance is the same. This group includes the following vegetables and commonly grown grains:

barley	lima beans
cowpeas	oats
endive	snap beans
escarole	soybeans
garden peas	tomatoes
lettuce	wheat

(Technically speaking, even these self-pollinated crops can cross-pollinate in from 0.1 percent to five percent of plant populations.)

These seeds, then, are the best bet for your early seed-saving endeavors, since you can be fairly confident that the plants grown from them will "come true."

Most other favorite garden vegetables will cross with other varieties of the same kind, to a greater or lesser extent depending on variety, weather, insect activity, and other conditions.

Cross-Pollination

Cross-pollination—the acceptance by a flower of pollen from a plant of the same species having a different genetic makeup—often results in seed containing genes that differ from those of the parent plant. Plants grown from those seeds, then, may have different characteristics from the parent plant.

The following plants are wind-pollinated. Their pollen is fine, virtually dustlike, and the number of grains produced is lavish, since vagaries of wind are sometimes more capricious than insect activity when distances are great:

beets	spinach
corn	Swiss chard
rye	

The pollen produced by these plants is so fine, and travels so far, that any plantings spaced more closely than one mile apart have a chance of crossing, with the exception of corn, which has relatively heavy pollen, and crosses rarely (if at all) at distances greater than 1,000 feet.

The large insect-pollinated group includes the following vegetables:

asparagus	eggplant
cabbage family	gherkins
cabbage	melons
collards	onions
kale	parsley
kohlrabi	parsnips
broccoli	peppers
Brussels sprouts	pumpkin
carrots	radish
celeriac	rutabagas
celery	squash
Chinese cabbage	turnips
cucumbers	

Flowers of these vegetables (some of which, you will remember, are biennials) may cross-pollinate within one mile, but one-fourth-mile separation is generally sufficient for home garden purposes. Cross-pollination is especially likely if several stands of different varieties of the same vegetable are located on the direct flight line of a bee colony. Bees generally collect pollen from one species at a time.

This crossing, however, can occur only within a species. When you know this, you can dismiss the old garden myth that you shouldn't grow cucumbers next to cantaloupe. It's amazing how many people still take this seriously. You'll even hear tales about the cucamelons or watercucumbers that someone grew, but they're just that—tales. If you're not saving seed, you can grow any of the cucurbits next to each other. Any close-relative crossing that *did* occur would show up only in the next generation planted from seed of this year's plants. I hope this is good news to the man who remarked to us last year that his wife didn't want him to plant zucchini since he had already planted watermelon and she didn't want to waste garden space on weird crosses!

Seed-Saver's Caveats

If you're saving seed, you just need to remember that squash, pumpkins, watermelons, cantaloupes, and cucumbers will cross-pollinate only within their own species. A pumpkin blossom won't accept watermelon, cantaloupe, or cucumber pollen; a cantaloupe can't be pollinated by a cucumber, squash, pumpkin, or watermelon; a cucumber won't mix with a zucchini, Halloween pumpkin, or watermelon. Like many myths, though, the one we're debunking has its origins in reality. Some kinds of pumpkin and squash *do* cross, with odd and sometimes picturesque results. The vegetables produced by such crosses are edible, but they may not always be as tender or delicious as the originals.

Here's a quick look at the cucurbit family tree to give you an idea of what to expect in your garden. The cucurbit genus is divided into various species. The species *C. pepo,* for example, includes Halloween pumpkins, spaghetti squash, and small gourds. All of these widely varied vegetables can cross, so you can see that there's plenty of potential for mischief within this group alone.

The species *C. maxima* includes the long-keeping winter squash like Hubbard, Buttercup, and Delicious. These will cross with *C. moschata* (Butternut), but they are less likely to cross with *C. mixta,* which includes the Cushaw and Japanese pie pumpkin, or with *C. pepo*—the large and diverse group mentioned above.

Corn, a member of the grass family, presents another special case. A cross between adjacent stands of, say, popcorn and sweet corn, field corn and sweet corn, or yellow corn and white corn, may affect the ears of *this* year's crop, depending on wind direction, tasselling time, and other variables. The result of such a cross is not always evident on eating the corn, since enough sweet kernels usually develop to cover any odd-pollinated less flavorful ones. When the kernels are dried, differences—if any—between kernels will be more pronounced.

If you intend to save seed of more than one variety of a certain vegetable, especially one that is easily cross-pollinated, you'll probably find it more practical to plan for seed development in alternate years to keep the strains as pure as possible. Since most seeds are good for two years after harvest, anyway, this plan should simplify our garden planning, especially for biennials.

27
Backyard Plant Breeding

Suppose you want to try making some controlled crosses of seed-bearing vegetable plants. How do you begin?

First, you select parent plants that have qualities you'd like to perpetuate and try to combine. See chapter 29 for selection criteria.

Then you must isolate your plants to prevent accidental wind or insect pollination from unknown sources. A well-anchored cloth cover will keep out wind-borne pollen; a screen-wire cage or cheese-cloth drape effectively deters insects. Self-pollinating flowers like that of the tomato must have their anthers removed before the pollen is ready to shed, to ensure that only the introduced pollen is accepted by the flower. The necessity for hand pollination is responsible for the relatively high price of hybrid tomato seed. Composite flowers and those of peas and beans and some other self-pollinating plants are difficult to hand-pollinate.

Having thus taken control of the flower to eliminate random pollination, it is now up to you to carry out the pollen transfer from one parent plant to another. If you will pinch off the blossom petals, when possible, you'll have a better view of what you are doing.

Hand pollinating a tomato flower with a paintbrush.
Flower to be pollinated has anthers and petals removed.

Then transfer the pollen from the parent plant you've chosen to be the fertilizing agent, to the stigma of the plant you want to bear the seeds. To do this, you can use a twist of paper tissue, a rabbit tail, a small paintbrush, a fingertip, a rubber pencil eraser, or a piece of ball fringe (a decorative curtain edging).

If one of your chosen parent plants blooms before the other one, you can save the pollen, according to Ken and Pat Kraft, authors of *Garden to Order,* by tapping it into a small dry vial and then drying it for about 24 hours under a light bulb or in any other spot where a fairly constant temperature of 90°F. (32°C.) can be maintained. Store the pollen in the freezer. Species vary, and pollen is often short-lived at best—some kinds are potent for only a few hours—but others have lasted for several weeks with this treatment.

Corn crosses are easy to make, because the pollen source, the tassel, is distinctly separate from the pollen receptors, the silks. Remove the tassels from the plants you want to bear seed. Leave the tassels on nearby pollinator plants. It is necessary, of course, for the pollen to be discharged while the seed plants are in the silk stage, in order for pollination to take place.

This is a quick look at a complex subject, but perhaps these few hints will help you to make a beginning if you choose to try some deliberate crossing. Don't hesitate to pull apart a few flowers so that you can learn more about their structure. If you become at all serious about this, you will of course want to do a lot more reading about plant genetics, flowering mechanisms, isolation and breeding techniques, etc. If you will label your experiments and record your procedures and results, you'll be able to learn and profit from what you've done.

28
Hybrids

Should you save seed from plants that you've grown from hybrid seed? Only if you have plenty of time and space to experiment. I certainly wouldn't rely on such seed for my main planting. The problem is that F1 hybrid seed, the kind usually sold, is the product of the crossing of two genetically different parent plants, both of which have been severely inbred in order to concentrate the desired characteristics. The first generation (F1) of a good cross is noticeably, sometimes outstandingly, superior to the parents—a phenomenon known as hybrid vigor (called heterosis by biologists). Succeeding generations grown from seed saved from the F1 plants will tend to revert to the highly inbred, lackluster-appearing recent ancestors. You can see, then, that you probably have more to lose than to gain from saving seed of garden hybrids. Still, there's no harm in fooling around with some of these second-generation crosses as long as you don't expect much. Some hybrid seeds are sterile. Do I save seed from hybrids, you ask? No.

Hybrid seed is available for the following kinds of vegetable plants. If you intend to save seed, you'd be wise to either note hybrids at planting or refer back to the seed catalog to check on varieties you've planted. Marglobe and Rutgers tomatoes, for example, are open-pollinated. Spring Giant and Big Boy are hybrids. Bell Boy peppers are hybrid. Vinedale and Staddon's Select are not.

Hybrid seed is commonly available for the following vegetables:

cabbage	spinach
cantaloupe	squash
corn	peppers
cucumbers	pumpkin
eggplant	sugar beets
onions	tomato
sorghum	watermelon
cauliflower	Chinese
carrots	cabbage
Brussels sprouts	broccoli

29
Selection

When you save garden seed, you can improve, as well as per-petuate, your vegetable crops. Simply by practicing careful selec-tion, without any deliberate cross-breeding or hybridizing, you can develop a strain of vegetables that is suited to your climate and that possesses some of the characteristics you find most desirable. Selec-tion won't introduce dramatic new improvements, but over the years the process can gradually intensify good qualities.

The Bases for Selection

Your aims in selecting vegetable plants from which to save seed will depend on the strain with which you're starting, the peculiarities of your local weather conditions, and your personal tastes. Here are some of the qualities you might want to consider in choosing your parent plants:

- Early bearing.
- Flavor.
- Size.
- Insect resistance.
- Disease resistance.
- Ability to germinate and thrive in cold weather.
- Lateness to go to seed (in leafy crops).
- Color.
- Storage life.
- Yield.
- Plant vigor.
- Fruit texture—tenderness, juiciness, seediness.
- Suitability for purpose, for example, paste tomatoes should be meaty, kraut cabbage should be solid.
- Special qualities—absence of thorns, spines, strings, etc.
- Resistance to drought, wind, smog, dampness, or other stressful atmospheric conditions.

Acquired characteristics like fanciful shapes or dwarfing due to drought cannot be transmitted to the next generation. Disease is not an inherited trait, but resistance or vulnerabiliy to plant ailments may be inherited. The seed-borne diseases, although they affect the next generation, are not genetically based.

Judging the Parent Plants

Even though you may not be collecting the seed until toward the end of the season, you'll want to observe the plants from the very beginning so that you have an idea of their overall performance. Although your first impulse might be to save seed from the largest single specimen of fruit that you can find, the best approach is to consider the plant as a whole. You might not want to intensify the characteristics of a giant tomato from a disease-prone or low-yielding plant. It is the entire plant—its vigor, resistance to disease and insect predation, yield, etc.—that gives you the best clue to the nature of the plants that will grow from its seed.

Biennials, which don't produce seed until the second season, should be selected for eating quality when stored in the fall, and then reselected for keeping quality in the spring after winter storage.

When saving seed from any plant that cross-pollinates, it's wise to collect from more than one plant, otherwise you may find yourself selecting increasingly inbred stock. Without sufficient genetic variety, the strain will lose vigor. This is especially true of corn. Pumpkins and squash, though, seem to maintain vigor even when inbred, so it's all right to save seed from a single fruit of these crops.

Self-pollinated vegetables like beans, peas, and tomatoes get along quite well accepting their own pollen. Since they are naturally somewhat inbred, you needn't worry about preserving genetic variety. Go ahead and save seed from exceptional individuals; it needn't be mixed with others to preserve its vigor.

Keeping seed from superior vegetable plants sometimes involves a bit of sacrifice. Particularly if you're selecting for earliness, and your family is counting the days until that first round of sweet corn or salad tomatoes, it's not always easy to let it be. Unfortunately, it's not often possible to eat the vegetable and retain the seed, since in order to produce viable seed the fruit must mature on the plant. Pumpkins and winter squash may be eaten at the same time their seed is collected, but most other vegetables must be left on the plant. Naturally, if you're selecting for some other quality or qualities such as yield, flavor, or size, you can indulge your hunger for the first fruits and wait to size up the plant's midseason performance before setting aside seed-bearers.

Even if you're not as absentminded as I am, you'll want to mark your chosen parent plants, especially if other family members do some of the picking. If that super, all-time champion cucumber gets put in the pickle crock, you might have to wait until next year to get another equally outstanding. Use a stake, chicken wire, a ribbon or string tie, a tag—anything that will stay in place and call attention to the plant's special purpose.

30
Care of the Seed-Bearing Plant

Having chosen and marked the plants from which you plan to save seed, you'll want to take good care of them throughout the growing season—mulching, watering, fertilizing, and controlling insects as necessary.

Stake, mulch, or otherwise protect the fruit from rotting ground moisture and bird or animal predation so that seeds can mature properly. Biennials, when replanted the second spring, develop a long seed stalk which sometimes needs to be staked so it isn't broken by strong spring winds.

When the plant is concentrating on vegetative growth, its carbohydrate content is relatively low in comparison to its content of nitrogen. With the beginning of seed production, as the plant becomes less sappy and more fibrous, the ratio of carbon to nitrogen starts to rise.

Conditions during seed development have considerable effect on the vigor of the matured seeds. Some influential factors will be beyond your control. For example, the prevailing temperatures 20 to 30 days and 30 to 40 days before maturity have a definite effect on the oil content of soybeans. A sharp rise in temperature affects the protein content and yield of developing wheat seed.

There are two ways of looking at this nurturing process. You certainly want the plants to be healthy. On the other hand, some gardeners feel, and I agree, that pampering the plant to the point of giving supercare that you wouldn't have time to give to your whole garden is self-defeating. Your aim, after all, is to raise a race of cucumbers or whatever that do well under ordinary garden conditions. So give the plant everything it needs. But don't hover over it with second helpings.

31
Collecting Seeds

As you remember, seeds depend on stored nourishment to carry them through their winter dormancy so they can live as green plants next spring. Seed that is harvested too early, even though it may look the same as other seed, may be either deficient in endosperm or embryonic development or immature in some way. Such seed is likely to deteriorate in storage. If it does survive, it may germinate unevenly or produce inferior seedlings. I proved this to my own satisfaction last year by saving seed from both red (ripe) and green (unripe, though good to eat) cherry peppers. The seed saved from the green pods had a very low germination rate, although as far as I could tell the few plants that *did* grow were normal. Germination of seed saved from the red pods was more rapid and much more complete.

Still, you must be sure to collect the seed before it rots or shatters. Harvest time is most critical for those plants which release their seed as soon as it is ripe (shattering). To make things trickier yet, certain plants that shatter readily also ripen seed one stalk at a time over a period of weeks—a valuable survival mechanism for the plant, but inconvenient for the gardener. If you're counting on saving seed from lettuce, onions, okra, or any of the cabbage family —all of which behave in this way—you can tie small paper bags over the heads of developing seeds to catch them in case you're not able to make daily seed-collecting rounds. Be sure to punch a few holes in the bag to admit air.

Plants that bear seeds embedded or encased in edible flesh—the cucumbers, eggplants, tomatoes, and peppers—should be on the overripe side before the fruit is picked. Let them develop just past the point where you'd want to eat them. Tomatoes should be soft, cucumbers yellow, peppers red and wrinkling. If the fruit actually begins to rot, though, seed may be damaged by the heat of decomposition. The flesh of the vegetable shouldn't be allowed to dry around the seed either, or it may form an impermeable covering that will cut down on the gas exchange necessary to the life of the seed in storage.

Plants bearing edible seed, especially corn and wheat, will

256

retain their fully matured seed for awhile. These grains may be left on the plant for several weeks, or until you have a chance to collect them. Snap beans and soybeans also retain their dry seed for some time, although they do eventually shatter. They are often cut when the seed is fully developed and piled in a dry, protected place to cure further before the seed is threshed out.

If possible, seed collecting should be done on a dry, sunny day when the seeds are free of rain or dew. Frost doesn't hurt most seeds, as long as they are dry. The danger in allowing seed to remain out in freezing weather is that the condensation of moisture that often follows a frost can be damaging to the seed if another frost follows soon.

It's awfully easy, I find, to get batches of collected seed mixed up, particularly if you are saving more than one variety of the same vegetable. Labeling each batch as collected (put it into a marked bag, jar, or envelope) can save a lot of confusion later on.

32
Preparing the Seed

So far, so good. You have good, fully ripe seed collected dry from healthy plants. The way you prepare the seed for storage can make a difference in its viability.

Cleaning the Seeds

The simplest seeds to prepare are those that you pluck directly from the seedhead of the plant. Such seeds as lettuce, endive, dill, sunflower, and the brassicas need only to be winnowed and then dried. Winnowing—pouring the seed from one container to another in a stiff breeze or in front of a fan—blows off the lightweight chaff. Screening—passing the seed through the holes in a piece of mesh—will separate coarser, heavier trash such as small sticks, pebbles, and burrs.

Snap beans, soybeans, limas, and peas must be threshed to remove the seed from the pods. Generations of gardeners have sought easier ways to accomplish this task. Some people simply whack handfuls of the plants, a few at a time, on a hard clean surface. This is an excellent way to spend those awkward aggressive impulses, but it's not too efficient. You'll find beans in the corners for years afterward. I've threshed soybeans by spreading the dry plants on a clean sheet, covering them with another sheet, and treading back and forth over the covered vines. The beans fall out on the bottom sheet. The plants may be lifted off and the chaff winnowed out in the next breeze.

Or you can swing handfuls of the dried plant stalks so that the seedheads strike a sawhorse set on a sheet or tarp, or the inside of a barrel. This works somewhat better with grains than legumes.

But no one has yet been able to improve on the flail, a long wood handle with a short stick (called the swingle) wired securely to one end. You can use an old mop or broom handle if you have one. In the traditional peasant household in Poland, Mike recalls, the flail handle would be made from a strong hazelnut shoot which, unlike many tree saplings, does not taper much from one end to the other. The swingle is always made of hardwood.

You beat the plants with the swingle to release the seed from the brittle pods. If you remembered to spread a tarp or sheet down first, you'll find it easier to gather the dry seed. Vigorous as this method is, it injures few seeds. You wouldn't want to use anything heavier or rougher to extract the seed, though, because violent treatment *can* injure the embryo, with the result that the seed, if it sprouts at all, may be stunted. Such internal damage is not always evident on the surface of the seed.

Small lots of seed may, of course, be shelled out by hand.

Still other seeds, those of the tomato, cucumber, squash, pumpkin, and melon, must be separated from the flesh that surrounds them. Pumpkin, winter squash, and melon seeds may simply be washed to remove all traces of pulp, then thoroughly air dried.

Dealing with Seed-Borne Diseases

Tomato seeds will be protected against bacterial canker if you let the seedy pulp ferment for a few days. Just spoon the tomato pulp into a jar, cover it with water, and set it where you'll remember to check on it. In several days you'll notice that the good, heavy seeds have sunk to the bottom, while the pulp and the lightweight dud seeds have risen to the top. Good. Pour off the goopy band on top and strain out the good seeds. You might want to follow the same procedure with cucumber seeds. Many gardeners do.

Farmers in England noticed two centuries ago that seed wheat that had been immersed in seawater was free of bunt infection. Observations by Jethro Tull in 1733 led to the fairly routine use of a saltwater soak in areas where this fungus was prevalent.

Other simple ways to control seed-borne diseases include the following:

- Wash seeds in plain water.
- Steep seeds in hot water, 122°F. (50°C.) for 15 minutes.
- Steam seeds.

These measures are seldom necessary for the home gardener, whose diversified plantings are not likely to build up serious seed-disease problems. They must be carefully carried out to avoid overheating the seeds. But they are reasonably effective when they are needed.

Lightweight seeds, which are also often abnormally thin, are likely to contain an imperfect embryo or deficient endosperm. They'll never make it through the winter. Even your hens will probably ignore them. Toss them on the compost pile.

Drying

Seed should go into storage as dry as possible. Green seed, or seed that has accumulated moisture, will heat when heaped in a pile. Moisture also speeds up the seed's metabolism, causing it to use up its stored nourishment too quickly. Moisture content should be kept at 8 to 15 percent, the lower the better, down to a minimum of about two percent, below which viability is impaired. Studies done by Dr. James Harrington have shown that with each one-percent reduction in seed moisture, below 14 percent but not under five percent, the life expectancy of most vegetable seeds doubles.

You won't be able to determine the exact moisture content of seed you're storing, of course. The important thing to remember is to give all seeds a thorough postharvest drying period of at least a week, no matter how dry they already look. Seeds of most vegetables may simply be spread on newspapers in a dry, well-ventilated place. Change the papers once or twice if the seeds were damp at first.

If you live in a damp climate and want to be sure that your seeds are drying rather than absorbing moisture from the air, you can subject them to very gentle heat, like that of a light bulb or pilot light. Keep it around 90°F. (32°C.). Temperatures over 110°F. (43°C.) will damage the seed. If seeds dry *too* rapidly, they are likely to shrink, crack, and develop a hard seed coat. Rate of drying is more rapid at first when moisture content is high, and slower later.

33

Storing Seeds

The *genetic* vigor of your saved seed has already been determined by its parentage. Environmental conditions affecting the parent plant during seed formation—temperature, available moisture, weed competition, nutrient supply, etc.—help to determine the *physiological* vigor of the seed. Once harvested, the seed can't be improved upon,* but its vigor can be drastically reduced by poor storage conditions. In fact, Barton and Crocker, in their excellent book *The Physiology of Seeds,* go so far as to say that storage conditions are more influential than the age of the seed in determining viability—the ability of the seed to germinate.

Keep in mind that the seed is a living being, with its life processes barely humming. Even in its dormant state, it reacts with its environment. The seed absorbs moisture from the air and carries on the exchange of oxygen and carbon dioxide that is characteristic of life, combining the nutrients in its stored food with the moisture it takes in to make a soluble form of plant food. Oxygen in air taken in from the atmosphere then reacts with this soluble food, with the resulting release of carbon dioxide, water, and heat.

Your aim when storing the seed, then, should be to keep its metabolism operating at the lowest possible level, to keep the seed on "hold," neither jarring it into premature internal activity which would use up its stored food supply, nor slowing it so drastically that its embryo deteriorates.

To do this, you'll need to keep out as much as possible some damaging influences.

Heat

It turns seeds on. Seeds stored at home at temperatures between 32° and 41°F. (0° to 5°C.), not freezing but cold enough to retard enzyme activity, usually keep well. Under laboratory

---

* Except for maturity induced by afterripening of certain seeds in storage. The following food seeds afterripen in *dry* storage:

barley • cucumbers • lettuce • melons • mustard • oats • pumpkin • rice
• turnips • watermelon • wheat

conditions, seed expert Dr. James Harrington has found that for every 9°F. the storage temperature can be lowered, between 32° and 112°F. (0° and 44.5°C.), the seed's period of viability will double. Seeds have even been successfully stored at 0°F. (−18°C.).* If you do want to try keeping some seeds in your freezer, be sure that they are good and dry. High moisture in frozen seeds will spoil them. Immature seeds don't freeze well.

Moisture

Moisture revs up seed metabolism. In some cases, it can be even more damaging than heat. Studies at Cornell University, for example, have shown that increasing the moisture content of lettuce seeds by 5 to 10 percent resulted in more rapid loss of viability than an increase in temperature from 68° to 104°F. (20° to 40°C.). Tests on clover seed yielded similar results.

It is important not only to have the seed well dried when putting it away, but also to *keep* it dry. Seed that has gotten damp and then been redried suffers irreparable damage.

Important as it is to seal out moisture, it is worse to seal it in; if seed is not thoroughly dry, it will keep better in open storage than when sealed.

Although as a home gardener you can neither measure nor control seed moisture exactly, you might find the following recommended levels useful as a guide. Seeds vary in the permeability of their seed coats, and thus in their ability to take in moisture and oxygen, even under equal temperature and humidity. Legumes, for example, have a relatively impermeable seed coat. Peas and beans will last well in storage with a moisture content as high as 13 percent (but no higher), as will corn and most other cereal grains. Soybeans have an upper limit of 12.5 percent moisture, flaxseed 10.5 percent, and peanuts and most other vegetables even less—9 to 10 percent. Seeds to be stored for long periods of time will fare best

---

* Here's a handy formula for converting Fahrenheit to Celsius (formerly called Centigrade): subtract 32, multiply the answer by 5, and divide the product by 9. Example: 212°F. − 32 = 180. 180 × 5 = 900. 900 ÷ 9 = 100°C.

To change a Celsius reading to Fahrenheit, multiply the Celsius figure by 9, divide the product by 5, then add 32. Example: 10°C. × 9 = 90. 90 ÷ 5 = 18. 18 + 32 = 50°F.

if moisture is kept around four to six percent, but no lower than one to two percent, or the embryo may be damaged. In most climates, you'd need to heat-dry your seeds to get the moisture content this low.

Dr. Harrington, whose storage temperature studies I have already mentioned, has also determined that each reduction in moisture (between 5 and 14 percent) doubles the storage life of the seed.

If a seed is very dry, it can withstand extremes of both heat and cold that would deteriorate a damp seed. Relatively moist seeds must be kept cool. There is, in fact, a rule of thumb that should help most home gardeners, who can't always control conditions as they might wish: the relative humidity of the atmosphere and the number of degrees (F.) of temperature prevailing in the storage area should add up to less than 100. At 60 percent humidity, then, the storage temperature should be not a bit higher than 40°F., preferably less.

Where atmospheric humidity tends to be high, seed storage life may be prolonged by packing a dessicant powder with the seed. Calcium chloride (the anhydrous form) will absorb moisture that would otherwise enter the seed. Dried powdered milk, wrapped in absorbent tissue, has been suggested by Dr. Harrington as a convenient dessicant for the home gardener. Seal a rolled-up tissue of dried milk in a jar with your seeds. Check in midwinter and replace the milk powder if necessary.

Other life forms

In the process of carrying on normal respiration, fungi and bacteria produce heat which can damage stored seed. In addition, some kinds of microorganisms give off substances which can harm the embryo or soften the seed coat, thus making the seed vulnerable to invasion by other destructive microorganisms. Fortunately, both bacteria and fungi are inhibited by cold, dry conditions. Although individual species of bacteria vary in their temperature preferences, most groups function poorly in moisture levels below 18 percent. Fungi and molds flourish in a moisture content of 13 to 16 percent, but most of them require fairly warm temperatures: 85° to 95°F. (29° to 35°C.) preferred, 70°F. (21°C.) acceptable, 50°F. (10°C.) and below inhibiting.

Seed that is clean and free of trash, pulp, and rotten seeds will give bacteria, molds, and fungi much less encouragement.

Insects may impair seed viability by producing heat or by consuming the seed, or portions of it. Most insects need a moisture level of better than eight percent in order to breed. The majority of insects that are likely to infest stored seed need at least 40° to 50°F. (4° to 10°C.) of warmth to maintain activity. Some mites can reproduce at 40°F., but they must have 12 percent moisture in order to do so.

Animal predators—rats, mice, raccoons, birds, and others—can make serious inroads on your seed supply, especially the peas, beans, soybeans, corn, and other grains that are appetizing food even before they're planted. Prevent this loss by storing seeds in tightly closed glass or metal containers, rather than in cardboard boxes or paper envelopes which are easily broken into.

Seeds stored in bulk sometimes tend to heat and should be stirred and rotated periodically to keep them in good condition. Small packages of seed, on the other hand, are more quickly affected by changes in humidity and temperature. Purchased seed in foil packets shouldn't be tightly resealed in the foil after being open to damp air for a season, if you want to save them for another year.

Stored seeds are safest in securely closed containers such as the following:

- Cans with metal lids.
- Screw-top glass jars, or individual envelopes sealed in a large glass jar.
- Screw-lid metal film containers.
- Vitamin bottles.

Less desirable are wooden boxes or bins, or metal cans with plastic lids, either of which may be gnawed by rodents if the contents are inviting. I keep my garden seeds from one season to another in individual envelopes inside a large, tight-lidded lard can, in a cold back room.

It's easy to forget, during the growing season, that seeds you're holding over for another year may deteriorate if not protected from extremes of heat and humidity during the summer months. Move them to the coolest, driest spot possible while you're busy hoeing and harvesting outside.

Last but not least, LABEL. Mark each batch of seed with the variety name and date collected, or you'll have a grab-bag garden next year!

To sum up, store your seed cool, clean, dry, covered, labeled, and insect-proof. And let the frost sparkle in the grass and the winds blow. You're ready . . . already . . . for the next planting time.

34
Viability

Most garden vegetable seed will remain viable (capable of germinating) for several years after harvest, if kept in cool, dry storage. Even the exceptions, onion and parsnip seed, which ordinarily deteriorate rapidly after ripening, will sometimes last longer than a year under ideal storage conditions.

The following table will give you some idea of what to expect of your seeds. Perhaps it will help you to plan your plantings of biennial seed crops so that you can grow enough cabbage seed, for example, in one season to last for several years. It is, of course, impossible to be absolute about the keeping qualities of seeds, for differences in ripening, drying, and storing procedures affect viability. You may find that some seeds will give satisfactory germination for even longer periods than indicated here. That's nice when it happens, but I wouldn't count on it. Even when germination is low, seed can be used if it is planted thickly, or, as in the case of lettuce or carrots, which are difficult not to overplant, old seed may be mixed with new to "dilute" it.

Testing Germination

Sometimes you can tell simply by looking at a seed that its quality has deteriorated. One lot of cabbage seeds that I had kept under less-than-ideal conditions for three years looked wrinkled and dented rather than plump and smooth. Sure enough, when I planted them in flats they germinated *very* thinly. Peas, corn, and a good many other seeds are either normally wrinkled and flaky or tiny and hard; they may *look* as good as new when past their prime, but any seed that is ordinarily smooth and round or plump is not likely to germinate well if it has become pocked or wrinkled.

To get a reasonably clear idea of the growth prospects for a particular lot of seed, you can run a germination test. Count out at least 20 randomly picked seeds. Fifty is better and 100 is the professional way to do it. If you want to be very scientific, mark a paper towel into a grid of squares and place a seed on each square.

Seed Viability

Approximate age at which seed of good initial viability stored under cool dry conditions still gives satisfactory stand of vigorous seedlings with a normal rate of seeding.

Seed	Years	Seed	Years
Asparagus	3	Lettuce	5
Beans	3	Martynia	1 to 2
Beets	4	Muskmelon	5
Broccoli	5	Mustard	4
Brussels sprouts	5	New Zealand spinach	5
Cabbage	5	Okra	2
Cardoon	5	Onions	1 to 2
Carrots	3	Parsley	2
Cauliflower	5	Parsnips	1 to 2
Celeriac	5	Peas	3
Celery	5	Peppers	4
Chard, Swiss	4	Pumpkin	4
Chervil	3	Radish	5
Chicory	5	Roselle	3
Chinese cabbage	5	Rutabaga	5
Ciboule	1 to 2	Salsify	2
Collards	5	Scorzonera	2
Corn	1 to 2	Sea kale	1 to 2
Corn-salad	5	Sorrel	4
Cucumbers	5	Southern pea	3
Dandelion	2	Spinach	5
Eggplant	5	Squash	5
Endive	5	Tomatoes	4
Fennel	4	Turnips	5
Kale	5	Watercress	5
Kohlrabi	5	Watermelon	5
Leeks	3		

Since the seeds tend to shift around when they're checked, though, I don't bother to mark the paper, but simply spread the seeds on several layers of premoistened paper towels or paper napkins, roll them up carefully in the paper so they stay separate, tuck the rolled paper (or papers) in a plastic bag, and keep the incubating seeds in a warm place (70° to 80°F.). Be sure to label each roll. Check the seeds in two or three days, and every day thereafter for a week or so, for evidence of germination. If a root or cotyledon protrudes through the seed coat, the seed has germinated. When some seeds have sprouted, and a one-week wait indicates that no more are about to emerge, you can calculate your rate of germination. Ten seeds out of 20? That's 50-percent germination. Forty out of 50? Eighty percent. Five out of 100? (After all that counting!) Five percent.

Prompt germination (within limits for the particular species, of course, meaning that 18 days would be prompt for parsley, late for corn) indicates vigorous seed. Allow three weeks at the outside for most seed varieties to germinate.

Seed Size

Is large seed better than small seed? The answer depends on which scientist or seedsman you ask. There doesn't seem to be conclusive proof that large seeds produce better plants than medium-sized ones. Runts and lightweights, though, are undesirable.

In tests reported by the USDA in *Seeds, the Yearbook of Agriculture* (1961), small seeds, planted in separate plots but at equal distances, performed as well as plantings of large seed made at the same population density. In mixed plantings of small and large seeds, though, the plants that grew from large seed tended to shade out those that grew from small seeds.

Commercial growers often plant sized seed, both for ease of mechanical planting and for a uniform plant population. While these considerations are less important to home gardeners, you might find it worthwhile, if you like to experiment, to separate certain seeds such as corn or soybeans, for example, according to size and see what kind of results you get.

Other studies, mentioned by Barton and Crocker in *The Physiology of Seeds,* indicate that mutations, caused by the deterioration of embryo cell nuclei, have been found to occur in old seeds. While it doesn't seem likely that the incidence of mutations would be very high, you might remember this if you discover an off-type plant in a stand of vegetables grown from aged seed.

After you've been at this for a few years, selecting and saving your own garden seed, you might like to try what seedsman Rob

Johnston calls "quality control." Plant a packet of purchased seed of the same variety preferably side-by-side with your home-saved seed, and evaluate the differences—if any—between the two stands of plants.

35
Seed-Saving Tips for Specific Plants

Artichokes, Globe (perennial) Commonly considered a fussy exotic vegetable, this delicacy has been successfully grown in several New England states, although it is doubtful whether seed would ripen there. Adventurous gardeners in warmer climates might like to experiment with saving seed from these cross-pollinated blossoms (the "choke" *is* the blossom bud). Victor Tiedjens, author of *The Vegetable Encyclopedia,* writes enthusiastically about the possibilities for selection and experimentation with this vegetable. Apparently seed-sown plants exhibit a wide variety of characteristics.

Asparagus (perennial) It's easy to save asparagus seed—in fact, the plants volunteer rather readily from seed. Seed saved from wild plants, which are usually bird-planted escapees from kitchen gardens, generally produce plants that look and taste just like their cultivated ancestors.

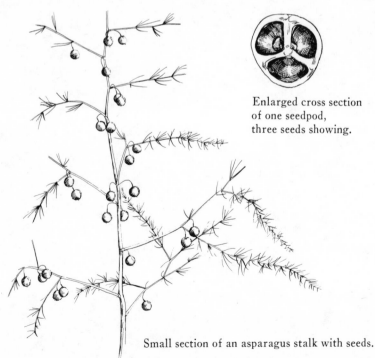

Enlarged cross section
of one seedpod,
three seeds showing.

Small section of an asparagus stalk with seeds.

Asparagus flowers cross-pollinate. The seedy red berries are borne only on the female plants, which tend to have thicker, but less numerous stalks. The thinner, more plentiful male shoots produce the pollen-contributing blossoms.

To save seed, cut the ferny plant top when berries are red and it starts to bend, and hang it in a well-ventilated place to dry. Soak the berries in water to soften the skin, then wash them and rinse off the pulp. Air-dry the seeds for a week before packaging them for storage.

Although soil and moisture conditions often account for differences in yield, you might want to try selecting seed from especially productive plants. If possible, choose seed that is formed early in the season.

Lima bean flowers and beans starting.

Beans, Lima (annual) Although limas are self-fertile, having both pollen-shedding and pollen-receptive organs in the same flower, they will cross-pollinate when visited by bumblebees. To save seed, treat like snap beans. After removing seeds from pods, air-dry indoors for a week or two, but store before mice or insects find them.

Beans, Snap (annual) Beans self-pollinate almost entirely; in fact, pollination usually takes place even before the blossom opens. Occasionally, though, two different closely planted varieties will cross to some extent. If it's important to you to keep the strain unmixed,

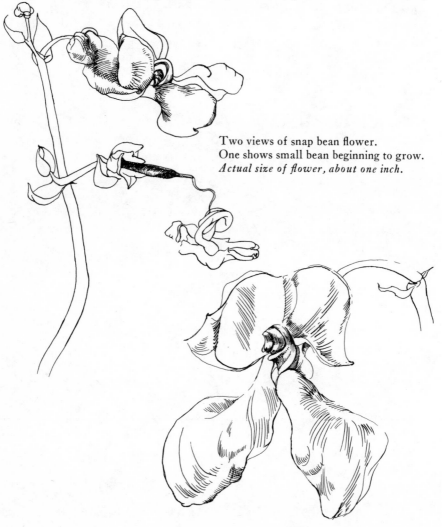

Two views of snap bean flower.
One shows small bean beginning to grow.
Actual size of flower, about one inch.

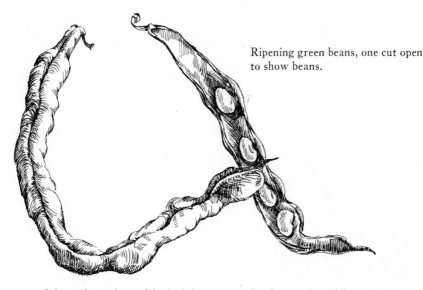

Ripening green beans, one cut open to show beans.

as with an irreplaceable heirloom strain, keep the different varieties 100 feet apart. A good supply of zinc in the soil is needed for healthy seed formation. Suspect zinc deficiency if the seeds mature slowly or irregularly. Leave the pods on the plants until they're dry and brown and the plants are nearly leafless. Seed is usually mature six weeks or so after the beans were tender and good for eating. The Vermont Bean Seed Company recommends biting a sample dry bean to determine whether the crop is dry enough to harvest. You should scarcely be able to make a dent in a bean that has dried properly. Pull the whole plants and stack them loosely in a dry place to cure further. Shell small lots by hand. Thresh out larger lots by beating or flailing.

Beets (biennial) Beets cross freely with Swiss chard and sugar beets. Their fine, air-borne pollen can travel for great distances; plantings less than one mile apart that blossom concurrently are likely to cross. Bees sometimes transfer the pollen too, if the plantings are lined up with their flight path. During the first season of vegetative growth, of course, it's not necessary to isolate different varieties. And you can grow second-season seed beets next to Swiss chard as long as you don't let the chard go to seed.

Select eating-size roots that aren't too large, and treat them gently to prevent rot-prone bruises. You needn't store a whole row of beets—six or eight roots should yield enough seed. Cut off the

Enlarged seed cluster
(still green).
Actual size, ⅛ to ¼ inch.

Ripening beet seed stalk (one of many on a beet).

tops, leaving a one-inch stub. Chilling (33° to 45°F. [1° to 7°C.])
is necessary for seed-stalk formation, but long periods of below-
freezing weather will spoil the beets. Most gardeners who save
beet seed harvest the beets before black frost, store the roots in
sand in a root cellar during the winter, and replant them in spring.
Where winters are mild, seed beets may be fall-sown to winter-over
in the garden, and thinned to 18 inches apart for spring seed-stalk
formation. As soon as the seed at the base of the stalk has ripened,
you can pull the plants.

Broccoli (annual) If you get an early start with your broccoli by
raising seedlings indoors, you'll be able to harvest seed the first
season. Choose an early-bearing plant of good type, and let the
tight green flower bud clusters—the part you ordinarily eat—de-

Portion of broccoli seed stalk
showing maturing pods.

Small broccoli head flowering, *and enlarged flower*.

velop into yellow blossoms. Since broccoli flowers aren't usually self-fertile, you'll need at least two closely spaced plants for pollination, but these two plants should yield plenty of seed for you and your neighbors. The flowers are cross-pollinated by insects.

Cut the whole plant when the pods are dry, and let it continue to dry in a well-ventilated place. Pods from just a few plants may be put in a paper bag, crushed, and winnowed to remove chaff.

Brussels Sprouts (biennial) Practice first on a few of the easier vegetables, but don't be afraid to try saving seed from this hardy member of the cabbage family. The plants often survive cold—though not severe—winters and go on to produce seed stalks, which you should treat like those of cabbage. Storing the plants in a cold root cellar over winter for spring replanting would be a bit chancier, but by no means impossible.

Cabbage (biennial) Cabbage, like its cousins broccoli, Brussels sprouts, kale, kohlrabi, and cauliflower, is cross-pollinated by insects and will cross readily with these other members of the species *Brassica oleracea*. For home-garden purposes, keep flowering stands of the seed crops 200 feet apart, or plant a row of tall-growing plants between varieties to throw the bees off course. Commercial plantings must be much more widely separated.

Select firm, ready-to-eat heads in the fall. Pull them root and all, trim off the largest outer leaves, and store the heads either in the root cellar or in dirt trenches well covered with soil. Keep cellar-stored roots damp and cold.

Replant the heads two to three feet apart in early spring. They'll send out a long seed stalk, which springs directly from the cabbage core. Many growers slash the top of each head one inch deep so that the seed stalk can make its way more easily to light and air. Pick the thin, dry pods when they're brown, or harvest the whole plant when pods are yellow and let it dry further if you're saving a lot of seed. Cabbage seed ripens gradually and tends to fall off promptly when it's ripe.

Cantaloupe (annual) They won't cross with cucumbers or pumpkins, no matter what you may hear over the back fence. Different varieties of melons *will* cross, though. The results might be odd, but they should be edible and good. To be pretty sure of maintaining

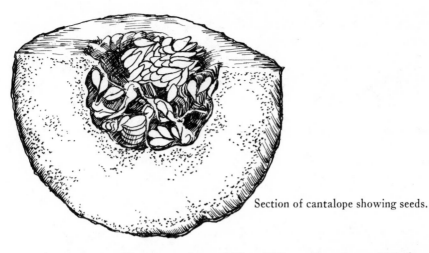

Section of cantalope showing seeds.

a pure strain, you'll want to keep hills of blooming plants 200 feet apart. Commercial growers maintain a distance of one-fourth mile to insure purity. Male and female parts are on separate blossoms, which are pollinated by insects, usually bees.

You needn't sacrifice good eating to save melon seed; the seed is ripe when the melon is ready to eat. Just spoon out the seed, rinse off the pulp as thoroughly as possible, and air-dry for a week. Rob Johnston of Johnny's Selected Seeds recommends letting the seed pulp mixture ferment at room temperature for several days. After fermentation the pulp rinses off more readily, and most of the good seeds sink to the bottom.

Carrots (biennial) Cross-pollination by insects makes it necessary to keep blossoming stands of seed carrots at least 200 feet apart. Even then, you'll get a small amount of crossing. For strict purity, keep plantings 1,000 feet apart. Carrots have a close wild relative —Queen Anne's lace—with which they will cross freely. If you have a lot of this common weed around your garden, you'll need to keep it mowed when your seed carrots are going into bloom.

Small-cored carrots make good eating, but the large-cored kinds store better. You might want to try selecting a good-keeping strain of small-cored carrots, though. Dig the roots before black frost, store them in sand or sawdust in a root cellar (or leave them in the ground if winters aren't severe and mice tunnelling under mulch aren't a problem). Replant in spring, spacing roots one to two feet apart in the row.

Carrot flower and buds.

Pick the seedheads when the second set of heads has ripened. If you wait for the later-ripening third or fourth umbels, the first and second sets will shatter in the meantime. Shattering usually occurs about 60 days after flowering. Small lots of plants may be bagged to catch seed that would otherwise shatter. Dry the seed inside for a week or so after harvesting.

Cauliflower (biennial) Save this one until you've practiced on a few of the easier biennial vegetables. It's tricky. The problem is that cauliflower won't live over in the ground where winters are cold, and it doesn't keep in the root cellar either. Yet, like the other biennials, it does need exposure to cool weather to induce seed-stalk formation. Rob Johnston, who has been generous in sharing his seed-raising expertise with home gardeners,* suggests planting seed in a cold frame or unheated greenhouse in early fall, no later than October. The young plants that make it through the winter are then set out two feet apart after the last spring frost. The yellow flowers that develop from the cauliflower head are cross-pollinated by insects. For crossing and isolation specifications, see cabbage.

For small quantities, pick the seedpods when they turn brown in the fall. If you go into the cauliflower seed business in a bigger way, cut the whole plants when the majority of pods have dried and cure them under cover. Don't let the seed freeze before it is thoroughly dry.

Celeriac (biennial) Slightly easier to store than celery, celeriac otherwise needs the same treatment. Store as you would beets. Varieties will cross up to 200 feet and even to a small extent beyond, as celery will.

Celery (biennial) Although considered a biennial, it *can* bolt to seed the first year if seedlings are chilled. Usually this happens when you don't plan on it. The umbels of white flowers, a clue to its kinship with carrots, fennel, and parsley, are cross-pollinated by insects. Celery will cross with celeriac.

Select fine, firm, thick-stalked plants in the fall and dig them carefully. Bruises and cuts hasten spoilage. Store the plants in soil in the root cellar and keep them moist. Even if outer ribs rot in storage, the plant may be used as seed stock if the roots are sound. Just cut off spoiled parts and plant the celery in rich, moist, but well-drained soil. You may need to stake the seed stalk. The seed shatters very readily. Either make frequent seed-collecting rounds or spread a "fall-out" cloth around the base of the plant to save the seeds that drop.

Collards (biennial) Treat this hardy, leafy cabbage relative as you would cabbage itself, although it will sometimes live over in the row if winters aren't severe. Storage may be a problem; it may do better

* In his booklet *Growing Garden Seeds,* self-published, December 1976.

in a cold frame than a root cellar. The blossoms are insect-pollinated. Isolate and harvest like cabbage.

Comfrey (perennial) Although comfrey flowers, it hardly ever sets viable seed. It's so easy to propagate by plant division or root cutting, though, that you won't even miss the seeds.

Enlarged comfrey flowers, post flowers, and buds.
Actual length of flower, ¾ inch.

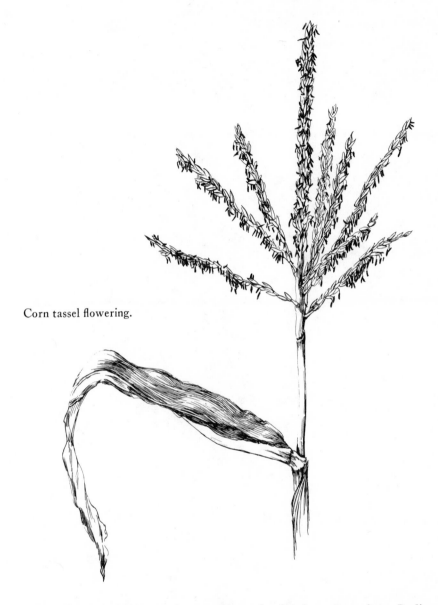

Corn tassel flowering.

Corn (annual) Through centuries of selection, American Indians developed six kinds of corn: popcorn, sweet corn, flour corn, flint corn, dent corn, and pod corn. These varieties have been refined by further selection, but the only really new developments added by European immigrants during the last 450 years of cultivation have been hybridizing and the selection of new kinds of dent corn.

281

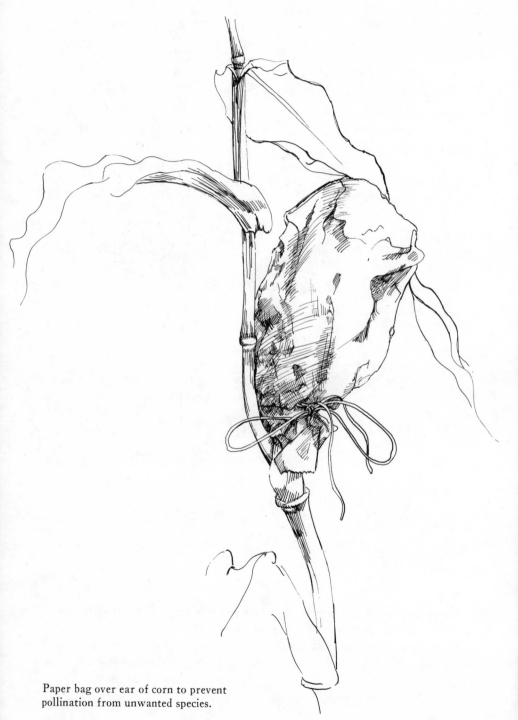

Paper bag over ear of corn to prevent
pollination from unwanted species.

Open-pollinated varieties like Country Gentleman, Golden Bantam, and White Evergreen come true as long as different kinds are separated by at least 200 feet at tasseling time. Early and late varieties which will not tassel at the same time may be planted closer.

Corn is wind-pollinated. The pollen, which is shed by the tassels and received by the silks, is fairly heavy, but you'll still get *some* crossing, even at this distance. For more complete control of crossing, keep plantings 1,000 feet apart. Don't bother saving seed of hybrid corn unless you have time and space to burn. It's often sterile, anyway.

Dried ear of sweet corn.

Save the fullest, most perfect ears from several of the earliest-bearing plants. To avoid inbreeding, be sure to mix seed from several different plants, even if you don't need that much seed.

Let the seed corn ripen on the plant. It should be ready to harvest about a month after the corn was right for eating. Well-dried seed corn won't be hurt by frost. Continue drying after harvest by peeling back the husks and hanging the ears in a well-ventilated place. Incompletely cured corn may heat in storage and won't germinate well.

Cucumbers (annual) Your picklers may cross with your slicers, but be assured your cukes will have nothing to do with your zucchinis! The separate male and female blossoms transfer pollen through insect activity. As with many other insect-pollinated plants, you can expect a certain minimal amount of crossing with 200-feet separation, but half-a-mile is necessary for absolute seed purity.

Leave the fruit on the vine until it turns yellow and grows fat. Frost won't hurt it, but pick it before it rots. Cut the cuke in half

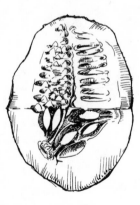

Two views of seed formation in a mature cucumber.

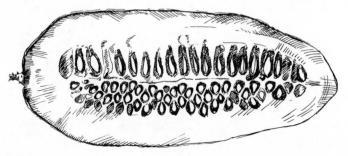

the long way, scrape out the seed pulp, rinse until the seeds are as clean as possible, then dry. Or, to ferment off the pulp and cull worthless seeds, let the pulp stand in a glass for several days or up to a week. The thick pulp will subside to an easier-to-rinse thin liquid and the heavy, good seeds will sink. Strain them off, wash and air-dry them.

Umbel of dill seeds and one enlarged seed.

Dill (annual) Technically an herb, but practically indispensable to many cucumber growers. I couldn't pickle cucumbers without it. One of the easiest kinds of seed to save. Just let the seeds dry on the plant and cut the heads off. (If you pull them you'll lose a lot of seed!) I keep my harvest of dill heads in an open paper bag in a warm room for several weeks before rubbing off the seed and storing it.

Eggplant (annual) When saving eggplant seed, remember that some of the newer varieties like Jersey King or Early Beauty are

Two views of an eggplant flower,
and an eggplant beginning to grow.

hybrid. For best results, stick to the open-pollinated kinds like Black
Beauty, Early Black Egg, or Early Long Purple. Although the
flowers self-pollinate, they may also be cross-pollinated by insects,
up to one-fourth mile or so.

The eggplant that has escaped your attention and gone beyond
the firm, glossy stage to turn somewhat dull and perhaps a bit
wrinkled on the bush is a good candidate for seed harvest. An
eating-ripe fruit that has spent several days on the kitchen counter
will yield viable seed too. Scrape out the seedy pulp, rinse the seeds

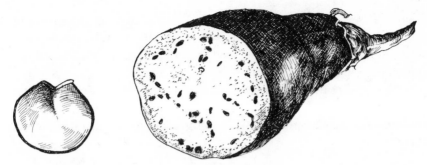

Eggplant with end cut away, showing seed formation.
One enlarged seed.

clean, and float off any lightweight seeds. Some gardeners ferment the pulp before extracting seeds, but according to several seed-raising specialists, this isn't necessary. I don't know about you, but I'm only too glad to follow the simplest procedure possible, especially when it has the blessing of the experts.

Endive and Escarole (biennial) These may perform like annuals if planted early and midsummer heat causes bolting; otherwise they are biennials. Plants to be carried over winter can be protected by a cold frame or heavy mulching and snow. Don't cover with mulch when the crown of the plant is wet. The cornflower blue blossom is self-pollinated. Harvest and store seed as for lettuce.

Fennel (annual) Florence fennel, which produces a delicious semi-crisp bulbed stalk, forms umbels of seed that follow the tiny cross-pollinated flowers. Warm weather hastens seed production. Select seed from slow-bolting, large-bulbed plants. The seedhead formation resembles that of dill and shatters as readily. The seeds are good to eat, but save a handful for planting next year's crop!

Grains (annual) Such small grains as barley, wheat, oats, and rye may be grown in small plots and hand-threshed to provide bread and cereal for the family. The old practice, which still makes sense, was to set aside a portion of the best grains for the next season's seed right before harvest, before any of the grain was eaten.

Grains don't shatter as readily as lettuce, onion, or cabbage seed, but you do want to harvest the seedheads before rain beats them down. A cold rain may make the grains sprout while still in the head. Warmth usually induces dormancy. Grains should be well dried before they are picked, with a moisture content of no more than 20 percent. Of course, you won't be able to tell exactly how much moisture remains in the seed, but if you go by the following guidelines you should get good seed.

Barley—ready to harvest for seed when the inside of a grain you've bitten open has a chalky appearance and the grain snaps readily. Too much springiness or doughiness in the grain indicates unripe seed.

Barley.
Enlarged kernel.
Actual size, about ¼ inch.

Wheat—Bend and shake the head. If the seed is ripe, 75 percent of the grains should fall off after shaking.

Rye—Pinch or bite seed to determine whether it is still doughy. Rye pollen is very fine and travels for one mile or more on the wind.

Oats—Wait till a week after grains have assumed a dry appearance.

Dried wheat stalks.
One kernel of wheat with husk removed.
Actual length of kernel, ¼ inch.

Seedheads of winter rye.

Emerging oat seedhead.

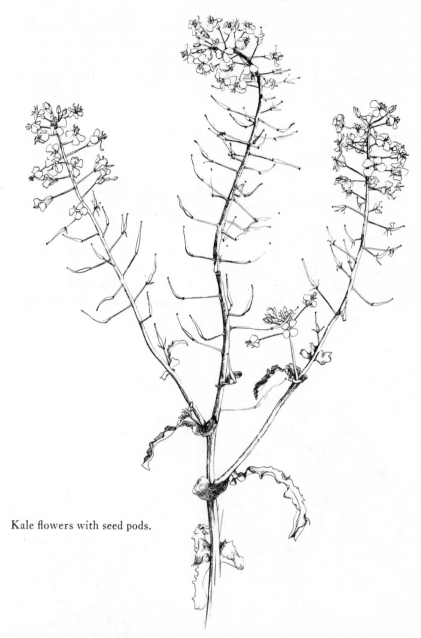

Kale flowers with seed pods.

Kale (biennial) Kale was first imported from Scotland, along with rhubarb seed, by Benjamin Franklin. It is insect-pollinated, like the other brassicas mentioned here, with which it will cross over distances up to 1,000 feet or so. And, like broccoli, the flowers are

291

often self-sterile, so you'll need at least two neighboring plants for adequate pollination. Since kale winters over, with some protection from mulch and/or snow, even in cold northern climates, you have a good chance to select your seed stock for hardiness. If the plants have long stems, they'll probably need staking in the spring to support the seed stalk.

Mature kale seed pod.
Actual size, four inches.

Lettuce (annual) Begin your seed-saving efforts with this easy annual. Lettuce flowers self-pollinate, so you can pretty much count on its coming true, although wild lettuce growing quite close to the garden will sometimes contribute pollen. Save seed from the plant

Flowers and buds of Buttercrunch lettuce.
Actual diameter of flower, ¾ inch.

Buttercrunch lettuce bolting.

that is slowest to bolt to seed. Leaf lettuce is the easiest to handle. Head lettuce matures somewhat later and must often be cross-cut (slash a one-inch deep X) to encourage the seed stalk to emerge from the head. When the yellow flowers have changed into downy white seedheads, pull or shake off loose seed, winnow it, and dry it indoors for a week. For larger quantities, cut the whole plant when enough seedheads have formed, and cure it in an airy place, then thresh out the seeds by shaking and rapping them on a hard surface. A single vigorous plant may bear as many as 30,000 seeds.

Buttercrunch lettuce flower having gone to seed,
and one seed with its parachute.
Height of flower, ½ inch; length of seed, ⅛ inch.

Okra (annual) Usually self-pollinated, okra is only too anxious to go to seed in a warm summer. Select pods from plants that bear early and heavily. Let the pods ripen completely on the plant unless frost threatens. Shell small lots by hand and dry the seed for a week before packaging for storage.

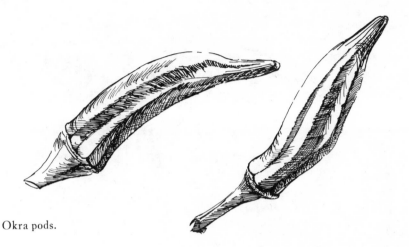

Okra pods.

Onions (biennial) You don't want to propagate an onion that will bolt to seed early the first year. Insects pollinate the balls (umbels) of small white flowers. Different kinds should be planted at least 100 feet apart. Store good, sound, fall-harvested bulbs in a cold, dry place over winter. Replant in spring, close together, or leave bulbs in the ground where winters are not severe, although then you won't be able to select for storage life. The flower-bearing stalk

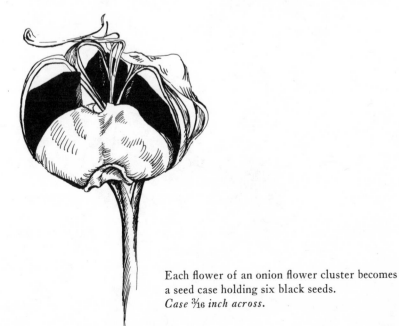

Each flower of an onion flower cluster becomes a seed case holding six black seeds.
Case 3/16 inch across.

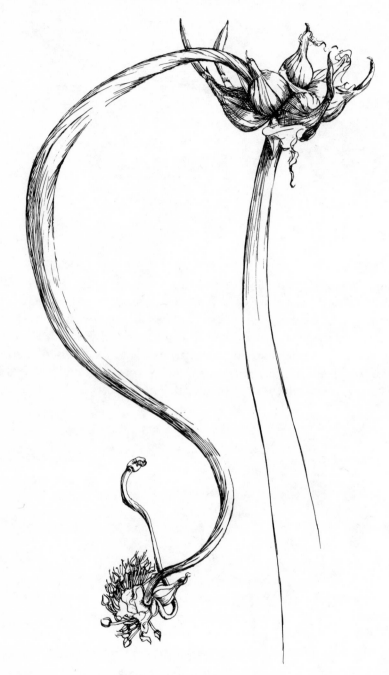

Head of Egyptian onion forming sets and flowering.

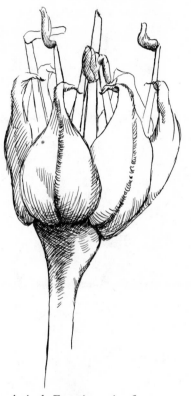

Flower head of Egyptian onion.

A single Egyptian onion flower.
Actual size, ¼ inch across.

breaks easily, so keep rows wide enough to allow for ease in weeding. If you're growing only a few seed onions, you can support the stalk with a stake. Harvest the umbels as soon as you see the black seed. They shatter readily. Cure the seedballs for several weeks, then gently rub off the seed.

In studies reported by Barton and Crocker in their book *Physiology of Seeds,* the best yields of onion seed were obtained by giving the plants ample nitrogen at first, then low nitrogen for two months, followed by a final period of high-nitrogen feeding. Onion seed is particularly vulnerable, in storage, to high temperature and moisture. When well sealed, it has been kept as long as 12 years.

Parsley (biennial) The delicate flowering umbels reveal parsley's kinship to carrots, fennel, and parsnips. Insects pollinate the blos-

297

Parsley flowering.

soms, which form in spring the year after planting. Parsley winters over fairly well, either under mulch or in a cold frame. Where snow cover is sparse or winds are fierce, you might want to pot up a young plant or two before the taproots grow deep, bring them inside in the fall, and replant in the garden in spring.

Umbel of parsnip seeds.
Single seed enlarged from approximately ¼ inch.

Parsnips (biennial) One of the easier root vegetables for home seed-saving, because it keeps well under mulch right in the garden row even in a bitter cold winter. Insects pollinate the blossoms, and cross-pollination with other parsnip varieties is likely up to 200 feet. How many home gardeners save more than one kind of parsnip seed, though? Or have neighbors who save another kind?

Overwintered roots send up leaves and then flower stalks in early spring. The seed shatters soon after it's ripe, so keep an eye on the seedheads and gather the light, dry, browned seed as it matures. That's about the end of July in my Pennsylvania garden.

Peanuts (annual) Like other legumes, peanut blossoms are self-pollinating. Spanish peanuts are easier than the larger varieties, which are more sensitive to an undersupply of calcium in the soil. The developing seed needs plenty of moisture, but harvest should take place during dry weather. Dig the vines and pile them loosely on a rack in an airy but not brightly sunlit place where they can cure gradually. Dampness in a closely stacked pile may bring on blight and mold. Strong direct light, though, often overdries the nuts to

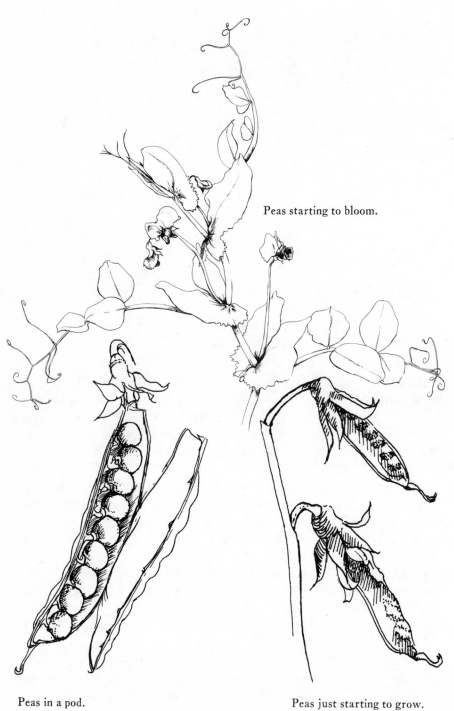

Peas starting to bloom.

Peas in a pod.

Peas just starting to grow.

the point of brittleness. "Hollow heart" of peanut seedling cotyledons is caused by a boron deficiency in the soil.

Peas (annual) Although the blossoms are usually self-pollinated, insect activity may produce a few crosses. Sugar peas shouldn't cross with regular peas, though. Pea vines tangle so that individual plants are often hard to identify. The most practical way to save pea seed is to set aside part of a row and let all the plants in that section ripen pods. You'll need about 15 feet of row to produce a pound of seed, or a shorter, wider, five-foot row. Zinc is necessary for pea formation. Peas should dry thoroughly in the pod. If in doubt, pull the vines and stack them in a well-ventilated spot to ripen for a week or two. If vines are tightly piled or damp, seed quality will suffer. Thresh or hand-crack the dry pods. Seed grown in manganese-deficient soil may have an area of dead tissue on the cotyledon and a damaged tuft of true leaves.

Peppers (annual) Self-pollinated, but since insects may sometimes transfer pollen, you might want to keep hot and sweet or small and

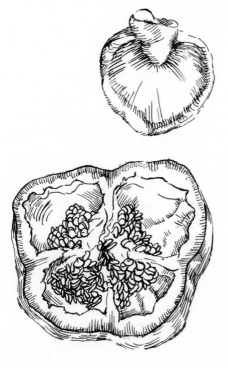

Green pepper, outside and inside
(showing seed cluster).
One seed enlarged.
Actual size about ⅛ inch across.

Green pepper flower.
Actual size, about one inch across.
Greatly enlarged here to show that ovary looks like a small pepper.

large varieties about 50 feet apart, or as far as is practical in your garden. The seed is ripe when the fruit is red. If you live where summers are too short for peppers to turn red, you can pick them before frost and let them ripen in a warm room indoors.

To save seeds, simply cut off the stem end of the pepper and tap the fruit to dislodge the seeds, or spoon them out. They seldom need washing. Dry them for about two weeks before storing. Soaking the seeds in warm water (122°F. [50°C.]) for 25 minutes helps to control seed-borne bacterial diseases, but I wouldn't do it unless I'd had a disease problem with my peppers, which I haven't. Be sure to rinse the seeds with cool water and dry them well after such a treatment.

Potatoes (annual) Seed potatoes are the tubers themselves, either large ones cut so that each piece has an eye, or preferably, small whole potatoes saved from last year's crop. Egg-size potatoes are recommended, but I usually plant a good many that are somewhat smaller. Cherry size is too small, though.

Some gardeners reserve an end row for their seed potato crop, planting there all their many-eyed seed potatoes and pieces and using seed with no more than two eyes—which will produce larger tubers—in the rows planted for eating. Others simply collect all the small potatoes that sift to the bottom as the family consumes the year's harvest, and replant the "littles" next year as seed. When harvesting a lot of potatoes strictly for seed purposes, cure them in the sun for a week or two. It doesn't matter if they turn green, as long as you don't intend to eat them. Potatoes keep best at 34° or 35°F. (2°C.).

Potato flowers.
Actual width, 1½ inches.

Then there is potato seed, which is what Luther Burbank planted in his quest for new and better potato varieties. The seed-ball, which follows the usually self-pollinated flower on some, but not all, plants, and resembles a tiny green tomato but is poisonous, may be dried and the seed planted early the following year, if you want to follow in Burbank's footsteps. Spring-planted seed, which may be started indoors in March and transplanted to the open garden in

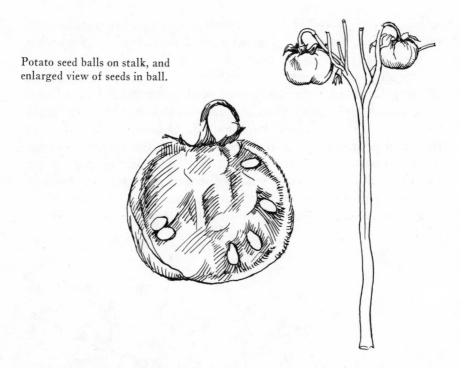

Potato seed balls on stalk, and enlarged view of seeds in ball.

June, will form egg-size tubers by fall. Dig them on a dry day, sun-cure them as suggested above, and replant them the following spring for eating potatoes. Consider this a just-for-fun project; many seedling plants, perhaps most, will be worthless. That's not to say you can't get a good one, though; you might. Perhaps you'll end up more than ever awed by the plant wizard's perseverance and powers of observation.

Pumpkins (annual) The longer-stemmed male flowers produce heavy pollen which is carried to the female flowers by insects (mostly bees) over distances of up to one-fourth mile, although a separation of 100 feet or so is satisfactory for most home-garden purposes.

Pumpkins in the species *C. Pepo,* which includes small Halloween pumpkins, will cross with the other members of the species, zucchini, acorn squash, patty pan and yellow crookneck squash, and in some studies with other species in the gourd family: *C. mixta, C. maxima,* and *C. moschata.* They will not cross with melons or cucumbers.

Male pumpkin flower, and with petals cut away.

Female pumpkin flower, and with petals cut away.

Collect seed from fully ripened fruits that have developed a good hard rind. Halve the pumpkins, fork out the seeds, wash off the pulp, and dry the seeds for a week or so indoors. You'll notice a few flat seeds. Since these lack embryos, they'll never grow. You can winnow them off or pick them out at planting time next year, if you're handling small batches of seed. British horticulturist Lawrence Hills declares that pumpkin seed improves with age. Up to a point, of course!

Radish flowers, and one flower enlarged.

Radish (annual—summer radishes; biennial—winter radishes) The summer radish is one root crop from which seed may easily be saved. Early-planted radishes produce crisp green seedpods by midsummer.

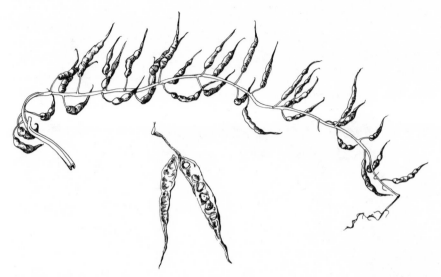

Radish seed stalk (one of many coming from one radish), and enlarged open seed pod.

When the pods turn yellow, pull the plants and stack or hang them in a dry place to cure. Small lots of the rather tough pods may be crushed in a paper bag or split by hand to release the seeds. The insect-pollinated flowers will cross up to one-fourth mile or so. Winter radishes should be treated like beets, stored and replanted the following spring.

Rhubarb (perennial) Division of roots is easy and dependable; in addition, seed stalks should be clipped off to conserve the plants' strength. If you *do* save rhubarb seed, collect from a plant that

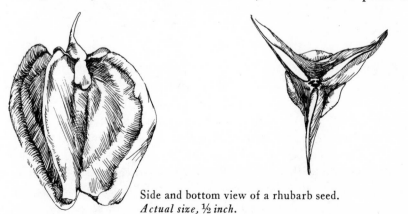

Side and bottom view of a rhubarb seed.
Actual size, ½ inch.

Rhubarb flower stalk and bud.

Rhubarb seedhead.

bolts to seed late rather than early, or you may find yourself raising
a strain that sends up a flower stalk with the first spring shoots.
Seed saved from your backyard rhubarb patch will produce rhubarb
plants, all right, but they may not be as good as the originals. If
you have the space and time to experiment, though, there's no harm
in trying. The seed is dry and flaky, resembling that of wild dock.
In a good season with plenty of rain, seed-grown rhubarb started
early will grow to picking size by summer. The plants should be
rigorously culled, however, to eliminate early bolters.

Rutabagas (biennial) Insects cross-pollinate the flowers of this large-rooted biennial, which should be replanted the second spring 200 feet from other flowering varieties for home gardening purposes—not a large stumbling block, for there aren't many different strains of rutabagas. Save firm, well-shaped roots from the fall harvest, gathering them before severe frost. Trim the leafy tops to a one-inch stub and store the roots in a cold root cellar. Replant in spring, reselecting for keeping quality. Or where winters are mild, mulch the roots and thin them in spring to stand 12 inches apart for seed production. Gather the pods when they've turned brown and dry. Watch them—they shatter readily like other brassica seed.

Salsify (biennial) This vegetable is easily stored over winter, even by the northern gardener, right in the garden row under mulch. Salsify is self-pollinated, but the problem of crossing is strictly academic, since only one variety of the vegetable is commonly available. The seed crop may be treated like that of the parsnip. The

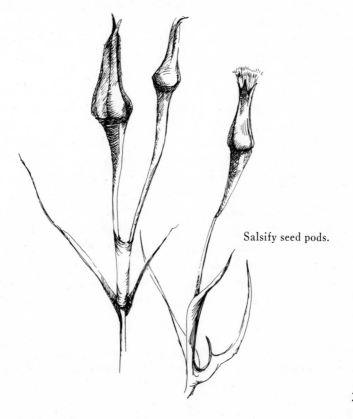

Salsify seed pods.

attractive purple spring flowers are followed by a large fluffy seed-head that looks like an overblown dandelion (similar to goatsbeard, which is a wild relative of salsify). The heads ripen successively and should be picked individually as they ripen, then dried on a rack or shelf for a week or two.

Sorrel (perennial) Save seed from the plants that go to seed late. Since flavor is better before seed-stalk formation, you don't want to develop an early-seeding strain.

Soybeans (annual) The self-pollinated flowers appear when days begin to grow shorter. Northern gardeners should choose an early-maturing variety like Altona (100 days). Although some selection is possible, in practice the soybean seed I save each year is what is left after I've picked as many green soybeans as possible during the 10 to 14 days in September when they're at their peak. When the beans start to turn yellow and toughen, I let the rest hang on the plant until they're dry and cut the whole plant when some of the dry pods begin to break open. Mice like the beans, so they should be threshed promptly and dried on a screen indoors for two to three weeks. I thresh all I need for seed and soup by treading on the vines sandwiched between two clean sheets, on a cement floor.

Spinach (annual) The inconspicuous wind-pollinated flowers occur in varied combinations on different plants. A row of spinach will usually include some plants that bear both male and female flowers; others that are only female; small, early-bolting extreme male plants; and larger, leafier vegetative males which produce the dust-like pollen that travels in the wind for as far as a mile.

Spinach may be selected for leafiness and late bolting, though, without identifying each graduation of gender. Just look for the undersized, early-seeding plants and grub them out. Most plantings of spinach tend to go to seed, spurred by warm weather and longer days, before the gardener has a chance to get his or her share, but at least selection should help to eliminate any genetic-linked early bolting. Pick the seeds in the summer after they've ripened on the plant.

Squash (annual) Since the species *C. Pepo* includes a variety of squash types—both hard-shelled winter and tender summer squash,

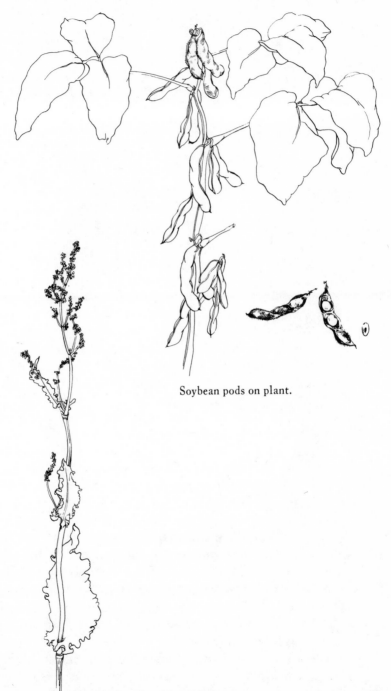

Soybean pods on plant.

Sorrel flower stalk with buds.

Female flower of Buttercup squash.

Female zucchini blossom.

as well as acorn squash, small gourds, Halloween pumpkins, and vegetable spaghetti—you can see that the possibilities for odd and interesting crosses are considerable. In my garden, Halloween pumpkin and gourd volunteers often come true, but since insects may carry the heavy pollen for at least 100 feet, different kinds of squash from which you want to be sure of fairly pure seed should be grown no less than 100 feet apart.

Squash won't cross with cucumbers or melons, but pollination of a zucchini by a gourd or an acorn squash can produce a hard-shelled summer squash that isn't too acceptable on the table. All

312

such crosses are edible, though. Some are palatable. Those that aren't make good stock feed; the animals relish the seeds.

Butternut squash (*C. moschata*) generally keeps to itself, but some crosses with *C. Pepo* or *C. maxima* (winter squash) may occur.

You can harvest seeds of hard-shelled winter squash when preparing them for a meal, but zucchini and other summer squash should be allowed to ripen and harden for about eight weeks after

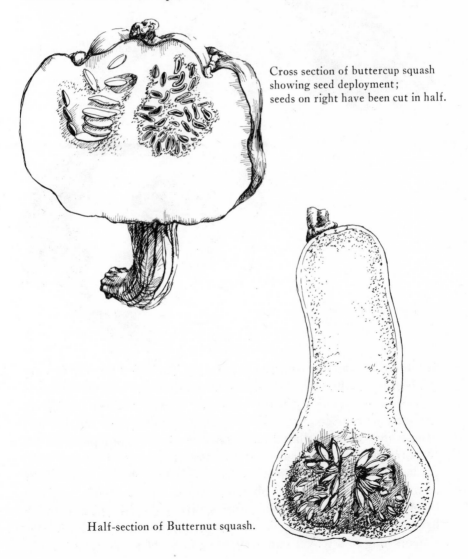

Cross section of buttercup squash showing seed deployment; seeds on right have been cut in half.

Half-section of Butternut squash.

they've reached the good-eating stage. Split the squash, rake out the seeds with your fingers or a fork, and rinse off the pulp. Eliminate lifeless seeds by floating them off in water; the good ones sink. Spread the seed on screens or newspaper pads to dry for two weeks or so.

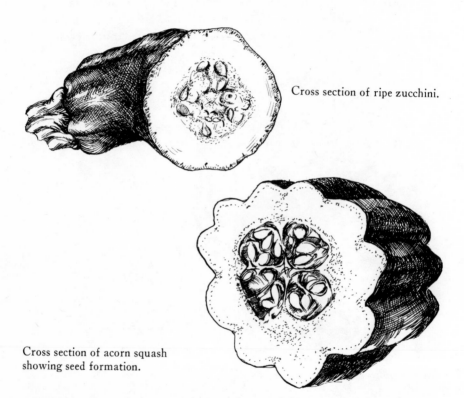

Cross section of ripe zucchini.

Cross section of acorn squash showing seed formation.

Sunflowers (annual) Watch the ripening heads and tie netting over the best ones when the seeds have formed but are still immature—otherwise the birds may beat you to the harvest! Cut the head from the stalk when seeds are dry but before they begin to fall off, and hang it in a well-ventilated but relatively mouse-proof place to dry for a few weeks. Then rub off the seeds and screen and winnow them to eliminate chaff. We sometimes select seed for next year's crop by setting aside the largest, plumpest seeds as we snack our way through them. For larger quantities, sift out small seeds through hardware cloth. Package promptly after drying; it doesn't take rodents long to discover and decimate a cache of sunflower seeds.

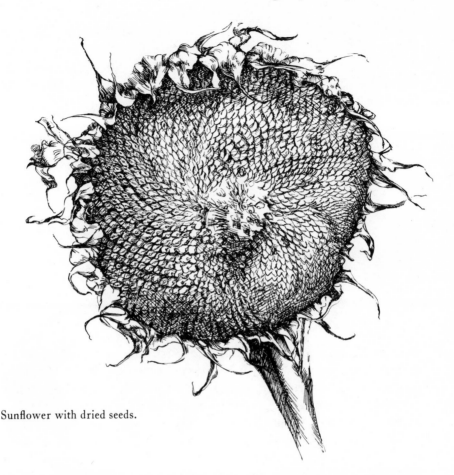

Sunflower with dried seeds.

Swiss Chard (biennial) The fine, dustlike, wind-blown pollen will carry as far as a mile, crossing varieties of chard with each other and with beets and sugar beets. Chard survives the winter in all but the most northern gardens, and even there a blanket of mulch will often pull it through. The deep, strong taproot stores energy for a second season of growth, when the plant will flower and produce summer seed.

Tomatoes (annual) Seed saved from open-pollinated (nonhybrid) varieties can be counted on to come true, since the self-pollinated flowers are only rarely visited by bees. (In their native Peru, where they are perennial, tomatoes are cross-pollinated by native insects.)

Pick the best fruits from your outstanding plant when they are

315

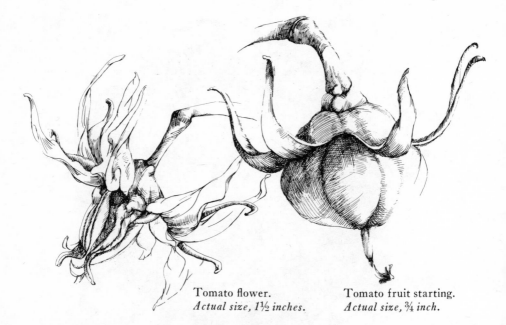

Tomato flower.
Actual size, 1½ inches.

Tomato fruit starting.
Actual size, ¾ inch.

fully ripe, perhaps a bit overripe. Squash the seeds and pulp together into a jar with one-fourth cup of water and let the mixture
ferment at room temperature. It's best not to put the jar in an
especially warm place. Fermentation develops in two days at 80°F.;
at 70°F. it takes three days. Leaving the seeds in the working
mash for the longer period permits more complete control of bacterial canker, a seed-borne disease. Stir the brew each day and pour
off the liquified pulp and the floating seeds on the second-to-fourth
day, retaining the seeds that have sunk to the bottom. Rinse the
pulp from the seeds and spread them on paper to dry for three to
seven days.

I've always liked the story (a true one, too) that Peter Tobey
related in an editorial in the magazine *House and Porch Gardens*,
about the man who grew a tomato plant from the seed in his BLT
sandwich.

Turnips (annual, sometimes biennial) Early-planted turnips will
form seed the same season. Fall-planted turnips will live over a
fairly mild winter and produce seed the following spring. The yellow flowers are cross-pollinated by bees, and they'll cross with other
blooming turnip varieties, as well as with mustard and Chinese

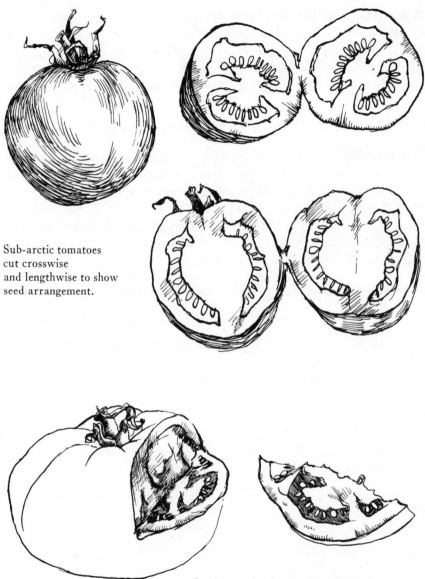

Sub-arctic tomatoes
cut crosswise
and lengthwise to show
seed arrangement.

Scotia tomato, showing seed formation.

cabbage, within 200 feet or often farther. Harvest the dry pods
individually and bag them for threshing in small amounts. Larger
seed harvests may be handled by cutting the plants when the pods
are mostly dry, and stacking them lightly in a dry place to cure
further.

Watercress (perennial) Well-established plants will form seed-heads by summer's end. Designate a clump from which you will refrain from harvesting leaves. These plants will form seed sooner. Ducks can eat a small planting of watercress down to the nub in late fall when other greenery fails, so you may need to put chicken wire around your seed-stock clump so that it can ripen seed un-molested.

Watermelon (annual) The separate male and female blossoms are cross-pollinated by bees, so plantings of different varieties may cross within 200 feet. Since the seed is mature when the fruit is ripe, you can keep the seed of especially good melons as you eat the flesh. Melons that remain in the field until they're a bit overripe can also be used as seed sources, if they are still sound. Just rinse the seeds and spread them out to dry for a week.

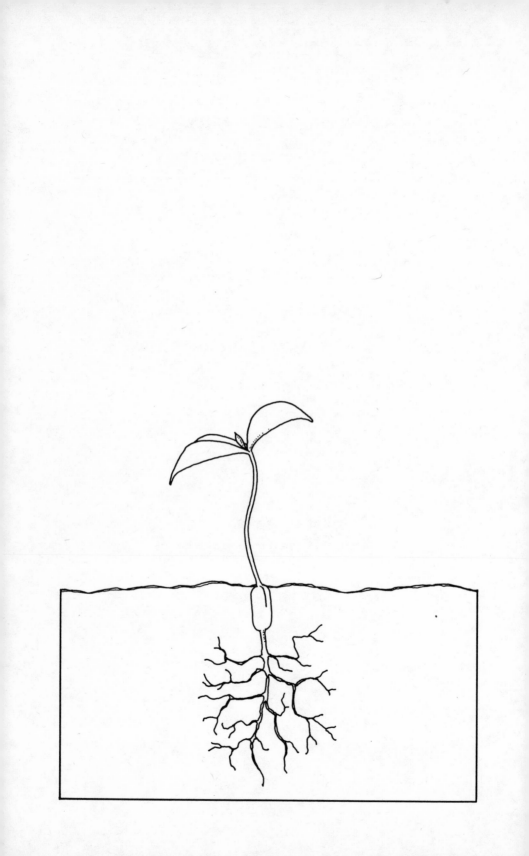

Section Five

What we call poor is someone who has no animals and no garden.

Patrick Kagoda of Uganda, in an interview with
Kathy Duncan of the *York Daily Record*

36
The Garden Diary

I keep a running record of our gardening activities and results, partly, I guess, because I'm a compulsive note-taker, but mostly for curiosity, comparison, planning, and improvement. The record is a useful tool that helps me, each year, to avoid at least some of the mistakes of years gone by. Garden notes need not be elaborate, or even terribly well organized, as long as you can find them.

My own system smacks of the patchwork theme that has become the trademark of our homestead. The heart of the system is a calendar that has space for notations on each day of the month. This is where I record planting dates, both indoors and outdoors, dates of first harvest, peak harvest times for different vegetables, yields, weather and insect problems (excuses, excuses!), notes to remind myself to save seed of certain vegetables, the phone number of the man who shells peas by the bushel (we gardeners always were an optimistic lot!), and kinds and amounts of manure and rock minerals spread, where and when.

The calendars differ from year to year, but they follow a basic pattern. Notations during the dead of winter center around ordering seeds and planting seed flats. Spring notes proclaim, "Ate first spring onion tops today!" (April 22), "peepers back," "planted out head lettuce," "hard freeze at night." By June the page is scrawled up and running into the margins: "make smaller, more frequent leaf lettuce plantings next year," "mammoth melting sugar peas better than dwarf kinds," "first zucchini today" (June 19). Late summer and fall are crowded with pickling, canning, and freezing tallies, as well as references to prime foraging dates, mushrooms and nuts to watch for, up to and well beyond the day when "black frost . . . 25 degrees last night" proclaims the certain turning of the seasons. (Interspersed with my garden notes, of course, are records of other homestead doings with goats, bees, hens, sheep, hay, and wildlife, as well as odd tidbits that just should not go unrecorded: "toad returned to the barn today," "found bottle gentians near swamp," "bluebirds nesting," "geese going south," "nine fall ducklings hatched by Crazy Lucy.")

Comparing harvest times from year to year helps me to determine how far back I can push certain planting dates in spring, and which varieties work best with this kind of gamble. Yield notes influence the amounts and kinds of vegetables we'll grow next year. Notations of food quantities put into storage, averaged over 5 to 10 years, tell me in a general way how much is enough. Since food quality is highest during the first year in storage, I prefer to can and freeze for one year only, considering the carried-over surplus from previous years to be second-rate nutritionally.

If we have an extra load of manure and decide to divide it between the corn patch and the grapes, I make note of that fact because I know I'll forget, by the next barn cleaning time, which piece of ground got the bonus.

Two other record sheets figure in my yearly planning guide. One is the garden diagram, that much-revised, out-of-scale sketch of the garden rows and what they grew, including intercropping tricks that worked (like the long row of beans that bore several bushels before the squash and tomatoes planted on either side of it closed in), succession plantings, and last-minute replacements of row or plant wipeouts. (*Who* ate the early beets? I'll never know. Whoever it was never made it back to gobble the chamomile and basil I put in their place, though.)

The other list I keep from year to year is the sheet of scrap paper on which I record kinds and amounts of seed under the name of the company from which I ordered it. This saves time when ordering next year. Short-top Scarlet Globe radish, for example, is one of my favorites, but only one seed company (di Giorgio) carries it. Or I may want to try a different strain of Butternut squash from a new seed house.

Experiments in plant breeding, seed saving, insect control, and the like will be of lasting value only if recorded: what did you do, when, to what, how long did it take, what were the results?

Taking notes on the garden gets to be a habit. Keeping the calendar handy, with a pencil nearby, insures that it's not a chore. And referring to the notes of other years helps me to determine, from the record of past successes, failures, omissions, and luck-outs, where to start and how to proceed this year. "More kale, more leeks, less broccoli" reads my command to myself. If I ignore it this year, I'll have to record it in red next year. And so the years cycle into one another, each one different, yet grounded in the year before. To leave them unrecorded is to miss a lot.

37
Seed Exchanges

Think of all the mountain hollows, city plots, small-town homesteads, isolated ranches, where people may be saving seed of an heirloom bean or a special meaty tomato or a slow-bolting lettuce. Simply keeping these varieties alive, and occasionally improving on them, is a good thing. Perhaps the seed is passed around the family or the neighborhood. But often the strain remains in a relatively restricted pocket, going round and round each year but not spreading.

Suppose, though, that some way was found to bring some of these people together, to let them know about each other and the seeds they save, to make it easy for a gardener in Iowa to try seed raised in a Georgia garden, to facilitate the sharing of seed that might otherwise peter out, with people who care about such things. Just imagine all the possibilities that would be generated by such a network!

Now for the really good news: The network exists! Gardeners who save their own nonhybrid (true) seed now have the opportunity to trade seed with other gardeners, through membership in a seed exchange. These people-to-people exchanges, which have started quite recently as one-man grass-roots ventures, are growing in size and scope. Their potential for good is tremendous.

How It Works

How does a seed exchange work? Let's take a look at the True Seed Exchange, designed by its originator Kent Whealy to be a "communications network for serious gardeners," devoted to spreading as many good, nonhybrid (and especially old, rare, or highly localized) vegetable varieties to as many gardens as possible. Beginning in 1975 with 29 members, the exchange listed 141 members in 40 states in 1976; current membership in True Seed Exchange numbers around 300.

Members pay $2.00 a year dues, which helps to cover printing and mailing costs. In return, they receive a mimeographed list of members' names, addresses, and the vegetable seeds offered and wanted, by each member. A member may change his or her wish/ want/have list each year to correspond with current needs.

Rules are few, but necessary to keep all dealings fair. When requesting seeds, members must enclose a $.13 (or current first-class rate) stamp. Nonmembers may order seeds from a member for $1.00. Postage on packages must be paid back to the sender by the recipient. To make possible the widest possible dissemination of seeds, only a few seeds, enough for a hill or a few feet of row, are sent to each person requesting them. Vegetable seeds are of primary importance; no all-flower listings will be accepted, and members are asked to limit flower listings to a minimum. "Please don't use the exchange as just a source of free seeds," Kent adds, "because it could easily be ruined by more taking than giving. This should be an exchange among seed savers. Let's save extra seeds from our best . . . and then share them."

In the exchange's latest catalog, listings range from high-protein corn, mung beans, Crenshaw melon, Vietnam basil, Sweet Spanish onions, and Swedish pole beans, to hop vine, broom corn, sea onion, and sugar cane seeds, with many strains of tomatoes, sweet corn, squash, lettuce, and other standbys as well. Membership forms for the True Seed Exchange are available from Kent Whealy, RFD 2, Princeton, MO 64673.

Another exchange, Abundant Life Seeds, is devoted to preserving and sharing open-pollinated, untreated seeds, especially those of the Pacific Northwest. The nonprofit Abundant Life Seed Foundation also offers workshops on seed raising and sells—at prices ranging from $.30 to $.60 a packet (1977 catalog)—seeds of vegetables, herbs, ornamentals, wild flowers, trees, and shrubs. Their address is: Abundant Life Seeds, PO Box 30018, Seattle, WA 98103. Catalog is $.50.

The following quotation from the 1977 catalog will give you some idea of what the Foundation is about:

> The Foundation needs seed-folks—people who can see the seed in the flower. There are thousands of plants, both native and naturalized, that could appear in this list but for lack of a grower or collector, and dozens of those listed are being obtained commercially at present (especially vegetables). We envision a more comprehensive listing of exclusively hand-collected and homegrown seeds.

You are encouraged to be a part of this endeavor. Here is what you can do:

—Survey the flora in your range. Look for extensive, healthy stands, know and observe the flowers, and look for the ripe seed seven weeks later. Seek also the rare plant and take care not to overharvest.

—As you prepare a garden, consider those species with which you have affinity as possible subjects for seed-raising.

—Consult with us on your prospects as a seed resource.

—Let us know if you have biennials in the ground or in your cellar that can be let seed this spring.

What the Foundation can do:

—Suggest where to concentrate your seed-energy so that our efforts are unified.

—Supply Foundation seed for increase under your care.

—Quote prices for needed items if you wish to raise bulk seed for sale or exchange.

—Share our sense of wonder in this work, and provide technical expertise. We are glad to come before any interested group to talk seeds.

Wanigan Associates, Inc., a nonprofit organization founded by John Withee of Lynnfield, Massachusetts, specializes in beans, especially old or rare varieties. Of the 5,000 known varieties of beans, Withee and his associates plant, eat, and perpetuate 300 varieties between them. (The name Wanigan is an Indian word used by the Algonquin or Abnaki tribes to designate the raft-borne cooking shanty that provided food for logging camps, in which beans were a staple on the menu.)

Wanigan publishes a catalog of their bean seeds, available from Wanigan Associates, 262 Salem Street, Lynnfield, MA 01940. Gardeners who wish to join in the effort to save old bean varieties from dying out may send $5.00 (tax deductible) to Wanigan. They will then receive their choice of two bean seed varieties, plus an additional two varieties selected by Withee for seed renewal. In return for saving and returning seed from the renewal beans, member gardeners receive, at season's end, their choice of two more varieties for next year's garden. Members also receive a bean newsletter.

The Henry Doubleday Research Association, a British-based

alliance of gardeners, is named for Quaker homesteader Henry Doubleday, who introduced comfrey to Britain in the mid-nineteenth century. The association sponsors research into "cheap, simple and effective answers to garden problems," gives away helpful leaflets, publishes gardening books, tests new vegetables, and is now compiling an index of existing and available varieties of vegetables and fruits in an effort to save good old varieties from extinction.

Dues ($8.00 a year in the United States and Canada, £5 a year in Great Britain) entitle a member to gardening advice; a quarterly newsletter, in which he or she may advertise without cost; and access to books and natural gardening supplies not commonly available elsewhere. In addition, of course, membership supports gardening experiments that are outside the scope of large university, government, and industry grants, yet hold much promise of helping backyard gardeners like you and me to raise better food and more of it.

38
Seed Banks

There is a still larger dimension to this business of selecting, saving, and exchanging seeds. Although this concern may seem remote from our neatly bounded backyard gardens, it is a matter that I believe every gardener should be aware of. The prosperity of our future food crops, the corn, soybeans, wheat, millet, barley, rice, beets, and other seed-sown foods on which our agriculture is founded, may well depend on the maintenance of primitive strains of these vegetables.

How can this be? Consider what has happened during the 10,000 years since people began domesticating plants. We have, largely through selection, produced races of food plants that germinate uniformly, yield better than their primitive counterparts, and often taste better. Only very recently, within the last 200 years, has deliberate crossing been used to improve plants. In the process, though, we have made these plants completely dependent on us for their continued survival. Few domesticated food plants could survive in the wild. Moreover, the lack of genetic diversity caused by deliberate inbreeding to produce high-yield hybrids has made some of our primary food crops vulnerable to crop failure, since disease, if it strikes, is likely to affect all the highly inbred plants which lack resistance. The Irish potato famine of the 1830s and the destruction of one-fifth of the corn crop in 1970 by the southern corn blight (which affected only T-cytoplasm corn) are both examples of the disastrous effects a blight or fungus can have on a crop with a narrow genetic base.

After the 1970 corn blight epidemic, the National Academy of Sciences studied the genetic make-up of the major food crops currently being planted. The results were scary. Dr. Garrison Wilkes, writing in the *Bulletin of the Atomic Scientists* (February 1977) reports: "For hard winter wheat, about 40 percent of the acreage was planted with just two varieties and their derivatives. In soybeans, the genetic base was limited to just six seed collections. For sorghum, like corn prior to the blight, all then current hybrids used the same cytoplasmic sterility component."

Let's go back, for a moment, to the primitive relatives of our

Japanese millet forming seedhead.

important food crops, those irreplaceable varied strains to which scientists have returned even in recent years for help in strengthening a certain quality that they wanted to breed into a crop. For example, research in developing a frost-resistant tomato, being done by Dr. Richard Robinson of the New York State Agriculture Experiment Station in Geneva, depends heavily on the use of wild tomato varieties from the Andes as sources of the desirable genetic traits. We'll be needing these reservoirs of genetic diversity for qualities we may not at present recognize as important. Where can we find them?

The food crops that have become most important to humankind were developed, over the years, in certain ancient seats of civilization. First described by the Russian geneticist N. I. Vavilov, the nine major centers are:

1. *Ethiopia* (barley, coffee, flax, okra, onions, sorghum, wheat).

2. *Mediterranean* (asparagus, beets, cabbage, carob, chicory, hops, lettuce, oats, parsnips, rhubarb, wheat).

3. *Asia Minor* (barley, cabbage, carrots, lentils, oats, peas, rye, wheat).

4. *Central Asiatic* (Afghanistan–Turkestan) (cantaloupe, carrots, chick-peas, cotton, grapes, mustard, onions, peas, spinach, turnips, wheat).

5. *Indo–Burma* (amaranth, cucumbers, eggplant, millet, oranges, lemons, black pepper, rice, sugar cane).

6. *Siam, Malaya, Java* (banana, coconut, grapefruit, sugar cane).

7. *China* (buckwheat, adzuki bean, Chinese cabbage, millet, radish, soybeans, rhubarb).

8. *Mexico–Guatemala* (amaranth, beans, corn, cashews, red pepper, squash, tomatoes).

9. *Peru–Ecuador–Bolivia* (beans, red pepper, potatoes, squash [*C. maxima*], tomatoes).

Minor centers are:

1. *Southern Chile* (potatoes, strawberries).

2. *Brazil–Paraguay* (cashews, cacao, peanuts, pineapple).

3. *United States* (sunflowers, blueberries, cranberries, Jerusalem artichokes).

Until very recently, considerable acreage in each of these areas was devoted to the native varieties of the old traditional crops.

Perhaps their yields were something less than spectacular, but there was enough variation in the individual plants grown from seed to insure that, even under poor conditions, at least *something* would grow.

Today, though, as Dr. Garrison Wilkes describes the situation:

> Mexican farmers are planting corn seed from a Mid-western seed firm, Tibetan farmers plant barley from a Scandinavian plant-breeding station, and Turkish farmers plant wheat from the Mexican wheat program. Each of these classic areas of crop-specific genetic diversity is rapidly becoming an area of seed uniformity.

It's a small world. Too small to allow the loss of native strains to continue. Wilkes writes:

> The only place genes can be stored is in living systems. And extinction of a native variety can take place in a single year if the seeds are cooked and eaten instead of saved as seed stock. Quite literally, the genetic heritage of a millenium in a particular valley can disappear in a single bowl of porridge. The extinction of these local land forms and primitive races by the introduction of improved varieties is analogous to taking stones from the foundation to repair the roof.

What are we going to do about it? "Positive steps," Wilkes maintains, "must be taken to bank and preserve this genetic wealth for the future." The banking of our plant heritage is taking two forms:

1. Collections of seed from "unimproved" native varieties are being built up and maintained by the National Seed Storage Laboratory in Fort Collins, Colorado, the N. I. Vavilov Institute in Russia, and in other regional, national, and individual collections. The International Board for Plant Genetic Resources, established in 1974, helps to coordinate plant-conserving efforts in various countries and to initiate new programs.

2. In situ conservation—the establishment by individual nations of centers for the protected growth of irreplaceable plant races—is a valuable concept on which work has begun, but much

more work needs to be done.

While all this may seem very far from the mulched paths of your own backyard plot, it seems to me a matter of the greatest practical importance to appreciate how interdependent we all really are on this small planet. You buy seed. No doubt you vote. Perhaps you contribute to organizations established to help Third-World countries improve their agriculture. And, as a gardener who has perhaps begun to save open-pollinated seed and exchange it with other gardeners near and far, you are making your own personal contribution to genetic diversity in a small but significant way.

39
Selling Your Seedlings

More than one experienced gardener has found it possible to pay for the season's gardening costs—fertilizer, rock powders, mulch, seeds, pots, a new hoe—by selling well-grown seedlings. A really thriving seedling operation might, in a few years, even pay for a greenhouse. (The trick is that you'd need the greenhouse to make it possible!)

Here are some points to consider if this good excuse for raising more plants appeals to you.

What to sell Plan your stock around the basics that many people want to buy, the tomatoes, lettuce, cabbage, and peppers that are staples in most household gardens. But grow special varieties of those vegetables—yellow tomatoes, say, and high-vitamin-A tomatoes, sweet, delicious Jersey Queen cabbage, Buttercrunch and Tom Thumb lettuce, burpless cucumbers, vegetables that often can't be found outside a seed catalog. Then, to keep things interesting, offer a few plants that are different, but easy to grow. Things like leeks, potted chives, cherry peppers, collards.

Listen to your customers, watch what they buy, take special orders, and you may find that you're able to develop a specialty and a loyal following of busy, space-short gardeners who depend on you.

Managing your growing space You'd probably need at least a three-tier, double-bank, 48-inch fluorescent light setup or a small greenhouse, good sunporch, or sun pit, to raise enough plants for yourself and your customers. A few cold frames, in which you can harden off early-grown plants, can double your seedling-producing capacity. I've been able to grow repeat orders of red cabbage and broccoli by moving them outdoors under glass quite early to make room for succeeding flats of tomatoes and eggplant.

Advertising Once you become known for quality plants of special varieties, good old word-of-mouth may bring you as much business as you can handle. If not, or if you're beginning your venture, a little publicity can help a lot. Advertising can be as simple as a sign on your mailbox or front door, a sentence in the classified section of your local paper, or a notice posted on the supermarket bulletin board. Craft fairs may offer you a chance to set up a table of your wares. A newspaper feature story on your operation would provide free publicity if you have an interesting angle or specialty that would catch the reader's eye.

Expenses You can pare expenses by using nonhybrid seed, which generally costs less, by buying seed in bulk, once your volume of business justifies such a step, or by using home-saved seed if you are *sure* it will run true to type. Mix your own potting soil in volume. Use recycled plant containers as much as possible, as long as they are fairly uniform, neat, and provide good growing conditions for the plant. Don't stint on fertilizers, but try substituting manure tea for the heavy feeders in place of the more expensive fish emulsion fertilizer. And remember that the extra electricity used to run your fluorescent light should be figured into the costs of doing business.

You'll want to keep good records of expenses and income, obviously, so that you can tell whether your seedling business costs or pays. Naturally, expenses in setting up will keep the ledger red for the first few months. It's unlikely you'll get rich at this, but often a little extra effort and space, spent at something you enjoy doing anyway, will help to pay for some household necessities.

40
Seed Catalogs

Recently I read an article by a man who maintained he'd received an excellent education by observing and asking questions in his local hardware store. I couldn't agree more; Mike and I have also learned a lot in this way. I feel the same about seed catalogs. In between the vegetable descriptions there is helpful information on planting, insect control, harvesting, even cooking.

As you look for the varieties of vegetables which will be most suitable for your garden, you'll learn too to evaluate the offerings of the different seed firms.

Disease resistance, for example, is important, especially with cucumbers and tomatoes, if you have had previous disease problems in your patch. You must know, though, what your problem was so that you can choose a variety with specific resistance. Even then, resistance doesn't guarantee immunity, and a pea that is resistant, say, to fusarium may still come down with downy mildew, or scab-resistant cucumber may succumb to anthracnose or mosaic. Generally, a resistant strain is less vulnerable to a disease than one that is termed "tolerant." Breeding for disease-resistant vegetable varieties available to home gardeners will increase considerably in the near future.

When shopping for early-producing vegetables, check out the catalog claims for flavor. Some early vegetables are fine flavored, but in others taste is sacrificed to a certain extent for quick harvest. Here again, early varieties are being improved and you'll find, more and more, that they taste as well as look good.

Should you buy pelleted seed? I did. Once. The bentonite clay often used to coat fine seeds is sometimes slow to admit water. The pelleted carrot seed I planted as an experiment last year cost more and produced less than a comparable number of regular seeds.

If your garden area is small, look for bush varieties of some of the cucurbit space-grabbers like acorn squash and even pumpkins. Flavor is not always quite up to that of the vining crops, but should still compete with anything you could buy.

If you've been bitten by the gardening bug half as badly as I have, I'm sure you'll need no urging to try something (or two or three things) new each year. While not every experiment will earn a permanent place on your garden plan, you're sure to find at least a few vegetables that you'll wonder how you ever did without. Even if it's just a new variety of tomato, one of the high crimson (extra red) ones perhaps, or the new Sweet 100 that bears so generously that it must be staked, treat yourself to something new. Even at today's prices, a packet of seed is one of the very best buys you can make.

Catalogs are different, too. Some are general, others specialize in northern-grown or open-pollinated seed, in herbs or cantaloupes or extra-large vegetables. I don't believe I've ever yet sent for a seed catalog that didn't have *some* different offering I found tempting. Adding to your catalog library might make your January fireside planning a bit more complicated, but I'll bet your June garden will be a lot tastier too.

Vegetables (and flowers) designated as All-America selections have been chosen for their high quality and ability to grow well in different parts of the country. The All-America selection trials have been set up as a nonprofit institution, managed by cooperating seed companies. Member firms have the privilege of selling seed for new selections introduced by other firms, as long as they offer seed obtained solely from the original grower—none of their own raising—for the first three years.

This eliminates a lot of the secretive hocus-pocus that formerly attended the introduction of new varieties. The effect is to protect the company offering a good new seed, to make it worth their while to share it, and to put good new strains in the hands of home gardeners sooner.

You'll often hear that you should buy seeds from a firm based in a climate similar to yours, or at least as cold in winter, in order to get plants that are acclimated to your regional conditions. That's good advice, as far as it goes, but it ignores the fact that these days most large seed companies buy seed on contract from large-scale growers. Some seedsmen, however, do raise most of their own seed, and indicate this in their catalogs. Seed that I've purchased from Maine, Vermont, New Jersey, California, Canada, England, Maryland, Iowa, North Dakota, and other states has performed well here in my Pennsylvania garden, leading me to conclude that, in this latitude at least, the geographical location of the seed source is not critical. It may be more important for cold-climate gardeners or for those in the Deep South.

One more thing. Keep those catalogs around after you've made out your order. With the exception of Stokes, whose seed packets are an education in themselves, planting information is usually more completely spelled out in the catalog than on the seed envelope, so you might want to refer to it again at planting time.

In the back of the book, in alphabetical order, is a list of companies selling mail-order seed. Unless otherwise noted, catalogs are free.

Glossary

Afterripening—Changes which take place in the seed after harvest, making it possible for the seed to sprout when conditions are right.

Allelopthy—The inhibition of one kind of plant by substances produced by a different plant growing nearby.

Annual—A plant that lives for only one year or growing season.

Anther—The pollen-containing tip of the stamen in a flower.

Auxin—A growth hormone produced by plants.

Biennial—A plant that blooms, bears seed, and usually dies the year after it is planted.

Blocking out—The practice of cutting around plants in a flat a week before transplanting them into the garden row.

Bolt—To send up a seed stalk, when vegetative growth is preferred.

Carpel—The individual female part of the flower, corresponding to the male stamens.

Cell—The smallest structural unit of an organism.

Chelate—To grab and hold (chemically) molecules of metal from the soil.

Cloche—Protective covers of glass or plastic, often a bottomless glass jug, used to protect growing plants from cold weather.

Cold frame—A plastic- or glass-covered frame used to protect plants from cold weather.

Companion planting—The practice of making purposeful adjacent plantings of plants that seem to enhance the growth of the other plants or confer some disease or insect protection.

Complete flower—One that contains both stamens and pistil.

Control—In experiments, the control is the untreated, standard plant (seed, soil sample, etc.) used to check performance of treated samples.

Cotyledon—The seed leaves or first leaves that emerge from a germinated seed, different in form from the later true leaves.

Crop rotation—The practice of planting a succession of different plants on a certain piece of ground to promote soil nutrient balance and prevent disease and insect buildup.

Cross-pollination—The transfer of pollen from the anthers of one kind of flowering plant to the stigma of a different variety of that plant.

Cutworm—Soil-dwelling beetle larva that encircles and nips off seedlings at soil surface.

Cytokinin—A growth-promoting plant hormone found in kelp.

Dessicant—A drying agent; a substance that absorbs moisture.

Dormant—Alive but inactive and, in some cases, incapable of growth until certain conditions (light, temperature, time, etc.) have been fulfilled.

Electrode—One of the two terminals of an electric source.

Embryo—The rudimentary plant contained in a seed.

Endosperm—The stored plant nourishment surrounding the embryo in a seed.

Enzyme—An organic substance produced by a plant (or animal) which causes chemical changes in other substances.

Exoskeleton—The external supporting structure of an insect.

Exudate—A substance which is produced and given off by a plant, as in root exudate.

Fertilization—The union of the male cell in the pollen with the ovule, or female cell.

Flea beetle—Tiny, very active black beetles, about one-sixteenth inch long, which eat small holes in the leaves of plants.

Fluorescent lamp—A glass tube coated on the inside with phosphorescent powder which glows when exposed to a stream of electrons from the electrode.

Fruit—Botanically, a ripened, seed-containing ovary.

Gibberellin—A growth hormone produced by plants.

Hardening off—The process of exposing young plants gradually to the stresses of outdoor life.

Heterosis—Hybrid vigor, exceptional vitality sometimes seen in a first-generation cross.

Hormone—A substance made by plant tissue which has the effect of stimulating certain plant functions.

Hotbed—A glass- or plastic-enclosed frame which is heated by buried manure or electric soil cable, used for raising early plants.

Hybrid—A plant grown from seed obtained by cross-fertilizing two different plant varieties.

Imbibition—The absorption of water by a seed.

Incandescent—A bulb which produces light (and some heat) when the filament it contains receives an electric charge.

Kelp—A sea plant.

Loam—A well-balanced soil consisting of approximately 40 percent sand, 40 percent silt, and 20 percent clay.

Metabolism—The chemical and physical processes necessary to maintain a living organism.

Mutation—A change in the gene pattern (and therefore characteristics) of a plant, which can be inherited by succeeding generations.

Open-pollinated—Referring to nonhybrid plants or seeds.

Ovary—The hollow chamber at the base of the pistil, containing one or more ovules.

Ovule—The female cell, or egg.

Pathogen—A disease-producing microorganism.

Perennial—A plant that bears flowers and fruit every year, surviving the winter. Some perennials live for 30 years or more; others die out after 5 to 15 years.

Perlite—Volcanic rock which has been "popped" (heat expanded).

Photoperiodism—The influence of the length of the daily period of darkness on the blooming habit of plants. Some plants need short nights in order to bloom, others need long nights, others (including most vegetables) are neutral.

Photosynthesis—The formation, by the living plant, of carbohydrates from water and carbon dioxide through the action of sunlight on the chlorophyll in the leaves.

Phototropism—The tendency of plants to grow toward a light source.

Phytochrome—The coloring matter in plants.

Pistil—The female part of a flower, consisting of an ovary containing at least one ovule, topped by a style and stigma. A carpel is a simple pistil. Compound pistils contain multiple carpels.

Pollen—Minute grains formed by the flower, which fertilize the ovule to produce the seeds of a new plant generation. Corresponds to the male element in plants.

Pollination—The transfer of pollen from anther to stigma. Precedes fertilization.

Respiration—The energy-releasing process carried on by all living cells, in which oxygen is taken in and combined with carbohydrates to form carbon dioxide and water. The chemical reaction is the opposite of what happens in photosynthesis.

Scarifying—The practice of scratching or notching the seed coat to hasten germination.

Seed—A fertilized, ripened plant ovule. A living embryonic plant.

Self-fertile—Able to produce fruit after accepting its own pollen.

Self-incompatible—Uneven maturation of pollen and ovule, sometimes necessitating cross-pollination if the plant is to bear fruit.

Self-unfertile—Unable to set fruit from the plant's own pollen.

Shatter—In seed saving, the prompt dispersal of seeds as soon as they are ripe.

Stamen—The male part of the flower, bearing on its tip the pollen-containing anther.

Sterile—Failing to bear fruit or viable seed.

Sterilize—To kill all living microorganisms (bacteria, fungi, etc.) as by heat.

Stigma—The pollen-receptive tip of a flower pistil.

Stratification—Chilling seeds to promote germination. Generally the seed should have absorbed some water before chilling.

Style—The slender part of the pistil, rising from the ovary and terminating in the stigma.

Succession planting—Sowing a second crop to closely follow the harvest of the first crop.

Synthesize—To combine separate elements into a new form.

Trace elements—Elements which are necessary for growth, but in very small amounts. Boron, manganese, copper, and zinc are trace elements.

Transpiration—The evaporation of internal water from plant leaves.

Ultraviolet—Light rays with short wavelength found just beyond the violet band on the visible spectrum.

Vermiculite—A form of heat-expanded mica used in soil mixes.

Vernalization—Chilling young plants in order to induce early flowering.

Viable—Capable of germinating.

Watt—A unit of electric power, measuring a current of one ampere under one volt of pressure.

Zygote—The single cell formed by the union of the male and female plant cells.

Bibliography

Barton, Lela. *Seed Preservation and Longevity.* New York: Interscience Publishers, 1961.

Cherry, Elaine C. *Fluorescent Light Gardening.* Princeton, NJ: D. Van Nostrand, 1965.

Crocker, William, and Barton, Lela. *The Physiology of Seeds.* Waltham, MA: Chronica Botanica, 1957.

Edmond, J. B.; Senn, T. L.; and Andrews, F. S. *Fundamentals of Horticulture,* pp. 3–167 and 361–429. New York: McGraw-Hill, 1964.

Hartmann, Hudson T., and Kester, Dale E. *Plant Propagation.* pp. 53–180 and 626–648. Englewood Cliffs, NJ: Prentice-Hall, 1975.

Hills, Lawrence D. *Comfrey Report.* Essex, England: Henry Doubleday Research Assoc., 1974.

————. *Save Your Own Seed.* Essex, England: Henry Doubleday Research Assoc., n.d.

Johnston, Rob. *Growing Garden Seeds.* Albion, ME: Self-published, 1976.

Johnston, Vernon (with Winifred Carriere). *An Easy Guide to Artificial Light Gardening for Pleasure and Profit.* New York: Gramercy Publishing Co., 1964.

Kingman, A. R. *Plant Growth Responses to Extracts of Ascophyllum Nodosum.* Clemson, SC: The South Carolina Experiment Station, Clemson University, 1975.

Knott, James Edward. *Handbook for Vegetable Growers.* New York: John Wiley and Sons, 1962.

Kozlowski, T. T., ed. *Seed Biology.* Vol. 1, 2, and 3. New York: Academic Press, 1972.

Krantz, Frederick H. and Jacqueline L. *Gardening Indoors under Lights.* New York: Viking Press, 1971.

Mayer, A. M., and Poljakoff-Mayber, A. *The Germination of Seeds.* New York: Pergamon Press, 1963.

McDonald, Elvin. *The Complete Book of Gardening under Lights.* Garden City, NY: Doubleday, 1965.

Myers, Amy. *A Manual of Seed Testing.* Sydney, Australia: New South Wales Department of Agriculture, 1952.

Rickett, Harold William. *Botany for Gardeners.* New York: MacMillan Co., 1971.

Roberts, E. H. *Viability of Seeds.* Syracuse, NY: Syracuse University Press, 1972.

Rodale, J. I. and Staff. *The Encyclopedia of Organic Gardening.* Emmaus, PA: Rodale Press, 1959.

―――. *How to Grow Vegetables and Fruits by the Organic Method.* Emmaus, PA: Rodale Press, 1961.

Schultz, Peggy. *Growing Plants under Artificial Light.* New York: M. Barrows and Co., 1955.

Senn, T. L., and Kingman, A. R. *A Report of Seaweed Research.* Clemson, SC: The South Carolina Experiment Station, Clemson University, 1975.

Stefferud, Alfred. *The Wonders of Seeds.* New York: Harcourt, Brace and Co., 1965.

Tannahill, Reay. *Food in History.* pp. 7–52. New York: Stein and Day, 1974.

Tiedjens, Victor. *The Vegetable Encyclopedia.* New York: Avenel Books, 1943.

USDA. *Seeds, the Yearbook of Agriculture.* Washington, DC: U.S. Government Printing Office, 1961.

Weatherwax, Paul. *Indian Corn in Old America.* New York: MacMillan Co., 1954.

Whitson, John; John, Robert; and Williams, Henry, M.D., LID. *Luther Burbank, His Methods and Discoveries and Their Practical Application.* New York: Luther Burbank Press, 1914.

Unpublished Papers

Booth, E. Frost Resistance and Insect Pests: Seaweed Has a Two-Way Benefit.

Brain, K. R.; Chalopin, M. C.; Turner, T. D.; Blunden, G.; and Wildgoose, P. B. 1973. Cytokinin Activity of Commercial Aqueous Seaweed Extract.

Brain, K. R., and Williams, D. C. Plant Growth Regulatory Substances in Commercial Seaweed Extracts.

Race, Susan. 1963. Seaweed in Horticulture.

Rosenour, Herbert. 1958. Seaweeds—Soil and Plant Food.

Pamphlets

Coleman, Eliot. *The Use of Ground Rock Powders in Agriculture.* Harborside, Me.: The Small Farm Research Association, n.d.

Fletcher, Robert F. Written with J. O. Dutt, includes correspondence with Professor Fletcher. *Vegetable Varieties for Pennsylvania.* University Park: Penn State University Press, n.d.

Lawrence, Eleanor. *The Conservation of Crop Genetic Resource.* International Board for Plant Genetic Resources, 1975.

Sheldrake, Raymond, and Boodley, James. *Commercial Production of Vegetable and Flower Plants.* Ithaca, NY: Cornell University Press, 1974.

Growing Vegetable Transplants. University Park, PA: Penn State University Extension Service, n.d.

Growing Vine Crops. University Park, PA: Penn State University Extension Service, n.d.

Plant Growth Lighting. Cleveland OH: General Electric, n.d.

Articles

Boland, Maureen and Bridget. "Old Wives' Planting Lore." *Country Journal,* April 1977, p. 68.

Brody, Jane E. "Upstate Scientist Is Trying to Breed a Tomato that Can Stand the Cold." *New York Times,* 14 May 1977.

Cox, Jeff. "Azotobacter: the Soil Bacteria that Can Increase Your Yields." *Organic Gardening and Farming,* April 1976, pp. 144–50.

Roughgarden, Rocky. "The Modular Coldframe." *Farmstead,* Spring 1977, p. 32.

Wilkes, Garrison. "The World's Crop Plant Germplasm—an Endangered Resource." *The Bulletin of the Atomic Scientists,* February 1977, pp. 8–16.

Recommended Reading

For more information about gardening specialities mentioned in this handbook, you might want to consult one of the following books.

Abraham, Doc and Katy. *Organic Gardening Under Glass.* Emmaus, PA: Rodale Press, 1975.

Bucaro, Frank (Chico) and Wallechinsky, David. *Chico's Organic Gardening and Natural Living.* Philadelphia, PA: J. B. Lippincott Co., 1972.

Campbell, Stu. *Let It Rot!* Charlotte, VT: Garden Way, 1975.

DeKorne, James. *The Survival Greenhouse.* El Rita, NM: Walden Foundation, 1975.

Farb, Peter. *The Living Earth.* New York, NY: Harper-Row, 1969.

Fisher, Rick, and Yanda, Bill. *The Food and Heat Producing Solar Greenhouse.* Santa Fe, NM: John Muir Publications, 1977.

Jeavons, John. *How to Grow More Vegetables than You Ever Thought Possible on Less Land than You Can Imagine.* Palo Alto, CA: Ecology Action of the Midpeninsula, 1974.

Logsdon, Gene. *Small-Scale Grain Raising.* Emmaus, PA: Rodale Press, 1977.

McCullagh, James C. *The Solar Greenhouse Book,* Emmaus, PA: Rodale Press, 1977.

MacLatchie, Sharon. *Gardening With Kids.* Emmaus, PA: Rodale Press, 1977.

Raymond, Dick. *Down-to-Earth Vegetable Gardening.* Charlotte, VT: Garden Way, 1975.

Riotte, Louise. *Companion Planting.* Charlotte, VT: Garden Way, 1975.

————. *Planetary Planting.* New York: Simon and Shuster, 1975.

Rodale, J. I. and Staff. *The Encyclopedia of Organic Gardening.* Emmaus, PA: Rodale Press, 1959.

Schroeder, Marion. *The Green Thumb Directory.* Garden City, NY: Doubleday & Co., 1977.

Skelsey, Alice, and Huckaby, Gloria. *Growing Up Green.* New York, NY: Workman Publishing Co., 1973.

Wilson, Charles Morrow. *Roots: Miracles Below.* Garden City, NY: Doubleday & Co., 1968.

Yepsen, Roger, ed. *Organic Plant Protection.* Emmaus, PA: Rodale Press, 1976.

List of Seed Suppliers

United States

Bash's Seed Store, 130 North Delaware Street, Indianapolis, IN 46204. Catalog 50¢ (credited)

Burgess Seed and Plant Company, PO Box 221, Galesburg, MI 49053.

Burnett Brothers, 92 Chambers Street, New York, NY 10007. Catalog $1.50 (credited).

W. Atlee Burpee, Warminster, PA 18974; PO Box B-2001, Clinton, IA 52732, and 6350 Rutland Avenue, Riverside, CA 92501.

D. V. Burrell Seed Growers Company, PO Box 150, Rocky Ford, CO 81067.

Comstock, Ferre, and Company, 263 Main Street, Wethersfield, CT 06109.

De Giorgi Company, Inc., 1411 Third Street, Council Bluffs, IA 51501. Catalog 35¢.

Farmer Seed and Nursey Company, 818 NW Fourth Street, Faribault, MN 55021.

Henry Field Seed and Nursery Company, 407 Sycamore Street, Shenandoah, IA 51602.

Glecklers Seedmen, Metamora, OH 43540. Brochure $1.00 (credited).

Grace's Gardens, 22 Autumn Lane, Hackettstown, NY 07841. Catalog 25¢ (includes free seeds).

Gurney Seed and Nursery Company, Second and Capital, Yankton, SD 57078.

Joseph Harris Company, Inc., Moreton Farm, Rochester, NY 14624.

The Charles C. Hart Seed Company, 304 Main Street, Wethersfield, CT 06109.

H. G. Hastings Company, PO Box 44088, Atlanta, GA 30336.

J. L. Hudson, Seedsman (World Seed Service), PO Box 1058, Redwood City, CA 94064. Catalog 50¢. Send first-class stamp for vegetable listing.

Johnny's Selected Seeds (Rob Johnston), Albion, ME 04910. Catalog 50¢ (credited).

J. W. Jung Seed Company, Randolph, WI 53956.

Kitazawa Seed Company, 356 West Taylor Street, San Jose, CA 95110. (Oriental seeds).

Earl May Seed and Nursery Company, North Elm, Shenandoah, IA 51603.

The Meyer Seed Company, 600 South Caroline Street, Baltimore, MD 21231.

The Natural Development Company, Box 215, Bainbridge, PA 17502. Catalog 25¢.

Nichols Garden Nursery, 1190 North Pacific Highway, Albany, OR 97321. Catalog 25¢

L. L. Olds Seed Company, 2901 Packers Avenue, PO Box 1069, Madison, WI 53701. Catalog 25¢ (includes free seeds).

George W. Park Seed Company, Inc., PO Box 31, Greenwood, SC 29647.

Pennington, Inc., PO Box 192, Madison, GA 30650.

The Rocky Mountain Seed Company, 1325 Fifteenth Street, PO Box 5204, Denver CO 80217.

Rohrer Seedsmen, Smoketown, PA 17576.

Roswell Seed Company, 115-117 South Main Street, Roswell, NM 88201.

Seedway, Inc., Hall, NJ 14463.

Shades of Green, 16 Summer Street, Ipswich, MA 01938.*

R. H. Shumway, Seedsman, 628 Cedar Street, Rockford, IL 61101.

---

* Sells seeds packed for current year at half price each June; list sent on request.

Stokes Seeds, Inc., PO Box 548, Buffalo, NY 14240.

Thompson and Morgan, 401 Kennedy Boulevard, Somerdale, NJ 08083.

Tsang and Ma International, 1556 Laurel Street, San Carlos, CA 94070. (Oriental vegetables).

Otis Twilley Seed Company, Box 1817, Salisbury, MD 21801.

Vermont Bean Seed Company, Way's Lane, Manchester Center, VT 05255.

Canada

Alberta Nurseries and Seeds, Ltd., PO Box 20, Bowden, Alberta T0M 0K0.

William Dam Seeds, Highway 8, West Flamboro, Ontario L0R 2K0.

Early Seed and Feed, Ltd., 198 Idlwyld Drive South, Saskatoon, Saskatchewan S7K 3S9.

Lindenberg Seeds, Ltd., 803 Princess Avenue, Brandon, Manitoba R7A 0P5.

W. H. Perron and Company, Ltd., 515 Labelle, Chomeday, Laval, Quebec H7S 2A6. Catalog $1 (credited).

Stokes Seeds, Ltd., St. Catherines, Ontario, Canada L2R 6R6.

Thompson and Morgan, c/o Canadian Garden Products, Ltd., 132 James Avenue East, Winnipeg, Manitoba, R3B 0N8.

T and T Seeds, Ltd., 111 Lombard Avenue, Winnipeg, Manitoba R3B 3A9.

Vesey's Seeds, Ltd., Little York, Prince Edward Island, Canada C1A 7N8.

Abroad

Sutton's, 161 Bond Street, London, England.

Thompson and Morgan, Ipswich, England.

Vilmorin Seeds, 228 Quai de la Megisserie, Paris, France 75001.

Sources for Some Items Mentioned in the Book

Soybean seed inoculant:

L. L. Olds Seed Company, 2901 Packers Avenue, PO Box 1069, Madison, WI 53701.

R. H. Shumway, Seedsman, 628 Cedar Street, Rockford, IL 61101.

Vermont Bean Seed Company, Way's Lane, Manchester Center, VT 05255.

Azotobacter inoculant:

Soil Enterprise Corporation, PO Box 128, Stoneville, MS 38776.

Seaweed extract:

Farmer Seed and Nursery Company, 818 NW Fourth Street, Fairibault, MN 55021.

Joseph Harris Co., Morton Farm, Rochester, NY 14624.

L. L. Olds Seed Company, 2901 Packers Avenue, PO Box 1069, Madison, WI 53701.

R. H. Shumway, Seedsman, 628 Cedar Street, Rockford, IL 61101.

Vermont Bean Seed Company, Way's Lane, Manchester Center, VT 05255.

Zook and Ranck, RD 1, Gap, PA 17527.

Leaf mold:

EKOL Corporation, PO Box 297, Ocala FL 32670.

Gibberellic acid:

Henry Field Seed and Nursery Company, 407 Sycamore Street, Shenandoah, IA 51602.

Gurney Seed and Nursery Co., Second and Capital, Yankton, SD 57078.

L. L. Olds Seed Company, 2901 Packers Avenue, PO Box 1069, Madison, WI 53701.

George W. Park Seed Company, PO Box 31, Greenwood SC 29647.

Fifty-foot vinyl hose with watering wand and finger control for indoor use:

Brookstone Company, 5 Vose Farm Road, Peterborough, NH 03458.

355

Cytokinin standardized seaweed (SM-3 brand):

Atlantic and Pacific Research, Inc., PO Box 14366, North Palm Beach, FL 33408.

Index

L

M

N

O

P

R

S